DAMNED
BY
DESTINY

The second STOCKHOLM immediately after her launch.

DAMNED
BY
DESTINY

BY

DAVID L. WILLIAMS

AND

RICHARD P. DE KERBRECH

A complete account of all the World's projects for large passenger liners which, for one reason or another, never entered service. Some were still-born, some met with disaster after launching and some were diverted to other purposes during war. Potentially, some were the greatest liners ever conceived and would have surpassed the most famous, not only in speed and in splendour, but in their very size and appearance. They were victims of circumstance – a fate narrowly missed by a few of the most celebrated liners.

WITH A FOREWORD BY

ARNOLD KLUDAS

TEREDO BOOKS LTD
BRIGHTON
SUSSEX

MCMLXXXII

ISBN 0 903662 09 4

Filmset in 12pt Times Roman by
Planet Press Ltd., Brighton

*"The Worldly Hope men set their Hearts upon
Turns Ashes — or it prospers; and anon
Like Snow upon the Desert's dusty Face,
Lighting a little hour or two — is gone."*

(Rubáiyát of Omar Khayyám,
Edward Fitzgerald's translation.)

FOREWORD

A great deal has already been written on the history of passenger liners and, in particular, recent decades have seen a veritable flood of publications dealing with this subject. Undoubtedly, the steady decline of the vanishing lines and liners of the classical passenger trades provided the reason for this massive production, which included many outstanding books which have become standard works of reference. However, all these publications deal with ships which really sailed on the routes for which they were built.

Nevertheless, for as long as liners have been constructed, there have always been interesting projects which, for one reason or another, were not completed and the ships concerned were never commissioned on the services for which they were designed. Some of them would have made history for their notable exterior and interior designs alone.

David L. Williams and Richard de Kerbrech undertook the praise-worthy attempt to write the history of these 'liners which were never to be', and the result is a fascinating story. This is the more so as the authors not only trace the individual career of each ship and the stages of the projects, but they also tell us of the men of vision who proposed them and the marine architects who designed and, sometimes, created them.

Thus a really unique book has come into being: a book which deserves all the success that I can possibly imagine.

ARNOLD KLUDAS
Bremerhaven, July 1981

CONTENTS

LIST OF ILLUSTRATIONS

Plate numbers for coloured illustrations in **bold** fount.
Plans and diagrams shown in *italics*.

xv

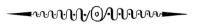

ACKNOWLEDGEMENTS

We should like to extend our heartfelt gratitude and acknowledgements to all those people, firms and institutions listed below for their kindness in contributing information or illustrations, or in providing other help towards the publication of this book. We are deeply indebted to them all but, because the subject of our theme seems to have struck so many chords from so many people in so many parts of the world, these Acknowledgements could run to a small book in themselves, were everyone to receive their just deserts. Since this is patently impossible, we trust that no invidious distinctions will be drawn if we list the names alphabetically by sections, viz:

Roy Anderson, Major Aldo Fraccaroli, Shizuo Fukui, J. H. Isherwood, Lt. Cdr. John M. Maber and A. J. Watts, who are all established nautical historians and authors.

High F. Munroe of American President Lines, G. Fouilloux of Chantiers de L'Atlantique, René Bouvard of Compagnie Générale Maritime, Robert Minton-Taylor of European Ferries, G. H. Murray of Swan Hunter Group Ltd., Edward K. Linen of Todd Shipyards Corp., T. Clark of Vickers Ltd. Shipbuilding Group and the Public Relations Managers of Achille Lauro Armatore, American Export Isbrandtsen Lines, Deschimag A.G. Weser, Howaldtswerke-Deutsche Werft A.G., Nippon Yusen Kaisha, Ocean Transport and Trading Ltd. (The Blue Funnel Line) and Verolme Dockyard B.V.

Robert P. Herzog of the Walter M. Ballard Corp., Mrs. C. J. Adamthwaite of the British Library, J. B. Moore and H. D. Williams of the Institute of Marine Engineers, K. J. Smith of the Public Record Office, Basil W. Bathe of the Science Museum, Stig Notini of the Sjöfartsmuseet, Göteborg, and the Librarians and Archivists of Fordham University, The Merseyside County Museums, Liverpool, the Southampton Reference Library, The Steamship Historical Society of America, the World Ship Society Central Record and the Secretary of the United States National Archives and Record Service.

The Canadian High Commissioner in London, the Naval Attachés of the German, Italian, Japanese, Russian and United States Embassies in London and Ronald K. Kiss and Edward S. Karlson of the United States Department of Commerce (Maritime Administration).

Much material and illustrative matter, otherwise not available, on the various projected liners was produced by the kind assistance of the following people, who also provided much support and encouragement which is deeply appreciated, namely: Frank O. Braynard, the late Col. Frank Bustard, the late Frederic H. Gibbs, of Gibbs & Cox Inc., Bob Hoare, L. L. von Münching and Arnold Kludas who unearthed so many original records of the German schemes and who so kindly agreed to write the Foreword to our work.

Equally we must record the names of Harvey Ardman, author of the forthcoming book *The NORMANDIE, her Life and Times,* Cedric Barclay of the London Maritime Arbitors Association, Ed. Bearman, Denny P. Beattie, Andrew Bell of Helston, Cornwall, Laurence Miller of the East Texas State University, Peter Thorne and Peter Wrigglesworth, who were all particularly valuable contributors of information and illustrations.

We are also especially grateful to R. L. Wheeler, Chief Designer and Technical Director of the British Hovercraft Corporation, East Cowes, I.o.W. for permitting access to technical publications TP 166 – *P192 – Passenger Cargo Airliner, March 1956,* to the Controller of Her Majesty's Stationery Office for permission to quote from Patent No. 2343 – *Improvements in Steamships . . . etc., 19 September, 1861,* to Graeme MacLennan, the Editorial Director of *Shipbuilding and Marine Engineering International* for invaluable cuttings and photographs from his archive material, to Trevor Lewis-Jones of the Society of Naval Architects and Marine Engineers (SNAME) of New York for allowing certain excerpts from SNAME transactions to be used in our text, and to the late William H. Tantum (IV) and the Titanic Historical Society for permission to quote from the observations of the *Britannic's* wreck.

For the illustrations in this book, we extend our thanks to the following persons or organizations, some of whom we have already mentioned above, viz (the numbers refer to the Plates): American Export Isbrandtsen Lines 146: Bassett-Lowke, Messrs. 134: B.B.C.-Hulton Picture Library 17-56-183 – rear endpaper: Ed. Bearman 20/1-119: Beken & Sons 42-57: Blohm & Voss 121: Frank O. Braynard 66-77/8-157: British Hovercraft Corporation 167: Brown, Boveri et Cie 50: the late Lt. Col. Frank Bustard 74: Chandris Lines 177: Chantiers de L'Atlantique 125: Cunard Line 19-61-130-166-168: Deutsches Schiffartsmuseum, Bremerhaven 14-122: A. Duncan 8-152: Barry Elliott 120-131: European Ferries 72: Theodore Ferris & Sons 153: Fordham University Library 106: Maj. Aldo Fraccaroli 47-92/4: German Atlantic Line 124: Gibbs & Cox 24/5-158: A.B. Götaverken 128: Hapag-Lloyd 16-75-109/10-182: Harland & Wolff 26/7-29/30-32/4-37-44-59-161: Bob Hoare 135: Alex. Hurst 1-4-9/10-13-15-36-48-70/1-73-79-108-192/3: David Hutchings 18-45/6-53/4-63/5-116/9-133-162/5-171/2-181: Ilcantieri S.p.A. 81/2-87: Imperial War Museum 28-40-114: J. H. Isherwood 62: Keystone Press Agency 22-60-160-169: Klosters Rederi A/S 179: Arnold Kludas, Front endpaper-Frontispiece-111/2: Michael D. J. Lennon 136-147/8-151: Lloyds, Trieste 84: *Marine Engineering* 51-67/8: Mariners Museum, Newport News 107-159: Roy Miller 7-76-154/6: E. Mione 88/91-95: Mitsubishi Heavy Industries 97/8: National Maritime Museum 5/6-173: National Railway Museum 132: New York Times News Service 126:

Nippon Yusen Kaisha 96-174/6: *Norge Handels og Sjöfarts Tidende* 178: G. Packham 191: Pathé Cinema 101: Tom Rayner 2-35-41-58-137-141/2-149-159-170-190-194: Science Museum 129: *Schiffbau Magazine* 11: *Sekai no Kansen* 100: Roger Sherlock 3-80: Skyfotos 127: Larry Smith 38/9: SNAME 138-140-145-150: Peter Stahre 52: Swedish America Line 83-85/6: Ludolf Timm 195: *Towline* 69: United States National Archives 43-99-102/5-139: University of Baltimore (Steamship Historical Coll.) 31: Vickers Shipbuilding Ltd. 180: L. L. von Münching 23-49-113-115-143: Peter Wrigglesworth 55.

We should like to single out for particular thanks David F. Hutchings, a friend of long standing, who was responsible for all the line illustrations except for those credited otherwise in the foregoing paragraph, and whose assistance in this direction is warmly acknowledged.

Finally, for typing the manuscript, we should like to express our gratitude to Barbara Witham and Elizabeth Denham, and also make special mention of our wives, Jane and Fiona, for the enduring patience and dedicated support of a project for which they did NOT share our own enthusiasms!

D. L. W.
R. P. de K.

1. The DOG STAR, built for film purposes, was an exact replica of the 703-ton, wooden SIRIUS which normally ran between Cork and London but, in 1838, was the first vessel to cross the Atlantic under continuous steam power, taking 19 days at an average speed of 6.7 knots. Brunel's 1,320 ton GREAT WESTERN arrived later the same day 15 days out of Bristol, averaging 8.2 knots. That day heralded the demise of the sailing packet ship and years of intense steamship rivalry on the route.

2. It was a far cry from the SIRIUS to the UNITED STATES which, in 1952, eclipsed all previous passenger ship records by making the westbound crossing at 34.51 knots and the eastbound at 35.59 knots. By no means the largest ship on the run, she was the ultimate in terms of speed.

INTRODUCTION

Of all the tales of the 'might-have-been', there are few more intriguing than those of the great passenger liners which might have sailed the seas but which, for one reason or another, never did so. *Damned by Destiny* presents a chronological review of these unfortunate and unfulfilled passenger liner schemes of the past century and a quarter and, with one exception, deals with such projects as only reached the concept stage; those which progressed to the design stage but were never actually built, and also with those which were built but, for one reason or another, were never operated commercially on their intended routes or in their intended form.

From this prospectus, it might be assumed that such notoriously unlucky liners as the *Titanic,* the *Georges Phillipar* of the Messageries Maritimes or the Royal Mail Line's *Magdalena* of 1949 would be included in the roster of subject vessels. Nevertheless, they are not so included, and their absence serves to illustrate precisely the limits of the contents of this book since, having commenced just one commercial voyage – in these instances their maiden one – they do not qualify for inclusion. In their cases, and in similar instances, any element of 'might-have-been' applies purely to their careers, so sadly foreshortened, since they *did* exist in their design form – however briefly.

During the past 120 years, more than a hundred and eighty passenger liners of over 20,000 tons have graced the ocean highways of the world. Their names are mostly well-known, like the *Queen Elizabeth: Rex: Normandie: America; Kaiser Wilhelm der Grosse, Champlain* and *Empress of Japan,* to mention but a few of them. All these distinguished vessels have a history, an aura attached to them and a following of devotees.

The great passenger ships which fell by the wayside and which 'never were' numbered about seventy of comparable tonnages. Much less is known about them, and there is probably much information which even the most exhaustive research has been unable to exhume. For these ships there are no yarns; no romance, no atmosphere and no glory. There cannot be any memories because, with the exception of those few which became some sort of reality, they had no physical existence. Despite this, the story behind the conception and design of these projected liners is a fascinating one of immense interest, for it provides a revealing look behind the scenes at all passenger ship development, whether lucky or unlucky.

The foundation of the projected liners' stories can be said to have been laid as far back as 1859 when Isambard Kingdom Brunel built the *Great Eastern:* a veritable monster in her day, but still small when compared with many of the vessels in this book. Her appearance encouraged immediate competition and rivalry, with plans to build a vessel of similar size, the *Spirit of the Age.* Her construction was never fulfilled but, from that time onwards, the idea of creating successful ocean leviathans became the coveted dream of every ship designer and, presumably as a result of Brunel's experiences, the nightmare of as many shipping financiers. In the light of some of the proposals included in this work, the reader will find it interesting that Brunel, although building by far the biggest ship the world had then known, prophesied with confidence that 100,000 gross ton vessels would eventually be built and, at the same time, if he had not brought all his ideas to the refinement achieved by naval architects a century later, many of his principles involving technical considerations relating to hull form and movement were not only revolutionary, but adopted to form the basis of much of the most modern forms of naval architecture.

Throughout the hey-day of the passenger liner, the completion of really mammoth vessels was regarded as an achievement of great national prestige. It was in virtue of this, and of the persistent endeavours to construct the ultimate in ocean-going luxury and splendour, that there were so many ill-fated attempts to build super-liners. Such unfulfilled dreams were never more prolific than in the period of the 'roaring twenties and golden thirties' when everything was conceived on the grand scale. The 1950s were another active time when many fanciful but short-lived liner projects abounded. Vessels of all sizes were suggested, with the emphasis being placed on successful competition with aircraft.

While the giants stole the scene in consequence of their prestige value and because they were almost always intended for service on the most illustrious and competitive sea-lane, the North Atlantic, ambitious projects involving intermediate and small liners have also been a noticeable feature throughout the whole of this era. Compared with the schemes for super-liners, however, those for smaller vessels were far fewer in number. This was undoubtedly because they lacked the record-breaking glamour and appeal of the giants but, in more recent years, the development of an ideal intermediate liner has figured high in the challenge to the aeroplane's monopoly of international travel, albeit with little success.

Despite the apparent futility of some of these projects (if only when viewed with hindsight) which became the 'might-have-beens' in the history of the ocean passenger liner, they are worthy of favourable acclaim in their own right because, through their important relationship with ships completed subsequently, they are an integral part of the whole subject and a vital part of the jig-saw of this chapter of maritime history. More than anything else, these luckless projects have reflected both the signs of the times and the hazards and difficulties of ship operation.

The projects which never proceeded beyond the concept stage are high-lighted by the Hyman Cantor and Edgar Detwiler proposals. These liners of 90,000 to 120,000 tons gross were intended to carry people to Europe from the United States by sea in much the same fashion as Freddie Laker's 'Skytrain' operation in the early 1980s. Although brilliant ideas, such complex projects became involved in issues of a much wider nature. For instance, there were the enormous stresses that would have been encountered in the main strength decks of such long liners (1,275 feet*) when operating in high sea conditions. However, these men, although experts within their own particular fields, were not in the shipping business. They were enthusiasts with inventive, business minds and with a capacity to think 'big'. Nevertheless, their views were heard and, for a

*388.62 metres.

short spell of three or four years between 1956 and 1959, they livened up the passenger liner scene with talk of their 'dreamboats' and, for that short period, provided a little hope for the future.

Some of these projected liners were drawn up to their final design stages, ready to be accepted for building, like those of the naval architect and marine engineer, Theodore Ernest Ferris, in 1931. Unfortunately, the timing proved to be inauspicious because all aspects of shipping suffered badly during the great Depression. Consequently the concepts of the United States Lines' Ferris-designed sister ships, along with many others, were lost as a result of the ruthless rationalization policies then necessary. Other similar schemes suffered as a result of reluctance to provide financial support, or even of a sheer absence of its provision, from a disapproving or parsimonious administration or, as in the case of the *Flying Cloud* project, through the needless criticisms of short-sighted sceptics.

In 1936, following the Merchant Marine Act of that year, the United States Maritime Commission was set up. A part of its terms of reference was: '. . . *to create an adequate and well-balanced fleet capable of providing shipping service on all the essential routes and of serving as naval or military auxiliaries in time of war.*'

This programme was launched in 1938, but the U.S.M.C.'s first passenger liner designs, such as the P-4-P, were postponed due to the outbreak of the Second World War. Although revamped and reactivated in 1945, a lot of the designs were no longer viable because, in the intervening years, the cost of shipbuilding materials, especially steel and labour, had risen prohibitively. In conjunction with the U.S.M.C.'s post-war proposals, there was a privately submitted design, from which two of the three projected liners actually materialized to be operated on their intended routes. These were the *Independence* and *Constitution* which, for the reasons set out in Chapter XXIC, have been included in this work and which represent the only exceptions to our central theme of 'Liners which never Were'. Since some of the U.S.M.C.'s designs were never blessed with names, we have had no option but to refer to their code letters, which is unfortunate but inevitable. In order to simplify this matter for the reader, Appendix 3 is included to clarify this form of terminology which, despite its rationality, might otherwise seem to be so much mumbo-jumbo!

3. The FRANCE, as originally designed, was limited to the North Atlantic route.

Other designs, like Cunard's Q3 project, failed because they had been overtaken by other seaborne, passenger-carrying trends and because their designs proved to be so inflexible that they were limited only to trans-Atlantic ferry requirements: a state of affairs that was demonstrated so sadly by the *France* before she was withdrawn from service in 1974. Happily, the Q3 design begat that for the Q4, which emerged as the *Queen Elizabeth 2.*

Most of those few projected liners which were, indeed, built as planned, yet which still did not ply their intended routes, were prevented from doing so by the two World Wars, and these interruptions to normal trade took a particularly heavy toll of these ill-fated ships. Among the many victims of actual hostilities were the *Britannic* and *Justicia,* and the *Kashiwara Maru* and *Izumo Maru* (as the aircraft carriers *Junyo* and *Hiyo* respectively) which were all lost on active, or other war, service and thereby prevented from entering the passenger trade for which they were designed and projected. Another loss was the *Vaterland* which was destroyed before she could be fitted out, but the effects of war were various and far-reaching, and the *Bretagne* was only one of many projects cancelled for this reason, while the Swedish America Line's beautiful, Italian-built *Stockholm* was sequestrated by the Italians for their war effort.

Although, on the face of it, *Damned by Destiny* might seem to be little more than a catalogue of much fruitless effort, this would be a very superficial viewpoint, since such effort was far from being in vain, and therein lies the essence of the story. As is the case in all new building schemes, there were invariably plans for these ill-destined ships to improve shipboard standards or to further marine technology in some way, and many innovations which later became commonplace in passenger liners which followed after them had had their origins in some incompleted project. For example: turbo-electric propulsion for a giant passenger liner was proposed for the International Mercantile Marine's *Boston* and *Baltimore* some thirteen years before the *California,* of the Panama Pacific Line, which was the first large turbo-electric passenger ship, had such engines installed. The *Oceanic* was also very advanced where diesel-electric machinery was concerned.

The suggestion of dual-purpose passenger ships, suitable for conversion to full aircraft carriers in time of war, was another projected liner's 'first', as proposed in the scheme for the *Flying Cloud*. This concept was well appreciated later in the many escort carriers built in the Second World War, and was an idea fully exploited by the Japanese. Even the Germans considered converting the Norddeutscher Lloyd's giant *Europa* in such a fashion, although it came to be realized that, unless special provision had been made in the hull design, liners in general were not suited for such conversion, other than for an aircraft ferry, for training, or for an escort role.

The Swedish America Line's *Stockholm* did not introduce the idea of a purpose-built dual-role cruise ship, since this distinction belongs to the *Empress of Britain* of 1931, but, ten years before the advent of the Cunard Line's *Caronia,* the *Stockholm's* designers proposed the first permanent accommodation layout suited to this type of ship, whereby practically all cruising passengers would have outside cabins. Yet another example of the influence of a 'might-have-been' is the one-class tourist liner of the 1960s, which was originally envisaged in the 'Yankee Clipper', designed for Paul Wadsworth Chapman in the late 1930s, and it was in the same vessel, re-modelled in 1951, that the first proposal was made for a form of gantry loading, which is now a standard feature of container ship handling. For all these reasons, the intrinsic value of these abortive passenger liner projects is surely beyond question.

Perhaps the greatest bequest of these unfortunate schemes was less tangible. As lessons in business economics and management, and in research and development, as forms of trial and error examples, they aided the progress of healthy passenger liner operations, as well as advancing the pace of marine engineering.

The proponents of these grandiose liners, like their ill-starred projects, have all been laid to rest. There were naval architects, marine engineers and shipping personalities such as William Francis Gibbs; Paul Wadsworth Chapman: Theodore Ernest Ferris; Vladimir Yourkevitch, A. C. Hardy and Frank Bustard, O.B.E., whose names will appear throughout this book. These are the leading players in the dramas we shall unfold and, although they had frequently achieved major successes in other undertakings, their fame should not lie more lightly on those conceptions which form the burden of this work and which were 'damned by destiny'.

It is hoped that this book will provide an interesting source of reference for shipping enthusiasts, historians, marine engineers and naval architects alike.

David L. Williams
Richard P. de Kerbrech

4.   The first screw-driven vessel to cross the Atlantic was the GREAT BRITAIN in 1843, the year of her launching, seen above. Designed by Brunel, she was then the largest ship in the world, displacing 3,618 tons and being 289 feet in length. In some sense she was the precursor of his later GREAT EASTERN. The rig of the ship was altered twice during her career and her engines were finally removed and she then traded as a full-rigged ship. Her original engines had been replaced in 1847, but the vessel represented a tremendous step forward when she was built and almost a landmark in maritime history. She is now being restored to her former state at Bristol, where she was built.

I THE *SPIRIT OF THE AGE*
AND
THE NINETEENTH CENTURY

The origins of the projected liner story can be said to have originated in 1859 when Isambard Kingdom Brunel completed the enormous *Great Eastern,* ex *Leviathan,* which was the name originally determined for her. In speaking of an 'enormous' or 'mammoth' ship, we must consider her within the context of her times, since it is clear that what seems to be a gigantic vessel to one generation may not seem to be so to a later one, and the fact of the matter was that the *Great Eastern* was by far the largest vessel afloat when launched, at 18,915 gross tons, and, indeed, that she retained that distinction for almost half a century – 48 years to be precise – until she was finally exceeded in size by the *Oceanic.* This simple statistic serves to put the nineteenth century into perspective, since it was not until the end of it that 20,000-tonners were becoming a reality although, as will be seen, at least one ambitious idea which was far ahead of current construction targets was bruited at that time.

Although regarded as a failure in her day, the *Great Eastern* was the legitimate predecessor of the ocean passenger vessels of the twentieth century. Significantly, she was also the first liner to precipitate a competitive – albeit unsuccessful – reaction, amounting to a challenge not only to improve on her trading performance and potential, but to outdo the ship herself as well as her appointments.

This was the aptly named *Spirit of the Age,* planned in 1861 to challenge the *Great Eastern* for honours in size. In addition, patented features, which sounded as though they had come straight out of a Jules Verne novel, showed the intentions of her designers to surpass her in technical innovations for both the comfort and convenience of passengers.

The proposed dimensions and tonnage of the *Spirit of the Age* are not known, though the lithograph of her by T. G. Dutton suggests that she would have been of rather similar proportions to Brunel's ship. She was described as *'having great length in comparison with her breadth, and with a very small freeboard.'** This vessel would have been operated by the Trans-Atlantic Express Steam Packet Company, on the route alternatively chosen for the *Great Eastern,* which had been intended originally for the Cape route to India – hence her name.

The few details available tell us only a little of her designers' thinking with regard to this proposed vessel. A much better picture can be obtained from the patents registered on 19 September 1861 for *The Spirit of the Age,* under the title: *'Silver and Moore's Improvements in Steam Ships Etc.'* Silver and Moore, both with the christian name Thomas, were the designers of the liner and their invention, as it was described, consists of eleven parts.

The first deals with hull subdivision and bulkhead strengthening from the keelson to a hurricane deck.

The second part concerns special loading equipment which is imaginatively described as *'facilitating the loading or discharging of coals or cargo, by beam travellers or wheels, flanged or otherwise, running in suspended grooves or working to and fro on rails.'*

Sections three to six refer to the proposed engines and machinery layout, although no specific details of the type of engine are given. The machinery and boilers were to be fitted to the sides of the hull, thereby leaving the centre part free and uncluttered.

The engine arrangement was intended to drive two paddle-wheels, two screw propellers – one under each stern quarter, and a hydraulic steering apparatus.

Parts seven to nine of the patent deal with passenger comforts and safety provisions ranging from a fire-fighting arrangement based on the ship's hot water pipe heating system, to a ventilation scheme and a between decks lighting contrivance. The description of these latter

---

* *Mail and Passenger Ships of the Nineteenth Century.* H. Parker & Frank Bowen, 1928.

5. When one considers that it was not until 1878 that a steamer crossed the Atlantic without square yards, the SPIRIT OF THE AGE (like Darius Davison's LEVIATHAN, Pl. 6) was either ultra-optimistic or foolhardy. The conception of folding masts with no stays could hardly have proved to have been of much use in an emergency. Not only did steamship sails provide valuable 'Push' in days of high fuel consumption but, on a 'belt-and-braces' principle, they could provide manoeuvreability, or better means of heaving to, in the event of engine failure. Admittedly, the larger the ship, the less cogent is the argument. The lithograph is by T. G. Dutton and dated 11 November, 1861.

6. *A lithograph of the proposed LEVIATHAN – the cigar-shaped vessel – drawn by her designer, Darius Davison. The passengers on deck appear to be impervious to*

inventions is typical in style of the whole specification and it makes both interesting and humorous reading. For instance, of the air-conditioning proposal it says:

'The eighth part of our invention consists in ventilating the between decks and cabins in a manner more suited to insure health, by carrying off impure air. This we propose to do by inserting trap valves in the decks, communicating with pipes carrying the foul air below, where it will be forced upwards from the bottom of the ship, and taken up through pipes through the floors, and extending above the upper deck. The carbonic gases, which contaminate the atmosphere through the impossibility of their escaping, will be allowed to descend, as it is their nature to do, and be carried up by the upward draught of the ventilating pipes in the bottom of the ship. The trap openings will be covered by gratings. The traps will be made self-acting floats, to close up in the event of water rising underneath. The tops of the ventilating pipes above the upper deck to be in the form of a cap cone fashioned to increase the draft.'

Regarding the lighting arrangement, the patent states: *'The ninth part of our invention consists in lighting the between decks. We accomplish this by inserting honeycombed or iron-framed glass in all the corridors or passages throughout the vessel, these diffusers of light to have the appearance of a honeycomb, with conical cells and glass bull's-eyes, so shaped as to fit such cells, the upper part of the cells to have an iron projecting rim, so made as to form cavities for the reception of elastic or other suitable cushions to keep the bull's-eyes from being forced upwards.'*

Finally, parts ten and eleven describe the rigging and the deck and auxiliary steering equipment. Part ten goes some way towards explaining the novel appearance of the *Spirit of the Age* as depicted in Dutton's lithographed conception. It was proposed that all standing rigging be abolished, suggesting that Messrs. Silver and Moore had great faith in the contemporary development of the marine engine, in spite of the *Great Eastern's* débâcle during a terrible Atlantic storm during September 1861 when she had her steering shaft ripped off, together with both paddle wheels, leaving her almost totally helpless. However, for emergency purposes, the *Spirit of the Age* would have carried hinged spars, flat along her hurricane deck, to take fore-and-aft sails, although it may be difficult to reconcile this rather strange arrangement with the lack of standing rigging.

The impression gained from the patented design for the ship was that the ideas were as obvious in their objectives as they were absurd in their approach. Typical of most patent descriptions of the period, the specification offers nothing in the way of sound, mechanical explanation of how the desired improvements would – or could – be achieved. The *Spirit of the Age* was never built; the misfortunes of the *Great Eastern* probably having as much to do with this 'non-event' as the improbability of her design.

As the nineteenth century progressed, so marine technology advanced with it, and the conception of large passenger liners moved out of the realms of fantasy, although some quite bizarre craft were being propounded. Among the odd and peculiar suggestions put forward during the latter half of the nineteenth century for large ocean-going vessels was one for a huge cigar-shaped ship, and another for a so-called 'roller-boat', whose designer was within a hair's breadth of discovering the principles of tank propulsion without – it seems – realizing it. Indeed, had he applied his principles to land, instead of sea, propulsion, he might have become famous!

The cigar-shaped craft was the brain-child of a New Yorker named Darius Davison. Dating from 1852, this was the 'Vernes-ish' prediction of the future of ocean travel by a mid-nineteenth century engineer. Of 700 feet in length and 50 feet maximum beam, she was intended to carry 3,000 passengers across the North Atlantic in relative luxury at an average speed of 25 knots. Other cigar-shaped vessels were in fact built although the *Leviathan,* as she was named, was not amongst them, but those which were completed proved to be quite useless.

As for the 'roller-boat', this was invented by Frederick Augustus Knapp, a Canadian lawyer from Prescott, Ontario, in the 1890s. His idea was that a revolving outer cylinder around a stationary inner cylinder would create less water resistance and minimize sea-sickness. A model of the roller-boat, a scaled-down version of a planned 800 foot, 35-hour* trans-Atlantic roller ship, was tested in Toronto harbour on 27 October 1897, but was a complete failure. As the propulsive power of the craft was increased, it was driven deeper into the water rather than forwards, and it

*A figure that the inventor must be presumed to have plucked out of the air!

KNAPP ROLLER BOAT, 1897

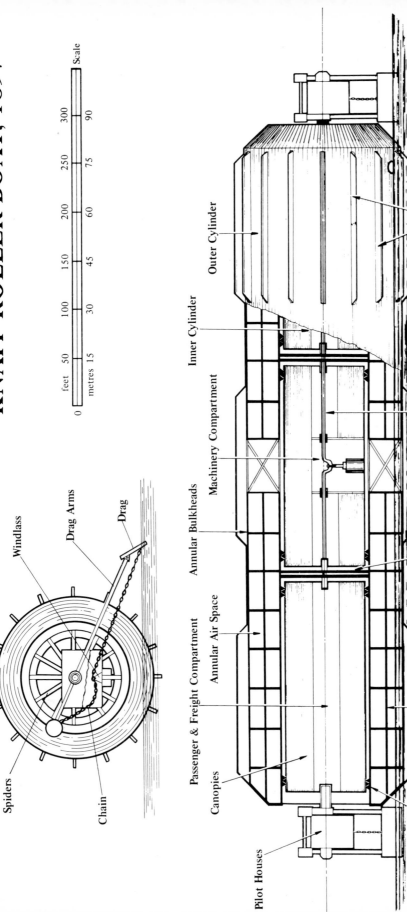

Scale

| feet | 50 | 100 | 150 | 200 | 250 | 300 |
| metres | 15 | 30 | 45 | 60 | 75 | 90 |

0

Windlass

Drag Arms

Drag

Spiders

Chain

Outer Cylinder

Inner Cylinder

Flanges

Drive Shaft

Machinery Compartment

Annular Bulkheads

Passenger & Freight Compartment

Annular Air Space

Spiders

Canopies

Longitudinal Bulkheads

Pilot Houses

Bearings

7. A midship sectional view, and an end elevation, of the Knapp Roller boat.

became quite unmanageable. The wreck of this model was broken up for scrap in the summer of 1921.

New passenger vessels, entering service in the late 1880s, benefited from the discoveries and inventions of the emerging scientific age, and the construction of even larger liners not only became more feasible but more economically practicable as well. This pioneering period of steam-powered ocean travel is distinguished by the very low number of liner schemes which were not fulfilled. With limited technical knowledge and experience on which to draw, most new ship proposals were eventually realized and lessons were learnt from their performances while actually in service – a potentially costly, though effective, procedure.

Around 1889 serious consideration was given to the design of another large liner and, as in the case of the *Great Eastern,* this vessel was also to be truly a monster when compared to her contemporaries. It was at this time that Sir Edward Harland, of Harland and Wolff in Belfast, produced a design of a 1,000-foot liner suitable for the White Star Line. It was a design which, although not pursued any further at that time, was retained for the next thirty or forty years, being perpetuated by Lord Pirrie, a later Harland and Wolff chairman, and setting a sort of symbolic size target for which to aim in all future giant passenger liner thinking. The design was revised from time to time to accommodate the latest improvements to marine engines, and it was said to have been used eventually as the basis for the design of the giant White Star liner *Oceanic,* laid down in the 1920s.

Whether there was any intention to build such a liner in the late 1890s is unknown, but it is unlikely as shipbuilding practice had not developed sufficiently at that time. Nevertheless, the feasibility of such large passenger ships had been endorsed by a respected authority in the ship-building world, and this was surely the main result – if not the object – of the exercise.

The eventual construction of a 1,000-foot floating palace had now been prophesied but, as realization became little nearer by the turn of the century, aspirations tended to moderate somewhat, and plans for new vessels were for ships of a more immediately practical size which tended to be natural progressions from the largest liners already afloat and in commission.

Politically, Great Britain and Germany faced one another across the North Sea as mighty contestants and, as the possession of the Atlantic Blue Riband record represented one of the highest national achievements and invariably attracted the greatest volume of passengers, besides reflecting increased business on the other ships of the company concerned and even, to some degree, on the nation as a whole, the major companies of both countries led the field with plans for record-breaking, modern sea-queens.

Meanwhile France, Italy and the United States were all emerging as important maritime nations in this field, and the first 20,000-ton liners were soon taking shape on the slipways in 1900/1901.

The years around the turn of the century also witnessed a revolution in marine engineering which was to have a far-reaching impact on the realization of many of the ambitions for future passenger liners. To cite but two instances, there was the public display of the *Turbinia,* introducing Parsons' marine turbine, at the Jubilee naval review in 1897, and the commencement of the Allan sisters *Victorian* and *Virginian* in 1903, these being the first passenger liners to be propelled by steam turbines.

A contributor to the *Scientific American* on 10 November 1900 offered his suggestions for a possible liner of the future — a six-funnelled extrapolation of the Hapag *Deutschland* (q.v.). He reckoned that a 30-knot, 4-day vessel could be produced by increasing the engine size to produce 110,000 horse-power on three screws, with proportionate enlargement to all other dimensions and capacities. On his own admission, however, the author concluded that the development he suggested would not be practicable in reality. Instead, he reasoned that the larger and faster ships of the type to which he referred would only come about with the development and adoption of the Parsons turbine. How right this prediction proved to be!

So the race was on, and an era of technological rivalry had begun!

8. *Fashions in liner design changed no less than in clothing, vide the people in the foreground going out to the KAISERIN AUGUSTE VIKTORIA in the first decade of the century. Laid down as the EUROPA, she was launched as the KAISERIN AUGUSTE VIKTORIA (p.26) and, after the first World War, became the Canadian Pacific's EMPRESS OF SCOTLAND.*

9. *Although designers of those ships which materialized, and of those which did not, made much progress in the elimination of funnel soot and, latterly, of smuts, the problem was never wholly solved. In earlier liners it was a very real problem. The White Star MAJESTIC, ex-Hamburg Amerika BISMARCK (P.25) is seen demonstrating this point.*

II NORDDEUTSCHER LLOYD'S FIVE-FUNNELLED LINER

Around the beginning of the twentieth century, the Germans were well established as the most superior country operating on the North Atlantic, and this was a most auspicious time for their Bremen-based company. Apart from the Hapag* *Deutschland* of 1899, the Norddeutscher Lloyd had held the Atlantic Blue Riband for five uninterrupted years with their two famous Stettin (Sceczin)-built liners, the *Kaiser Wilhelm der Grosse* of 1897 and the *Kronprinz Wilhelm* of 1901. Having nailed their flag to the top of the mast with these record-breakers, the N.D.L. intended to see it kept there by the commissioning of even speedier vessels.

So far as the Germans were concerned, their aim was a five-day vessel which would cover the distance between Bremerhaven and New York so as to arrive at the latter port no later than at 19.00 hours on the fifth day of the crossing. Such an arrival would permit the Customs and Immigration authorities to carry out formalities on the day of arrival. A ship which could travel at no less than 24.8 knots over the 3,558 miles of distance was therefore required.

Following the *Kaiser Wilhelm der Grosse* and the *Kronprinz Wilhelm,* a third, slightly larger liner, the *Kaiser Wilhelm II,* was begun in 1901 and, with her up-rated engines producing 44,500 i.h.p.,† was certain to be a 24-knot flyer, but she would still be unable to cross the Atlantic in the required five days. It was well appreciated by the N.D.L. designers that there was very little scope for obtaining further increases in output from

---

*Hamburg Amerikanische Packetfahrt Actien-gesellschaft. Shortened to HAPAG, by common usage, the company became known alternatively as 'Hapag'. This word may be taken as being synonymous with the Hamburg Amerika Line throughout this book.

†See Glossary.

10. *The KAISER WILHELM II. Note her array of cowled ventilators, which make an interesting comparison withthe KAISERIN AUGUSTE VIKTORIA (Pl.6).*

the steam reciprocating machinery installed in her. The Company, therefore, sought other means than just increasing engine capacity for the development of a faster vessel, and the projected ship which followed was conceived by their Chief Designer, Professor Dr. J. Schütte.

Professor Schütte saw other, more economical means of achieving the desired performance by improving the ship's hull form. In June 1902 he announced his plans for a new liner — a five-funnelled, five-day ship with a cruiser stern! Two important features had been incorporated into his new design, and both had their origins in contemporary warship construction.

The first was a much smaller length to breadth ratio, resulting in a far beamier ship. The second was the replacement of the usual counter stern with á cruiser stern: a feature soon to be adopted universally.* The 16,810 gross ton Canadian Pacific liner *Empress of Russia,* running across the North Pacific, which entered service in 1913, was the first large passenger ship to have a cruiser stern in the event, thereby launching the widespread change of fashion away from counter sterns.* It had already been demonstrated that cruiser sterns on fast warships were extremely successful. A model of the 5-funnelled liner was constructed and tested at Bremerhaven in the great German Experimental Towing Basin, which had also been projected and built under the supervision of Professor Schütte. These tests proved beyond question that the combination of a cruiser stern and more beam in relation to a smaller block coefficient†

*Preceding the *Alsatian* and *Calgarian,* which were the first such liners on the North Atlantic run, by nearly a year.

†See Glossary.

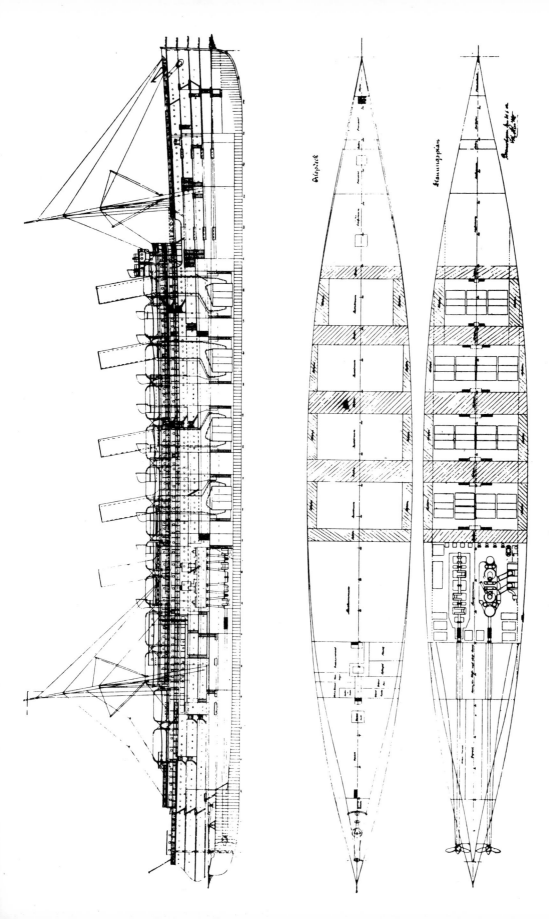

Abb. 1, 2a, 2b. 25 kn-Schnelldampfer-Projekt. Längeriss, Orlopdeck und Stauungsplan

11. *Drawings of the Norddeutscher Lloyd express liner, dated 24 June, 1902.*

12. *The KRONPRINZESSIN CECILIE, which followed the cancellation of the five-funnelled liner.*

produced a greatly improved hull form. With smaller engines, the 5-funnelled liner would be able to more than match the speed of the *Kaiser Wilhelm II.*

In comparison with the *Kronprinz Wilhelm* and *Kaiser Wilhelm II* one can see how great an improvement had been made in the plans for the new 5-funnelled vessel. She would have displaced only 21,069 tons with a gross tonnage of 20,689 and, in spite of her greater dimensions, would have drawn 3 feet less water than the much smaller *Kronprinz Wilhelm* whose draught was 24¼ feet. This was due partly to the influence of the greater beam on the ship's weight, but also to the intended use of a new type of steel in her construction. Her dimensions were planned to be 690.5 feet overall length and 89 feet beam, which compared with 706 feet and 72 feet for the *Kaiser Wilhelm II.* Thus her length/breadth ratio was 7.76 against 9.81 of the latter vessel. Her engines would have provided a horse-power of 39,000 against the 44,500 of the *Kaiser Wilhelm II,* but she would have been well over a knot faster with a continuous service speed in excess of 25.5 knots.

The contemplated 5-funneller not only had a hull form improved on that of the *Kaiser Wilhelm II,* but she also had a greater capacity with a complement of 750 first class passengers, 340 second class and 900 third class in contrast to the earlier liner's 775, 340 and 770 respectively.

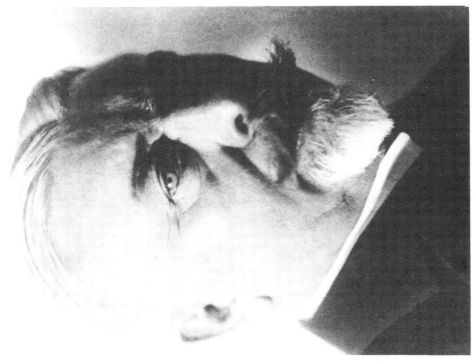

14. *Professor Dr. J. Schütte.*

13. *A bow view of the KAISER WILHELM II.*

24

Of her five funnels, the aftermost one was a dummy, but the number alone would have been a comfort to the superstitious emigrant passengers, for it was said that these simple folk were reassured of a liner's potential safety by the number of her funnels, and booked their passages accordingly! The only other passenger vessel to be designed with five funnels was Brunel's *Great Eastern* – 43 years previously.

Construction of this superior liner was probably due to start early in 1903 but, before any work could be begun, the Norddeutscher Lloyd became aware of the Cunard Line's intention to build two revolutionary turbine liners to wrest the Blue Riband from the Germans. In view of this, the Company re-appraised its building plans and, in the face of this new threat, considered it more expedient to build a second and improved vessel of the *Kaiser Wilhelm II* type. An up-rated version of the five-funnelled liner with bigger reciprocating engines or turbine propulsion might have been able to meet the challenge but, with time against them and with no operating experience of a ship of this type to guide them, the Norddeutscher Lloyd decided on the former course of action.

The five-funnelled liner could have been in service by 1905. Instead, there was a four year gap between the *Kaiser Wilhelm II* and her near sister, the *Kronprinzessin Cecilie,* and although the former vessel took and held the Blue Riband until 1907, the latter proved to be no match for the *Lusitania* and *Mauretania*.

15. *The LUSITANIA which, with her even faster sister, the MAURETANIA, eclipsed the German dominance of the quickest trans-Atlantic passages.*

III THE *EUROPA*

Following the cancellation of the five-funnelled liner, the Norddeutscher Lloyd had no ships bigger than the *Kaiser Wilhelm II* or the *Kronprinzessin Cecilie* under consideration during the late 1900s, with the exception of the 25,570 gross ton *George Washington,* which was completed in June 1909.

As for the White Star Line, they had answered this German challenge with their celebrated 'Big Four' which entered service between 1901 and 1907. Named *Celtic, Cedric, Baltic* and *Adriatic,* each of them was in turn the largest passenger liner in the world on completion, although the value of this distinction must be somewhat tempered when it is realized that, even with a gross tonnage averaging 22,500, they were still − after 45 years had elapsed − little bigger than the *Great Eastern.*

In the meantime, Cunard's reply took the form of exhaustive model tests on designs for two new liners of between 725 and 800 feet overall length; tests which resulted in the famous *Lusitania* and *Mauretania.* During this period, the position of the Hamburg Amerika Line (Hapag) was rather ambiguous.

Despite the limited success of their one record-breaker, the *Deutschland,* which was soon to be withdrawn from her scheduled service to ply eventually as one of the earliest full-time cruising liners, they appeared to have adopted the same policy as the White Star Line. Instead of building more 'racers', they began work on a trio of slower, but steadier and extremely luxurious vessels. As with their later triad of giants − the *Imperator, Vaterland* and *Bismarck* − each of these ships was to be a development of the previous one and, consequently, each was slightly

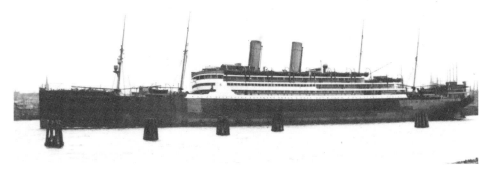

16. The KAISERIN AUGUSTE VIKTORIA in Hamburg. Insufficient data exists to produce a picture of the proposed EUROPA, which would have been extended from this design.

larger than the one she succeeded and had corresponding improvements to her appointments. The first of the three, the *Amerika,* was ordered from Harland and Wolff at Belfast in 1903, and she was followed soon afterwards by the *Europa,* which was ordered from the Vulkanwerke shipyard in Stettin, northern Germany (now part of Poland). While under construction the *Europa* was re-named *Kaiserin Auguste Viktoria* to honour the Kaiser's consort, and her original name was passed on to the third vessel which had been ordered from the *Amerika's* builders in 1906, as yard No. 391 with a delivery date set for 1909.

Essentially, the three ships were very much alike, though extra length and increased enclosed space made each of them about 4,000 tons gross bigger than her predecessor. The new *Europa's* gross tonnage was to be 29,700, with an overall length of 718 feet* and, like the two earlier liners, she was to have the same two-funnelled/four-masted profile which had become very popular between 1900 and 1909. However, in late June 1907, in the early stages of her conception, drastic alterations were incorporated into her design which were to raise her gross tonnage to 44,500 and her length to 780 feet,† while her passenger accommodation was enlarged to 4,250, comprising 550 first class; 350 second class, 1,000 third class and 2,350 fourth class. These plans included enlargement of the *Europa's* propelling machinery from twin to triple screw, driven by the Harland and Wolff combination of reciprocating engines exhausting

*218.85 metres.
†237.74 metres.

through a low pressure turbine. At this time, immigration to the United States was still increasing and presumably the additional capacity was to be utilized primarily for this purpose. Whether this dramatic change in size would have also altered her general external appearance drastically is uncertain.

Mr. Rupert Cameron, a former Harland and Wolff director, considered it unlikely that the new design for the *Europa* progressed very far and based his conclusion on the very brief interval which elapsed between the announcement of the ship's increased dimensions and her sudden cancellation in December 1907. Therefore, in the absence of pictorial records, her likely appearance as a larger vessel must remain a matter for conjecture but, with bigger engines and more boilers, she would almost certainly have had one more funnel. Indeed, Hapag-Lloyd's records suggest three funnels as a minimum.

The reason for her cancellation was a need for economic restraint, the causes of which were two-fold. There had been a temporary decline in the passenger-carrying trade in the early years of the twentieth century following the end of the Boer War, when additional tonnage, released from trooping activities, created a surplus of available berths, thereby depressing both passenger volumes and earnings per ship. Hapag's results, like those of everyone else's, reflected this trend. In addition, Albert Ballin, the Managing Director of the Hamburg Amerika Line, had experienced difficulties with the International Mercantile Marine Company which had been created to gain control of all the major trans-Atlantic lines. From April 1902, when the I.M.M. was formed by the millionaire steel magnate, John Pierpont Morgan from Hartford, Conn., many of the major North Atlantic companies were absorbed into this massive all-American finance corporation. These included the Dominion Line: Atlantic Transport Line: Leyland Line; Red Star Line, Inman Line and, most significant of all, the White Star Line.

Morgan aspired to cast his I.M.M. net even wider and also to acquire ('M-organize' was the term the press preferred to use) the major Continental lines as well as the Cunard Line – the most important British company to remain independent. Morgan had established something of a cartel with the concerns of which he had already gained control and used his vast reserves to finance almost irresistible boardroom take-overs of his victim companies. In the event, the French and British Governments intervened and provided sufficient monetary assistance to enable the Compagnie Générale Transatlantique and Cunard to remain autonomous.

As for the two great German lines, which wished to avoid any form of direct take-over, they agreed at an early stage to a ten year affiliation arrangement which involved mutual co-operation with the I.M.M. on certain joint policies. Notwithstanding this, the I.M.M. eventually acquired a substantial – though by no means majority – holding in both the Hamburg Amerika and Norddeutscher Lloyd Companies. Although their arrangement had relieved the pressure on Hapag to some degree, the fight to remain wholly independent of the I.M.M. had drained valuable funds, and financial constraints were therefore necessary in order to preserve liquidity. In consequence, the shelving of the *Europa* project, although well advanced, became unavoidable.

J. P. Morgan's ambition had been to dominate the North Atlantic shipping lines totally, but his failure to achieve this objective was pertinently illustrated in an example of what might pass for poetic justice at the time of his death in 1913, at the age of 75. Since he had died during a trip to Rome, arrangements had to be made to return his body to the United States for burial but, ironically, the vessel in which he made this last voyage was the *France,* the flagship of the C.G.T. – one of the few lines which had successfully resisted his challenge!

17. John Pierpont Morgan (Sr.)

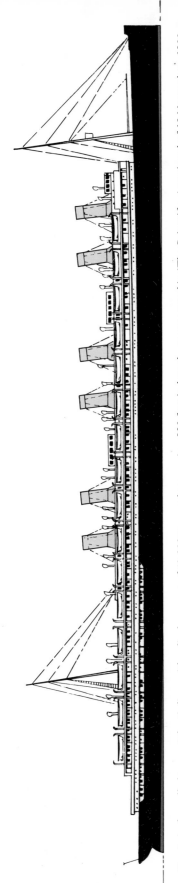

18. *A six-funnelled trans-Atlantic liner with a displacement of 40,000 tons and measuring 930 feet in length, as suggested in 'The Scientific American' of 10 November, 1900. See p.17).*

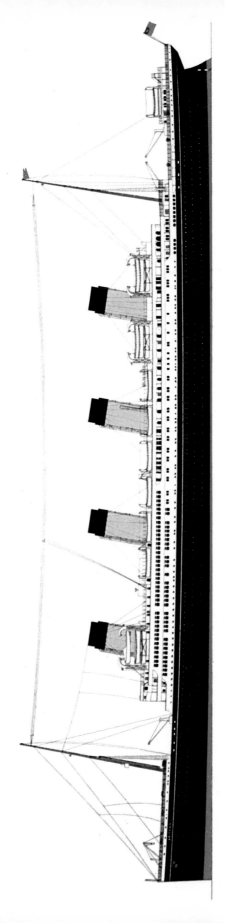

19. *An artist's impression of the BRITANNIC as intended for commercial service. (See Chapter V)*

20. A painting of the JUSTICIA in her capacity as a trooper . . . (See Chapter VI)

21. . . . and another of the BRITANNIC in hospital ship colours. (See Chapter V)

IV THE *BOSTON* AND *BALTIMORE*

Once international trade began to revive again, the major companies began renewing their fleets and replacing their worn-out units. The interval of decline had enabled naval architects to review and improve their ideas for new ships and, with the advent of the White Star's *Olympic* class, the Cunard's *Aquitania* and the *Imperator* trio of the Hamburg Amerika Line, each in turn being the world's largest ship on going into service, another step was taken nearer to achieving the goal of constructing a 1,000-foot long giant. It was, however, a period when the American presence on the North Atlantic was noticeably absent. This disturbing lack of enterprise concerned American people from many quarters, since they felt that there was a great need for the United States to establish itself as a powerful and progressive maritime nation, with a worthy fleet and an estimable naval presence to match her growing strength and prosperity.

It was with the intention of remedying this lamentable situation that the next two 'unfortunates' were conceived for, had they been completed, they would have been highly enviable vessels. With their proportions, they would not only have been the largest vessels in the world, but also the first to have exceeded the coveted 1,000-foot mark as well. These two liners, which would each have had a gross tonnage of 55,000, were designed between 1909 and 1914 by William Francis Gibbs and his brother, Frederic H. Gibbs, whose intended careers as lawyers were influenced drastically by a shared experience on 12 November 1894, when they were eight and seven years old respectively. This was the occasion of the launch of the *St. Louis,* coincidentally, as it turned out, herself a ship of the American Line which, with her sister vessel, the *St. Paul,* was destined to be the largest liner* to cross the Atlantic wearing the United States ensign for the next 23 years. Inspired as they were by this momentous event, the pair went on to dedicate their lives to naval architecture and, although basically self-taught for the task, their accomplishments have been considerable and their contribution towards the rebirth of the American Navy and Merchant Marine has made them renowned internationally.

William Francis Gibbs, the senior partner, was born in Philadelphia on 24 August 1886 and was the designer responsible for the reconstruction of *the Leviathan,* ex-*Vaterland,* between February 1922 and June 1923, but there is no question that his greatest success was the record-breaking liner *United States,* completed in 1952. His schemes and plans are a persistent feature throughout this book. After an eventful and successful career as a naval architect, he died in September 1967.

This brief resumé anticipates the events which concern us immediately, and it is necessary to go back to the year 1908, when the Gibbs brothers were embarking on their University careers and when they first conceived the idea of these two giant liners. Remarkably, they not only appear to have mastered the technicalities and intricacies of ship design concurrently with their university studies, but worked on the project at their own expense. Then, in June 1913, W. F. Gibbs was awarded two degrees as a Batchelor of Law and Master of Arts at Columbia University and, from then onwards, he financed his ship-design project from legal fees which he obtained.

The proposed vessels were to have been four-funnellers with graceful counter sterns. The funnels, similar to the Stettin-built German liners, were to have been in two widely-spaced pairs, perhaps with an eye to a Federal subsidy and their use as armed merchant cruisers or for other military activity, but they bore a general resemblance to the *Olympic.* Their overall length was planned to be 1,001 feet,† with a beam of 106 feet, a depth of 74 feet and a load draft of 35 feet when they displaced 57,000 tons. Accommodation for 3,000 passengers was to be provided, divided into 1,000 saloon-class, 800 second-class and 1,200 steerage class, with a crew of 1,000. The Gibbs brothers' liners were to be 30 knot vessels, this speed being produced by quadruple screws driven by 185,000

*11,629 tons.
†305.1 metres.

horse-power 'electric-drive' engines — the first consideration of this method of propulsion for an ocean liner of any size! Outlines for the machinery were prepared at the brothers' request by Mr. W. L. R. Emmet of Schenectady, New York State, the Chief Engineer of the General Electric Company. Mr. Emmet considered that electric propulsion was the only method by which the extra power to propel the ships at 30 knots could be attained.

These two projected 'speed-queens' were to be oil-fuelled with a cruising radius of 7,000 miles, so that they would only need to bunker in the United States where oil was so much cheaper. The presumption is that the architects had calculated that this saving more than offset the additional cost of energy, in view of the deeper draught which this entailed, apart from its obvious advantages if and when the ships might be diverted for war-time purposes. It was further intended to operate them from Fort Pond Bay, Montauk Point, on the eastern end of Long Island, with rail links to Manhattan on the Long Island Railroad. The promoters also aimed to involve both this concern and its parent company, The Pennsylvania Railroad, as business partners and as investors in the venture, whereupon booking offices for both railroad companies could become sales points for tickets for trans-Atlantic crossings in the two ships.

By dint of using the quick turn-round capabilities of spacious Fort Pond Bay, and thus avoiding the slow trip up the Narrows to Manhattan, it was hoped to save four hours on the crossing time, particularly in thick or foggy weather, enabling the two liners to make four-day passages — an attractive element which appealed to other, later proponents of trans-Atlantic vessels. Indeed, at that time the saving was very significant although the changes in the intervening years, and particularly in the last decades, may occasion the reader to pause to reflect on the relative merit of this saving of four hours to which the Gibbs brothers attached so much importance as a fundamental element of the *Boston* and *Baltimore* scheme. Today its value pales into insignificance when it is compared with the time of less than six hours that is now the *total* time taken to cross the Atlantic by modern jet airliners: in other words, a crossing time barely 50% more than the four hours which the Gibbs were hoping to save! The achievement of such a reduction in journey time of approximately 95% in barely half a century can only be described as a revolution and, as it took place, there was little that any passenger liner designer could do realistically to reverse the decline in seaborne passenger traffic which was precipitated thereby.

When they had developed the various elements of their scheme to the stage when it represented a technically viable form of package, the Gibbs brothers approached Mr. P. A. S. Franklin, President of the International Mercantile Marine Company, in July 1916, and he, in turn, introduced them to Mr. J. Pierpont Morgan, Jr., the son of the famous shipping magnate. He, for his part, was so impressed by the plans he was shown, which appeared to fit the requirements of the American Line, that he offered immediate financial backing and had the Gibbs placed on the I.M.M. payroll.

At this point it should be remarked that the predicament of the United States Government was that it had lacked a positive maritime policy for many years, and in consequence American businessmen had never really been encouraged to invest in shipping of any nationality with any degree of confidence. However, the formation of the International Mercantile Marine combine in 1902 indicated a significant change in attitude, although the emphasis was still on investment in foreign flag fleets as subsidiaries. Nevertheless, one important unit of this great shipping organisation was the American Line, which was entirely American-owned and then in need of new ships, and it was undoubtedly for this company that J. Pierpont Morgan Jr. intended these two giant vessels. Indeed, it is safe to assume that this had also been the expectation of the Gibbs brothers from the outset. This conclusion is given the greater weight by contemporary artists' impressions which depicted the two ships in American Line colours — black hull, white superstructure and black funnels with a single, broad white band, and it was now proposed to name them the *Boston* and the *Baltimore,* which was consistent with the American Line's system of nomenclature.

In the meantime, the two architects established offices at 11, Broadway, N.Y., and then had their design tested thoroughly with models at the United States Experimental Model Basin which, situated in the Washington Navy Yard, had been constructed under the supervision of David W. Taylor (later Rear-Admiral D. W. Taylor) and, at the time of the Gibbs' model tests, in November 1916, he was the Basin's Director. *En passant,*

22. John Pierpont Morgan (Jr.)

23. While the American presence on the North Atlantic was noticeably absent, European companies were entering the lists with fine new liners. This is Hamburg Amerika's IMPERATOR.

when a new and larger model basin was commissioned at Camp Carderock, Maryland, in 1937, it was named in honour of Admiral Taylor in recognition of his pioneering work in the fields of naval engineering and experimental mechanics.

The results of the tests on the Gibbs' design for a 1,000-foot liner were passed to the United States Government, complete with an exhaustive statement on the economic justifications for the project. By this time, however, the attention of Congress was focussed closely on the situation in Europe, and all Government funds were being directed into defence channels or being held in reserve for the anticipated national emergency which arose the following year, in 1917.

In view of the revolutionary idea of 'electric-drive' engines included in the two vessels, the *Boston* and the *Baltimore,* as they were so briefly named, it is both interesting and significant that it was not until 1928 that the first turbo-electric liner of any size was completed, and that she was built for the Panama Pacific Line, which was a subsidiary of the American Line Steamship Corporation, demonstrating that the idea had taken root within the power-house of the I.M.M. The vessel concerned was the *California,* the lead ship of almost identical triplets. Of approximately 20,500 gross tons and with 600 feet overall length, the three vessels, of which the other two were the *Virginia* and the *Pennsylvania,* served on the New York to San Francisco route via the Panama Canal until 1937. Later, re-named *Uruguay, Brazil* and *Argentina,* they operated .on Moore McCormack Line's South American schedule, linking New York and the La Plata ports, becoming known popularly as the 'Good Neighbor trio'. All three were broken up in 1964. Their engines consisted of two oil-fired steam turbines generating power for two direct-drive electric motors, one for each screw shaft. Their top speed was 18½ knots at 17,000 s.h.p. Perhaps reflecting their pioneer work in this field of marine engineering on the *Boston* and *Baltimore,* the three sets of turbo-electric machinery were supplied by the General Electric Company.

Meanwhile, another giant liner design was created by the Gibbs brothers for the I.M.M., incorporating the latest trends in appearance and including other novel features. In comparison with the *Boston* and *Baltimore,* this new ship's tonnage would have been about 40,000, although the long rows of lifeboats indicated a vessel of considerable

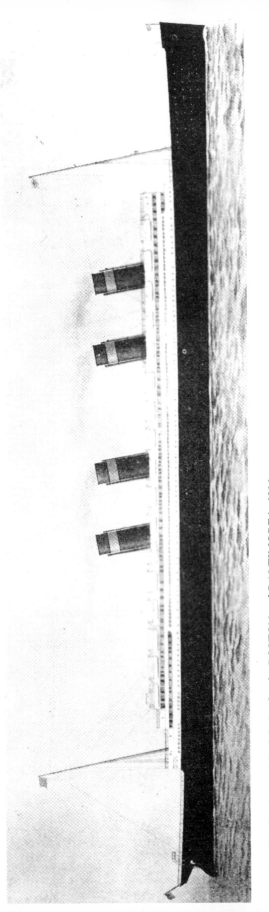

24. *The Gibbs brothers original design for the BOSTON and BALTIMORE in 1916 . . .*

25. *. . . and their revised design for a giant liner of approx. 40,000 tons for the International Mercantile Marine Company.*

length. She had three wide, capped funnels and a cruiser stern had been substituted for the conventional counter stern, while a slightly curved and raked bow complemented the liner's graceful sheer. Although this new design had many attractive and advanced features, no ships materialized from it.

When the War had ended and the next opportunity to present the original project occurred, the ships' design had been substantially re-modelled, putting an emphasis on military versatility. The space above the counter stern had been cleared and enlarged to carry and launch sea-planes for reconnaissance purposes. This was one of the ancillary features of the new design, but the most outstanding modification in this new concept was the complete reappraisal of the liner's fuel storage system and facilities. William Francis Gibbs had come to appreciate the potential of using large liners as commerce raiders during war-time from the German example but, realizing that fuel limitations had been their main disadvantage, he now gave his ships even more enormous volumes of fuel space. This made it necessary, in view of the additional tanks resulting from this exercise, to devise a new and carefully controlled ballasting procedure in order to maintain their stability in all conditions as the tanks were consumed. Simultaneously, it was also suggested that up to a total of four of these 1,000 foot liners should be built, and this pro-posal did indeed become part of the Shipping Board's Merchant Marine Plan of 1919 but, despite this support and the additional naval benefits in this modified design for the *Boston* and *Baltimore,* it was all too late. The post-war depression in the United States and the vast surplus of war-built emergency tonnage by then laid up in the United States Reserve Fleet now put any such scheme beyond realistic contemplation, and so these 1,000-foot super-liners were abandoned. Although his high hopes had been blighted, the basic principles of the giant liner concept remained in William Francis Gibbs' mind for the next thirty years, when he was finally given the opportunity to fulfil his dreams in the magnificent *United States*.

V THE *BRITANNIC* AND *HOMERIC*

While the Gibbs brothers had been persevering with their 1,000-foot passenger liner scheme, the outbreak of the First World War had come earlier in Great Britain, and with it had come the postponement of a number of liner projects. A number of these were, however, amended to be used in auxiliary capacities during the conflict. Some of the resulting vessels were to pass through it safely, earning fame and glory for their daring feats and gallant services. Others, less fortunate, were doomed to be 'sent to the bottom', either tragically or heroically as the case might be, and in consequence were prevented from ever operating in the peaceful role which they had originally been meant to fulfil. The *Britannic* was the first of twelve such vessels lost on active service in the two World Wars, and she was by far the largest British merchantman lost in the first of them.

Originally ordered for the White Star Line as the third ship to follow the *Titanic* and *Olympic,* the *Britannic* was laid down as yard No. 433 at Harland and Wolff's at Belfast in November 1911. The name *Gigantic* had been tentatively chosen for the new liner but, in the light of the *Titanic* disaster, it was abandoned. That calamity was, however, to have an even more profound effect on the *Britannic,* for construction of this third ship of the series had hardly begun when the *Titanic* collided with an ice-berg on her maiden passage and staggered the world with the terrible news of her death toll. Construction was halted immediately, and many additional safety measures were incorporated into her design following the Public Enquiry into the disaster. The *Britannic,* as she had now become, was given much increased watertight compartmentation, while she was also fitted with a double skin to her hull that extended up beyond her bilges.

The other alteration was in the provision for extra lifeboats. The *Britannic* was to be fitted with eight sets of a new form of girder crane davits which, it was said, would transfer their boats from one side of the ship to the other, as necessary. These would have enabled her to carry forty-eight boats, but even the five sets eventually fitted (together with other boats under conventional radial davits) looked grotesque and completely spoiled her appearance.

Many of the schemes described in this book never came about in any form, but others did reach fruition, and some even went into commission, if not for their designed purpose, namely: the carriage of passengers on a regular schedule. As to the former, no-one can state with certainty that they would have matched the claims made for them but, even if some of the entrepreneurs whom we shall encounter had little personal experience of nautical matters, it is undeniable that all of them employed very enlightened marine architects of sheer genius, and it would be presumptuous for anyone on a lesser plane to question their findings. However, in certain instances, as in the case of the *Britannic,* when vessels did see sea-service, certain of the claims made do give rise to doubts, and the matter of these girder davits is a clear case in point. Since the whole matter of lifeboats in passenger liners deserves comment, it may be well to quote first from various contemporary sources. A White Star brochure, for instance, stated:

'The vessel is equipped with the latest and most approved type of electrically-driven boat-lowering gear, by means of which a very large number of boats can, one after the other, be put over the side of the vessel and lowered in much less time than was possible under the old system of davits. . . . One of the advantages of the new system is that the passengers take their places in the boats expeditiously and with perfect safety before the boats are lifted from the deck of the vessel, and the gear is so constructed that the fully laden boats are lowered at a very considerable distance from the side of the ship, thus minimizing risk in bad weather. Moreover, the whole of the boats on board can be lowered on either side of the vessel which happens to be

26. *The BRITANNIC on the stocks just prior to her launch. At this time, the Harland and Wolff yard was plagued by countless myriads of starlings which roosted on the gantries at night. The mess from their droppings was not only extremely unsightly, but so slimy as to be actually dangerous to the squads of men working, so a gang was brought in early at about 5.30 a.m. each morning to wash it away with high-pressure hoses before the main labour force arrived. When work was suspended on the ship, she was soon in an indescribable state of filth. It might be supposed that the immense weight of bird droppings might have acted as an anti-corrosive sealant to the bare plates but, if such was the case, it was certainly not appreciated!*

clear, and the gear has been kept so far inboard as to give a wide passage at either side of the ship for promenading and for marshalling the passengers in the event of an emergency.'

42

The Harland and Wolff rigging plans show eight sets of gantry davits capable of handling six boats apiece. Provision was made to float twelve boats forward on the upper deck, twenty-four aft on the upper deck and twelve boats aft on the poop deck, making a total of forty-eight boats, some of which were motorized. The description 'gantry' davit may seem odd, but that is by the way. The *Marine Engineer and Naval Architect* of March 1914 carried quite a feature on the *Britannic's* boats and gear, much of which repeats the foregoing quotation, but it is worth recording part of it:

> '. . . *These boats, instead of extending right along the boat deck* are arranged in four separate groups with abundant space for marshalling passengers etc. The system of davits used differs from that in any other preceding ship. There are two davits on each side of the deck where the boats are placed. These do not slew, the space apart being sufficient to pass the boats through. They are of lattice girder construction with a swan-necked top turned towards each other in each pair. They more resemble sheer legs in their action than davits or cranes, being pivoted at their base and moving from a vertical position to a considerable angle inboard or to a considerable angle outboard. Indeed, the angle is so great that* **the davits command one half of the deck of the ship** *while, when outboard, they would enable the boats to be lowered vertically into the sea even if the vessel has considerably heeled over. The arrangement is such, too, that the* **boats may be traversed across the deck so that all of the boats may be lowered on the one side of the ship** *at the will of the captain. The davits are inclined inboard or outboard by means of powerful screw gear. The height and outreach of the davits enables the boats to be mounted one over the other in tiers and to facilitate the placing of several tiers in the width of the ship . . . limit switches are provided so that in the event of any accident, or any temporary aberration on the part of a man manipulating the gear, the motion of the davits, or both, will be arrested before damage can take place, thus making the gear practically mistake-proof. Another feature is the arrangement by which boats can be lowered on an even keel*

*As previously stated, this proportion was modified in the event.

27. With their boats slung conventionally, the BRITANNIC's sisters lie in Belfast – the ill-starred TITANIC (left) and the OLYMPIC which, the first of the trio, survived until 1935, although she experienced three collisions during her career.

28. Seen in hospital ship colours, the BRITANNIC's gantry davits may be observed.

> *even in the event of the ship being down by the head or the stern. A further advantage of this davit, which is made by the builders of this vessel, is the fact that the boats can be all open lifeboats of good type, thus dispensing with the troublesome collapsible type.'*

The bold fount is ours. First, if the *'davits command one half of the deck of the ship',* how, one asks, can they extend to lower boats on the opposite side? Even if they could do so, they must immediately foul the set on that side of the vessel. Thus, although the above descriptions may have seemed heartening after the *Titanic* débâcle, it is difficult to take very seriously the claim that all the boats could be lowered from one side of the ship. Indeed, although the *Britannic* was the first ship to be so fitted, others followed her and, if no photographs seem to exist showing close views of her boats, there are such pictures of other vessels, and it is abundantly clear that this claim was utterly impossible.

Nevertheless, their appearance apart, they were a tremendous improvement on the old form of radial davit with its falls consisting of three-fold purchases, since these were often difficult to handle, and in all those cases − all too common in certain companies (notably the C.G.T.) − where two boats were served by one set of radial davits, it was virtually impossible to overhaul the falls after the first boat had been launched even in ideal conditions, let alone in an emergency. If we accept the fact that the notion that all boats could be lowered on either side of the ship was impossible, the fact is that these girder davits represented a tremendous advance because, even when the later Welin davits, and later the vastly improved Welin-McClachlan type, became standard, there was still the often insuperable difficulty of launching a boat sufficiently clear of the ship's hull − especially on the high side if she was listing − and, in any sort of sea, from getting away from the weather side at all.

Ships' lifeboats were never handy in any sense of the word. They would not sail well and, when fully loaded, were the very Devil to row, whilst in any sort of poor or bad weather this was well-nigh impossible. Moreover, of the vast crews of big passenger liners, few men were seamen in any sense of the word, but composed of catering staff, firemen, trimmers, greasers or the like. In principle there were two Able Seamen or better (bos'n's mates etc.) to a boat: the one to lower and one as cox'n. In a ship with radial davits, the number was generally three, since two men were required to lower away. Yet, as sail gave way to steam; as the transitional sail-steam vessels passed to those which were fully powered from the late 1880s onwards, and as the years rolled by, a quite different class of seamen became born, who had less sea-sense or understanding of the very run of the sea. As a steamboat-man, albeit through no fault of his own, he was far less able to cope with emergencies, and he had none of that experience of boatwork which had been so much part and parcel of life in sail.

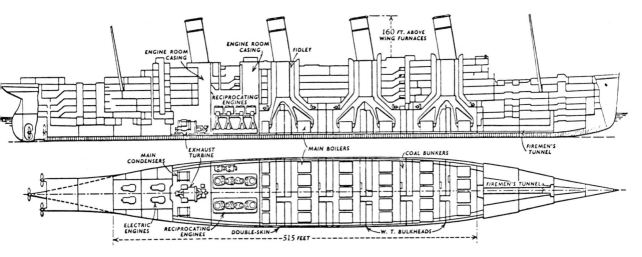

29. *The BRITANNIC's engine arrangement, showing combination reciprocating and turbine machinery.*

Many of the great passenger liners were in even worse case, since they tended, in the case of the British, to use Southampton as a terminal base, and the port became very much passenger ship-orientated, with the result that the majority of its seamen knew little of other types of vessels. For slightly different reasons, the same situation obtained in the big liners of other nations, and the passenger ship seaman tended to become a class of his own. Nor were such vessels popular with the run-of-the-mill merchant seamen, who preferred their dungarees, whether clean or dirty, to running about the decks in what they termed 'sailor suits', engaged in cleaning jobs which they tended to despise. At the same time they tended to look down on the so-called A.B.s in these prestigious vessels who, commonly enough, were unable to steer, to box the compass, to rig a stage or to perform so many of the common-or-garden duties expected of a seaman, and this was a reason why they were not generally welcomed aboard normal cargo vessels.

Thus, however good the equipment *might* have been, there must exist an over-riding doubt whether the men would have been capable of putting it to good use in emergency. Indeed, those who were in convoys hounded by wolf-pack submarine attack in the last war are under no illusions about the numerous occasions when men were lost due to the sheer ineptitude of boat-handling in one form or another by the modern steamship seamen who, as often as not, had not the slightest idea what to do, nor how to do it, despite his Lifeboat Efficiency ticket gained in the peace of a sheltered dock. It is a sad but indisputable comment. Lifeboat Certificates meant nothing when the operation was transferred from a placid dock to a stricken ship in a running seaway, and there is little doubt that, for all the thought and for all the regulations which have gone into lifeboats and all that pertains to them, their actual use in a large passenger liner, in which there might well be panicking passengers, was a spectre which haunted all who were immediately concerned with operating them: a spectre which became the bleaker with each decade that passed.

If we have diverted ourselves onto this subject of ships' lifeboats, we have done so because, in its wider context, it has a certain relevance to our theme. Enormous technical advances have been made in ships themselves, but men have not so advanced and, so far as practical seamanship is concerned – and even matters of discipline itself – there has been rather more of regress than of progress in those skills required in times of emergency. This is no criticism, since it is all part of the developments of the twentieth century, and it is not a question of attaching blame. However, it is pointed out elsewhere in this book that, when considering ships which never came into existence, one can but speculate on their careers had they actually come into being. Some would undoubtedly have become household names, on account of their very splendour and performances, but, by the law of averages – and an actuary could determine that average – a proportion of vessels meet with disaster.

The more people who are involved, the greater is the potential tragedy and, in the final analysis, when this sort of situation arises, it is not the ship, but her men, who will call the tune. Indeed, these very situations can be brought about by the failure of human judgement: by bad seamanship; by miscalculation, or by a variety of similar reasons. Although we shall not divert ourselves into the matter of great disasters, any reader will recall how the *Titanic* was steamed at full speed into a known ice-field: he may know that the pre-war *Empress of Britain,* in order to maintain her mail contract, steamed at excessive speed through fog and ice-bergs, and

30. When the *TITANIC* (above) was sunk, many instances of great heroism were recorded. Equally, many of her boats which got away could have held far more people and those in them could have made efforts to save others. Statutory regulations will never succeed in legislating for the unpredictability of human behaviour in emergencies.

even did so when beating her own record for the Northern crossing whilst the *Queen Mary* was capturing the Blue Riband on the New York route. How long she would have borne so charmed a life had the war not come to seal her fate by other means is anybody's guess, but he may consider the incidence of the human element in a variety of well-known and authenticated disasters.

Human behaviour, or human fallibility, is the one factor beyond the competence of entrepreneurs and naval architects alike, and is thus the one seldom taken into account. It can be demonstrated neither on a design plan nor in a financial forecast.

Bigger than both the *Olympic* and *Titanic,* the *Britannic* measured 48,160 gross tons on completion, and her overall length was 903 feet.* In common with the earlier pair, her engine installation consisted of a combination of steam reciprocating machinery which exhausted through a low pressure turbine driving a third, central propeller, which gave her a speed of 22 knots.

As a matter of comparison, it may be worth recording the passenger capacity of the *Britannic* and her earlier sisters. The *Britannic's* figures were 790 first class, 830 second class and 950 third class with a crew of 950. Against this, the *Olympic* could carry 1,054 first class, 510 second class, 1,020 third class and 860 crew, while the *Titanic* accommodated 905 first class, 565 second class and 1,134 third class with a crew of 900.

The *Britannic* was launched on 26 February 1914 but, before she could be completed, the world was plunged into war and, like so many other ships, she was then set aside until the termination of hostilities. However, in November 1915, with the withdrawal of allied troops from the Dardanelles, she was requisitioned for use as a hospital ship. The Dardanelles campaign had been opened up in April 1915 with the invasion of the Gallipoli Peninsula by Great Britain and France, the object being to force a supply route through to Russia via the Bosphorus and the Black Sea. At the same time, the Allies hoped to gain the allegiance of the Balkan States along the way. The operation turned out to be a costly blunder because not only was there a complete failure to achieve the prime objective, but Bulgaria actually joined the enemy. Indeed, it was Bulgaria's aggression against Serbia and Montenegro (now part of Yugo-Slavia) that precipitated the collapse at the Gallipoli offensive. When these small Balkan

*275.23 metres.

31. A magnificent model of the BRITANNIC, showing her gantry davit arrangement very clearly. Alongside her is a model of the White Star liner BRITANNIC of 1874 which was a famous ship in her day, breaking the Atlantic record with an average speed of 15.25 knots. She was of 5,004 gross tons.

countries were overrun in the Autumn of 1915, it became necessary to release French and Italian warships covering the landings in order to render assistance in the evacuation of Serbian and Montenegrin troops to Corfu. In consequence of this, there was no alternative to the withdrawal from Gallipoli.

The *Britannic* was ready for her first voyage by 23 December 1915 and then made five round voyages between Naples or Mudros (on the island of Lemnos) and Southampton, evacuating wounded soldiers from the battle zone. Lemnos, which lies about 50 miles west of the Dardanelles between Greece and Turkey, had been established as the Allied headquarters for the Gallipoli campaign.

Leaving Southampton on her final voyage on 12 November 1916, the *Britannic's* eventual destination was scheduled to be Salonika (Thessaloniki), where she was to embark more casualties. She called at Naples *en route* to re-bunker, arriving there on the 17th and remaining for the next two days as she was delayed by a severe storm. On 21 November, at about 08.00 hours, when nearing the end of the voyage outwards, she struck a mine off Port St. Nikolo, the principle port of the small island of Kea which is situated south-east of the Gulf of Athens, in the Aegean Sea. At first there was some dispute about whether it was a mine or whether she had in fact been torpedoed. However, in spite of the unrestricted submarine warfare by then practiced by the Germans, it was considered to be unlikely that she had been torpedoed. The vessel was painted quite clearly in the Internationally-accepted hospital ship colour scheme – white with a green band interspersed with large red crosses – and the probable cause of her loss was indicated later by Lieutenant-Commander Siess of the submarine *U73,* who stated that his vessel had laid mines in the Kea Channel, through which the *Britannic* had been passing, only one hour before the fateful explosion occurred. As if to confirm this, the *Braemar Castle,* another hospital ship, also struck a mine in the same area two days later and was only saved from sinking by being beached. The *Britannic,* so it seemed, had almost certainly struck a mine.

During 1976, Jacques Cousteau and his team located the *Britannic's* wreck in an attempt to establish once and for all the true cause of the liner's loss. The resultant film investigation was released for television viewing under the title *CALYPSO's search for the BRITANNIC.*

32. *A splendour which never came into being – an artist's impression of the BRITANNIC's first-class main stair-case . . .*

33.

34. . . . and her first-class smoking room (above) and the dining saloon.

Although it shed very little light on the actual cause of the sinking, it is nevertheless an exciting and informative documentary, highlighted by the eerie underwater views of the great ship's hull, vague and indistinct due to the depth and the poor light. Amazingly, much upholstery and furnishing remains to be seen, albeit decomposed by the effects of salt water and ready to disintegrate at the slightest touch.

There is an account from William H. Tantum IV, an American who was well known in the United States for the interest he engendered in passenger liners and for his involvement in schemes for the recovery of data from quite important wrecks of some of them. He went down to the wreck in the small, highly-manoeuvrable saucer-like submarine from the *Calypso*. On the whole, it is rather long and repetitive, but the fact of the matter is that a wreck which has lain on the bottom of the sea for some sixty years has neither the glamour of the original vessel, nor the interest of some ancient craft which may yield unsuspected secrets to archaeologists. Essentially, he reports steel, totally encrusted with barnacles and crustaceans, wherever they looked, but the following are a few extracts from his account:

'... we landed the submarine right on the side of the ship ... this small saucer submarine ... in diameter maybe 16 or 18 feet* ... this little thing ... its like taking an aspirin tablet and putting it against an Entex† model on the side of the hull. There I was on the side of the BRITANNIC, right near a porthole. Incidentally, all the glass in those portholes was completely gone ... the hull in that area was completely encrusted with barnacles and sea life and all kinds of growth ... I'd say two or three inches ... of growth. We ... proceeded around the stern. You can see her two propellers – her port side and centre propeller very well. Her starboard propeller is really down into the mud, into the sand, very deeply. The seabed is very smooth. It doesn't have as much as Atlantic sealife. Again ... everything is covered with barnacles and crustaceans. Some of them have colour, some of them are black or brown.'

'... we proceeded right along the main deck railing right past the first set of lifeboat davits – the large special lifeboat davits which she has – you could see them turned out. Some of them

*4.88/5.49 metres.

†A brand of model kit.

*still have the cable and gear hanging from them, others don't.
. . . As we proceeded along the promenade* (sic) *deck in that
area, we came to some more lifeboat davits, all of them turned
out and a great deal of crustacean on those. . . . some of the deck
area looks like it was put on yesterday, it's so smooth. Others are
rotting or breaking away, full of barnacles. . . . all of the doors
are actually rotted away or they have fallen into the hull or have
gone down to the seabed. There are no funnels up on this ship.
. . . the wooden sections of the bridge – the outer sections – are
all rotted away. . . . I saw quite a few Greek fishing nets from
fishing boats all over the hull, but nothing like the nets that are
spread all over the ANDREA DORIA.*

*From the No. 2 to the No. 3 bulkhead, right straight up to the
deck, she is opened up* (as if with) *a can opener. All her ribs*
(frames) *and sections of her keel are blown completely away –
they are not even there! The ribs* (sic) *that are there are bent and
blown out. It looks to me like either a mine or a torpedo hit her
in the reserve coal locker* (sic) *which . . . this voyage . . . they had
been using coal from Naples – and, as you know, coal dust is
one of the greatest explosives in the world – just blew her all the
way through. She's blown completely through, right from starboard to port, port to starboard! The only thing holding the
bow to the rest of the ship is the deck and some deck plates. Incidentally the bow is bent – it is not like the rest of the hull,
straight and laying on its side. It is bent at an 85° angle the other
way. In other words, when she first touched bottom with her
bow, it twisted and . . . as the survivors and witnesses stated,
that she first went* (listed) *to port, then . . . to starboard and then
. . . to port again and rolled over. The water rushed into the
funnels and the funnels broke off simultaneously and she went
down on that angle on her starboard side. So actually her bow
was already twisting in the seabed at this point and just holding
from the amount of metal of the deck area left.'*

'*We're down 330 feet to the side of the ship and it's about 360
to 370 feet to the seabed . . . the reason that you see very little
glass at this depth is because of the way she went down and the*

pressure immediately breaks the glass . . . even the closed port-holes. The glass, thick as it is, is smashed away . . . it's gone.'

'We proceeded again along the seabed. You see a lot of stern wreckage such as metal cots, rusting away. Again, no wood can be seen . . . some pieces of machinery can be seen as you move up, laying there . . . about 180 metres behind the BRITANNIC we found the third funnel flat − flat again, just completely laid out like the fourth funnel. . . .'

There is more in the same vein. It reads as though the author was giving a running commentary, which is precisely what he was doing − on tape, and one has the feeling that it represents the impressions of an interested observer rather than those of a seaman. The account may raise one or two queries in the mind of the reader, but we reproduce the foregoing excerpts without comment. Obviously, the authors have not had the opportunity of viewing the wreck in this manner.

In fact, the *Britannic* went down very quickly, sinking within an hour, and there were a number of relevant factors contributing to this. Captain Bartlett made an abortive attempt to beach his ship on the nearby coast, but it cannot be said with any certainty that the rapid forward motion of the vessel at this time caused the breakdown of any bulkheads which had not been damaged by the explosion. Certainly it was the only course open to him, failing the possibility of being towed in stern first − and even the advantage of this might be open to question. Perhaps the most salient feature of the events subsequent to the initial explosion was the failure of the forward watertight doors to operate, with the result that water was permitted to flood in unimpeded from between compartments 2 and 3 on the starboard side where the explosion had taken place and, before long, five compartments were flooded and the giant hospital ship was severely down by the head. Then, with a fast increasing list, the *Britannic* heeled over to starboard and sank. Like the *Titanic,* her stern disappeared below the surface last.

Of the 1,125 medical staff, R.A.M.C.* personnel and crew on board, 21 lost their lives and another 28 were injured. Most of the deaths occurred when two life-boats were smashed by the *Britannic's* still revolving propellers which had risen clear of the water as the ship's head had sunk deeper and deeper. The survivors were picked up by the cruiser

*Royal Army Medical Corps.

H.M.S. Heroic and the destroyers H.M. ships *Foxhound* and *Scourge*. Amongst those saved were two very remarkable individuals, a nurse named Mrs. Violet Jessop and a 29 year old fireman, John Priest. Four years earlier, both had survived the *Titanic* disaster, Mrs. Jessop in the capacity of stewardess, and with this second terrifying experience they were to be the sole witnesses of the tragic demise of two of the White Star Line's giant ships. Mr. Priest later came to be known as 'the man who couldn't be drowned', due to his numerous escapes from sinking and damaged ships. He had been aboard the *Olympic,* the *Britannic's* younger sister, when she had collided with the cruiser *H.M.S. Hawke* in the Solent on 20 September 1911 and, in February 1916, he experienced his second sinking when he was among the survivors of the former Royal Mail liner *Alcantara* which was lost in her duel with the German surface raider *Greif* in the South Atlantic. In spite of shrapnel injuries, he was able to join the *Britannic* for her last three voyages and, after surviving her loss, he was back at sea again in 1917, only to be rescued in April of that year from the British freighter *Donegal* after she had been torpedoed.

The loss of the *Britannic* was a tragic one, the more particularly since, as a hospital ship, she struck a mine and was not, by any stretch of imagination, a specific target of the enemy, and she was typical of so many fine resources wasted by the exigencies of war. She had been meant to enter the White Star's Southampton to New York service in the spring of 1915 but, as things transpired, she lasted less than a year as a hospital ship. Her furnishings and decorations which had never been installed were auctioned off on 4 July 1919. Although she has a number of claims to fame, not least of them being the mystery precisely surrounding her loss, the *Britannic* will also be remembered as the largest four-funnelled liner ever built, while her triple expansion steam reciprocating engines were the largest of their kind ever to be fitted in a ship.

Concurrent with the construction and brief career of the *Britannic,* another large liner was forecast for the White Star Line. Listed as a forthcoming new building in the Company's 1913 list of new tonnage, and already bearing the name *Germanic,* she was intended to be a replacement for the recently lost *Titanic.* Measuring 33,600 gross tons, the *Germanic* was also to be built by Harland and Wolff at Belfast, the traditional shipyard for White Star vessels.

35. The HOMERIC, built as the Norddeutscher Lloyd COLUMBUS.

Following the outbreak of war, the projected vessel's name was changed prudently to *Homeric* but, by the time of the Armistice, no progress had been made on the new liner. In 1921 the proposed vessel was abandoned in favour of captured or seized German tonnage.

At that time the *Columbus* was being completed at the Danzig (Gdansk) shipyard of F. Schichau, and was handed over to Great Britain under the War Reparations scheme and, on completion, she was passed over to the British Shipping Controller for disposal. The White Star Line acquired her, giving her the name of the cancelled vessel, and she entered service on 15 February 1922, sailing on her maiden voyage from Southampton to New York. Meanwhile the *Columbus'* former sister, the *Hindenburg,* one of the few half-built German ships not commandeered by the Allies, was completed for the Norddeutscher Lloyd, eventually sailing on her maiden voyage in 1924 under the name *Columbus,* the two ships rivalling one another to some extent.

So the *Homeric* project was replaced by an ex-German liner bearing the same name, but this simple statement of fact has been questioned, quite inexplicably, with suggestions that the original *Homeric* was either abandoned much earlier than 1921, or was instead completed as either the *Justicia* or the Red Star Liner *Belgenland,* two other passenger vessels

36. The Norddeutscher Lloyd COLUMBUS, completed in 1923, was laid down as the HINDEN-BURG, a sister to the vessel lost to the White Star Line. (Pl.29)

also building at Harland and Wolff's at that time. It has also been hinted that the *Homeric* may have become the Holland America Line's replacement *Statendam*. Certainly all four ships were of similar size, but construction of the *Homeric* as either the *Justicia* or *Belgenland* can be completely discounted. Articles in Liverpool newspapers, commemorating the White Star Line's Golden Jubilee, still announced the *Homeric* as a forthcoming new construction two years *after* the appearance of these two vessels.

So far as her becoming the *Statendam* is concerned, this cannot really be confirmed or denied, as Harland and Wolff did not introduce their 'History File' into their design offices until the late 1920s. This was an organ which would have established conclusively the *Statendam's* origin, because it contained a brief précis on each enquiry received by the shipyard, together with its subsequent outcome. The *Statendam* was, indeed, a particularly long time under construction, since her entry into service did not occur until more than ten years had passed since she was officially ordered on 29 January 1919, but there are a number of quite plausible explanations for this, principally the severe shortage of materials after the First World War. Besides this, her construction did not commence until after the *Homeric* had disappeared from the White Star's list of

37. *The Holland America's STATENDAM, as finally completed, was very much the same size as the COLUMBUS, but very different in appearance.*

forthcoming new ships. All things considered, it is most unlikely that the *Homeric* became the *Statendam,* bearing in mind the individual requirements of each shipowner in the design of new tonnage. As has been concluded previously by Roy Anderson in his book *White Star Line,* the only feasible explanation for the termination of the *Homeric* project is that the liner's design was hardly started at the beginning of World War I, and, at the end of it, was not developed further until the White Star had decided between a new ship and one of the sequestrated German vessels. Once a satisfactory replacement had been found, the *Homeric* was cancelled.

Whilst it does seem to be most unlikely that the *Homeric* became the *Statendam* or any other vessel, it must be admitted that there does remain a shred of doubt, if only because so many theories have been put forward. In normal circumstances, it would be highly unethical for builders to pass the plans, or even the basis for plans, commissioned by one company to another, but in these conditions, when all the companies concerned were under the umbrella of the I.M.M. as holding company, this argument would not have obtained, whilst arrangements made in war-time are never so easy to unravel as those in peace-time. Thus, whilst the possibility cannot be wholly dismissed, the authors feel that the likelihood is extremely remote.

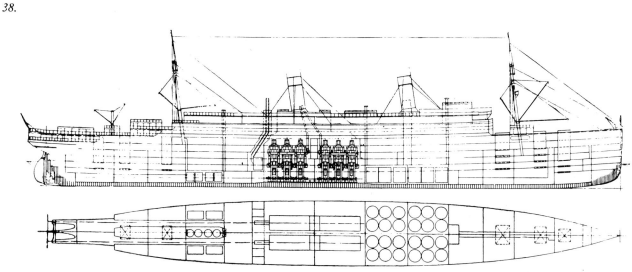

38.

39. *A pipe-dream which never even became a project. Two alternative proposals for a diesel-driven trans-Atlantic passenger lin*
   designed by Professor Ing. Giorgio Supino, the Italian engineer, about 1915. It was envisaged that the ship should be of 36,000 ton
   with a length of 750 feet and a speed of 21 knots with two Junkers engines (vertical in the top drawing and horizontal in the lower
   each having six double cylinders (cylinder diameter 820mm = 32.2 inches: stroke 2 × 820mm. = 32.2 inches), totalling 30,000 b.h.
   at 110 revs. per minute.

VI THE *JUSTICIA*

Yet another vessel which suffered a similar fate to the *Britannic* was building at Harland and Wolff's at the outbreak of the 1914 War. Given yard Number 436, this was to become the British troop-ship *Justicia*. Originally ordered as the *Statendam* for the Holland America Line in 1912, she was launched on 9 July 1914 but, after the war had started, work on her proceeded at a much slower pace. Then, following negotiations with her Dutch owners, she was requisitioned when almost complete for conversion to a troop-ship.

On 7 April 1917 she was handed over to the White Star Line who managed her for the British Government under the name *Justicia*. The original intention had been to award her to the Cunard Line to replace the lost *Lusitania,* and it was for this reason that she was given a name ending in *ia* instead of in *ic*. Cunard's initial choice of name had been *Neuretania* before they settled for the more topical — and possibly more comprehensible — *Justicia,* * but all this proved to be of little consequence because, in the event, Cunard did not have the officers and men with which to man her anyway. The *Justicia* was therefore re-allocated to the White Star Line, who had spare men from the lost *Britannic,* for them to manage for the duration of the war. It is uncertain whether the ship would have been returned to the Cunard Line after the war or transferred back to the Holland America Line who had ordered her in the first place.

Her gross tonnage was 32,235 and her overall length 776 feet.† In passenger service the *Justicia* would have carried 3,430 passengers in three classes: 800 first class, 600 second class and 2,030 third class, whilst the crew would have numbered 600. Although the Holland America

*Intended to replace the *Lusitania,* the word was to carry the connotation of 'Justice'.
†236.52 metres.

40. Seen from the ARLANZA, the JUSTICIA painted war-time grey, and . . .

Line's projected flagship was of modest proportions compared with the ships then being built or contemplated for the Hamburg Amerika, White Star and Cunard Lines, this was certainly not the case with regard to her public rooms and standards of internal décor. Indeed, it is widely held that, had the *Statendam* been completed for the express mail service as scheduled, the quality and spaciousness of her interiors would have far exceeded that of any of her contemporaries. For instance, she would have boasted a first class social hall over 20 feet high,* which would have been amongst the tallest of the day. Both her first class dining saloon, which would have been capable of seating 563 at one sitting, and the huge palm court, were designed with the kind of creative freedom more akin to the unfettered artistic expression of the 1920s.

Like all Harland and Wolff liners of the period, she was a triple screw vessel fitted with combination machinery. In the *Justicia's* installation the outer shafts were driven by four-cylinder triple expansion engines, and these exhausted into a large direct acting low pressure turbine which drove the centre screw, the maximum indicated horse-power (i.h.p.) being 22,000. Steam was supplied by twelve boilers, and her designed speed was 18 knots. The aftermost funnel was a dummy.

The *Justicia* commenced her first trooping voyage in April 1917 and, initially, she was painted all grey but later, some time in early 1918, she

*6.1 metres.

41. . . . here in dazzle-painted camouflage.

was given a dazzle-painted scheme. This camouflage idea had been contrived during October 1917 by an Admiralty working group under the leadership of Norman Wilkinson, the marine artist, and its application was soon widespread. Unlike later camouflage paint schemes, particularly those used during World War II, the principle of dazzle painting was not necessarily to conceal the ship against her background. Instead the aim was often to break up her silhouette by contrasting areas of light and dark paints, making it difficult to identify ships and, more particularly, their sizes and the direction in which they were heading, especially in poor visibility and, in general terms, to falsify perspective.* The *Justicia's* dazzle paint consisted of patches of black, blue and light grey and was intended to disguise her as a single-funnelled freighter.

It does not seem to be recorded how many trooping voyages she made, but she did not survive for very long. Her first brush with the enemy was on 23 January 1918 when she was attacked unsuccessfully by U-boats in the Irish Channel. The beginning of her end came on Friday morning, 19 July 1918, for, when she was twenty miles off the Skerryvore Rock in the Inner Hebrides, in a convoy bound from Liverpool to New York, she was attacked by the submarine UB64 and torpedoed in the engine room. Other torpedo attacks failed to sink her and, later in the same day, she was taken in tow for Lough Swilly on the north-west coast of Ireland.

*When viewed in retrospect, dazzle-painting did not seem to have had the desired effects although, notwithstanding, French merchantmen continued the practice in the Second World War.

Early the following day the attack was resumed, again unsuccessfully, by U54. However, a further strike by this submarine at about 09.00 hours proved to be decisive. With two fatal hits in her port side, she sank by the stern and finally disappeared below the surface at 12.40 hours.

The *Justicia* had no passengers or troops aboard at the time of the attack, but she was carrying a crew of between six and seven hundred men. Of these, fifteen engine room ratings and a 3rd Engineer Officer were killed when the first torpedo exploded in her engine room. The survivors were transferred to the escorting ships and, of these, the destroyers H.M. ships *Marne, Millbrook* and *Pigeon* succeeded in sinking a third submarine — the UB124 — which had not actually taken part in the attack and, under Lt. Wutsdorf, had developed so many leaks from the depth charges exploded around her that she had made a fruitless attempt to escape by diving right under the stricken liner.

The *Justicia* had taken a good deal of punishment and was quite a long time a-sinking. There is evidence to show that she was amongst the first vessels to be provided with protective net-defence, which was first introduced in that year, and it also seems that she had been attacked on previous occasions without success. Moreover, it is of interest to note that a contemporary newspaper* reported that the *Justicia's* gunners exploded four out of the ten torpedoes fired at their vessel by gunfire, which was no mean feat.

For their part, the Germans were said to be particularly jubilant over the sinking of the *Justicia,* having mistaken her for the ex-*Vaterland,* their wonder ship 'stolen' from them by the Americans. This vessel, which had been interned in New York for over two years, had been seized along with many other German ships on 4 April 1917. They felt that their actions, although preventing them from ever regaining possession of the monster vessel, would also effectively deny the Americans the use of her but, in the event, the *Vaterland* was to continue operating long after the war as the *Leviathan* and, indeed, carried American troops to fight the armies of Imperial Germany during the last months of the conflict.

As for the sunk ex-*Statendam,* hers was a great loss, for she was a fine-looking ship and would undoubtedly have been a profitable and popular liner had she been able to fulfil her destiny. Her owners were compensated for her loss with 60,000 tons of steel, from which a fleet of modern

*The Daily Mirror, 25 July 1918.

42. The VATERLAND was in New York when war broke out and was taken over by the United States when they entered the hostilities. It was this vessel, now re-named LEVIATHAN, that the Germans thought they had sunk when they torpedoed the JUSTICIA, thereby denying her to the Americans.

43. The LEVIATHAN (ex-VATERLAND) in dazzle-paint. It is interesting to compare this picture with the three preceding plates in the light of the German error in identification.

freighters was constructed, while a new and more fortunate *Statendam* was ordered to replace the original liner from the same builders in 1921. She was launched in 1924 at about the time that the United States promulgated laws restricting immigration into their country, and this had the effect of work on the new liner being suspended temporarily. When it resumed, Harland and Wolff were so plagued with strikes in their yard that the ship was towed over to the Wilton-Fijenoord shipyard at Schiedam, and was completed there, being the largest vessel it had ever handled, and was finally finished in March 1929.

44. A beautiful builder's model of the original STATENDAM, completed as the JUSTICIA.

VII THE *FRANCESCO CARACCIOLO* AND THE EBB AND FLOW OF GRANDIOSE SCHEMES

The next passenger liner over which the curtains of the maritime stage never rose was quite an unusual vessel in many ways. Conceived as a warship and intended on completion to be 'bristling with guns' and the many other devices of sea warfare, she was sold incomplete for mercantile employment following World War I in the event. Her discarded naval hull, expensively armoured and compartmented to naval specifications, was redesigned, perhaps with insufficient consideration of the cost factors involved, to be furnished with passenger accommodation and cargo holds. Had she been completed, she would certainly have been one of the safest merchantmen that ever to put to sea!

The *Francesco Caracciolo,* as she was named, was laid down at the Castellamare Dockyard (now part of the huge Italcantieri S.p.A. Shipbuilding combine) in October 1914 as the first of four super-dreadnought battleships for the Italian Navy.

Originally to have been christened the *Dandolo,* after the famous Doge of Venice, the name *Francesco Caracciolo* honoured the Neapolitan commodore (1732–99) who had served with such distinction in the British fleet but who, after joining the French Jacobin revolution against Naples, was court-martialled aboard Nelson's flagship by his own countrymen and hanged within the hour from the fore yardarm of the Sicilian frigate *La Minèrva*. The other ships of the *Caracciolo* class were the *Cristoforo Colombo* (ex-*Goffredo Mameli), Marcantonio Colonna* (ex-*Giuseppe Mazzini)* and *Francesco Morosini,* ordered from Ansaldo at Genoa and Odero, and Orlando at Leghorn respectively.

The four battleships were intended to have a full load displacement of 34,000 tons on an overall length of 691 feet.* They would have carried eight 15-inch guns (scaled down from the original intention of twelve) as their main armament and, with propulsion by steam turbines, they would have had a maximum speed of 25 knots. Engineer-General Ferrati was responsible for their design.

As a result of sudden alterations to Italian naval construction plans in early 1916, work on the four ships was suspended and the three latter vessels were cancelled and dismantled to provide materials for more urgently needed light craft. The construction of the *Francesco Caracciolo* was resumed in October 1919, but to a very much modified design as a high-speed battle-cruiser, which entailed her shaft horse-power being raised from 70,000 to 105,000, giving her 3 knots additional speed. Eventually, she was launched on 12 May 1920 and towed to La Spezia. Once again, work was halted on her while consideration was given to yet more plans to complete her as an aircraft carrier but, just five months later, on 25 October, her incomplete hull was sold to the Navigazione Generale Italiana Company (N.G.I.) for six million lire for conversion to a merchant ship.

Her new owners planned to reconstruct her extensively into a 25,300 gross ton, high-speed cargo-passenger liner, and this design work was also entrusted to Ferrati. The *Francesco Caracciolo* would have been a modest passenger vessel compared with many foreign liners then planned or already in commission, but for Italy, which at that time possessed no passenger liners in excess of 15,000 tons, she would have represented a considerable achievement. With twin turbines producing 20,000 horse-power, she would have had a speed of 18 knots. Presumably these would have been new or de-rated turbines on account of the vessel becoming a merchant ship. In November 1920 the hull of the *Francesco Caracciolo* was towed to Baia, near Naples, for work to begin, but early in 1921 the conversion was abandoned as being too uneconomical and the incomplete hull, already the basis of four quite different vessels, was scrapped the same year. In her place, the N.G.I. took delivery of the *Giulio Cesare* and

*210.62 metres.

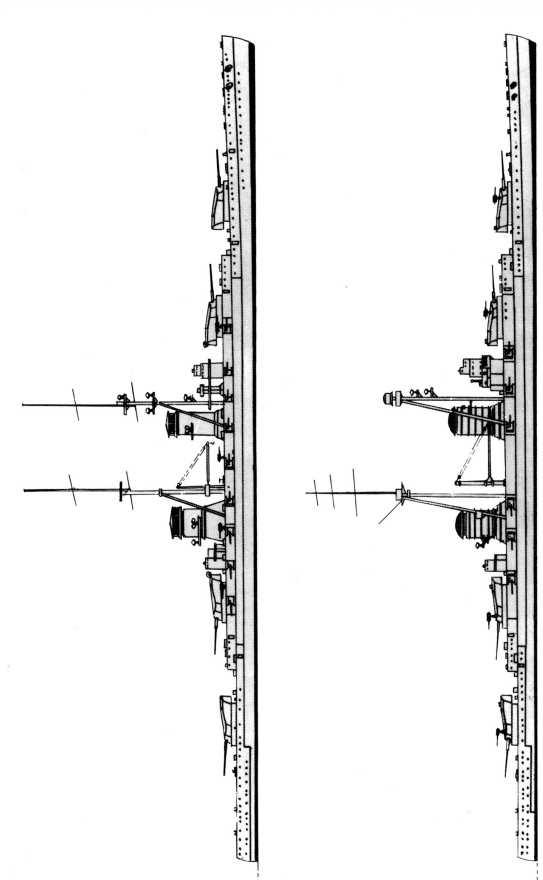

46. *The original design for the battleship FRANCESCO CARACCIOLO (top), and the modified design in 1919 (bottom) represented strange conceptions from which a large passenger ship project should emerge.*

47. The launch of the FRANCESCO CARACCIOLO – with quite an exceptional number of people aboard.

the slightly larger *Duilio*. The *Francesco Caracciolo* was the first of several projected liners whose construction proceeded some way before it was finally abandoned, and they were all discarded for one reason or another.

For the next eight years the realms of visionary new liner schemes lay in the doldrums, a state of affairs which was symptomatic of the times. There had been the large liner *Homeric* on order for the White Star Line, whose design work was apparently never completed and whose place had been filled by the confiscated German vessel *Columbus*. In a sense, this single incident summed up the whole indolent passenger shipping scene of the early 1920s with regard to large liners. The only new ones entering service were ships of pre-war design which had been laid up in a semi-completed state during the period of hostilities. Of these, the largest were in what is described loosely as the 'intermediate size range', being between 25,000 and 35,000 gross tons, and included, apart from the aborted *Homeric,* the French Line's *Paris* and the Red Star Line's *Belgenland,* both commenced in 1913, and the Norddeutscher Lloyd's *Columbus,* ex-*Hindenburg,* which was laid down in 1914. The slump in new building was especially reflected in the monster — so-called — 'liners of state', and there were a number of quite valid reasons for this. The general opinion then held in shipping circles was that the era of construction of truly massive passenger liners had passed with the Great War. This was in part due to a feeling that the rapid pre-war growth of passenger ships as symbols of national achievement did not have healthy competition as its root so much as a form of 'jingo-ism'. Some even went so far as to aver that it was one of the contributory factors that had finally kindled the flames of international conflict. Whether or not there was any substance in this latter contention, there was a strong feeling in the war weary years which followed the Armistice that such rivalry should not be allowed to recommence. Then, within three years of the peace, the world-wide economic slump was making itself felt.

These things apart, the other reasons behind this attitude to the building of large liners were two-fold. Most operators saw no point in building enormous ships when the volume of steerage passengers had been so drastically reduced by the new restrictions on immigration into the United States and they were not prepared to build vessels of relatively high speed for the new travelling public, the majority of whom were assumed to prefer a much more reasonable fare even at the expense of a slower crossing. The newly emerging Cabin ships, characterized by cheaper fare rates and considerably slower crossing times, seemed to be a far more practical solution to passenger needs. The feasibility of well-patronized giant liners with both high speeds and quite luxurious standards of accommodation for every class of passenger had not yet been appreciated and, as if to endorse this prevailing attitude, Italy's N.G.I. Company brought out yet another intermediate ship in 1926 — the *Roma.*

One place which saw considerable activity during this inclement period was the office of William Francis Gibbs, although here, again, it mostly revolved around small and intermediate liners. In 1924 he produced a remarkable design for a class of *George Washington*-type intermediate motor passenger ships. An attractive, one funnel/two mast silhouette was the outstanding feature of these liners that were never built. In appearance these ships hinted strongly of the later *Andes,* and they also had a close resemblance to the reconstructed Moore McCormack 'Good Neighbor' trio, already mentioned in Chapter IV, which were each reconstructed in 1938 with a single funnel replacing the original pair. About this time, Mr. Gibbs began his series of schemes for the re-commissioning of the United States Army Transports *Agamemnon* and *Mount Vernon* as passenger liners. Covering a period of seven years, these projects were eventually linked with plans for the successful operation of the *Leviathan,* and culminated in W. F. Gibbs' abortive attempt to gain ownership of the monster liner whose remarkable re-construction he had prepared and supervised so skilfully.

The *Agamemnon* was the former Norddeutscher Lloyd crack express steamer *Kaiser Wilhelm II* which had been interned in New York on the day that war had broken out in 1914. The *Mount Vernon* was her younger sister, originally built as the *Kronprinzessin Cecilie,* which had also been interned − in Boston − after running the gauntlet of the British naval blockade. This latter vessel had been carrying a cargo of gold bars valued at about 40 million marks and, in order to avoid capture, had been disguised as the *Olympic* by having the tops of her four funnels painted black. When the United States entered the war in 1917, the two liners were seized and converted into troop transports. From 1919, when their duties for the United States Government ended, they were laid up in Chesapeake Bay. In 1929 the *Agamemnon* was re-named *Monticello,* though this event had no influence on her enforced idleness or on that of her former consort.

Proposals for the *Agamemnon* and *Mount Vernon* included a suggestion that they be converted to turbine driven ships in 1926, and two more that they be given turbo-electric or diesel propulsion in 1927. Each scheme − and there were twelve altogether − was costed precisely and proven financially. In one effort it was proposed to use extra bunker space in the two smaller liners to carry 3,000 tons of oil for the *Leviathan,* whose own limited capacity forced her to purchase this essential and additional fuel at costly European prices.

Despite limited success in getting support for these proposals (one of which actually received President Coolidge's signature as authorization to proceed), funds were never available and nothing came of them. The *Monticello* and *Mount Vernon* were still rusting at their anchorages in

48. Comparison between this photograph of the OLYMPIC with that of the KRONPRINZESSIN CECILIE (Pl. 12) will demonstrate that their profiles were utterly different and that painting the tops of the latter vessel's funnels black would have deceived nobody.

Chesapeake Bay at the outset of World War II in Europe and were finally sent for scrap in mid-1940 when the need for them could hardly have been greater.

A rude awakening ended the confusion and lack of direction concerning the future for large passenger liners with the entry into service of the *Ile de France* in 1927. The French had appreciated clearly before anyone else that a large liner could still pay its way without reducing the standards in the first class, and by offering the old steerage spaces with a vastly improved décor to a smaller number of Tourist passengers. Besides this, the emergence of the *Ile de France* revived talk on the possibility of a two-ship weekly service: an idea which had been advanced in Great Britain before the First World War as a logical development of the then newly inaugurated three-ship express service. Consequently, following the commissioning of the *Ile de France,* the race for both size and speed was under way again. The immediate reaction was a close examination of their respective fleets by all the major companies, and a flourish of ideas from less established shipping interests, most of which never came to fruition.

On the Continent, the germinating seed of totalitarianism was already manifesting itself. In Germany a rapid and determined reconstruction of industry, to cover the social upheaval, was in progress, and the Norddeutscher Lloyd was soon to set the pace on the passenger shipping front

74

49. The REX.

with the introduction of the record-breaking sisters *Bremen* and *Europa*. Meanwhile the Italians, who were already experiencing the policies of a repressive dictatorship under the domination of Benito Mussolini's *El Fascisti,* had their shipping services reorganized on some sort of nationalized basis, and the construction of two similar-sized ships – the *Rex* and the *Conte di Savoia* – was soon in hand.

50. Dr. Walter Boveri.

VIII THE *FLYING CLOUD*

The response to this sudden upsurge in German and Italian giant liner interest came from English, American and French sources in five separate projects, each of which had outstanding and interesting features of its own. Of these, two were successful, culminating in the three largest passengers liners ever built: the *Normandie* and the two *Queens,* which elevated luxury ocean travel to its highest peak. The remaining three proposals were not so fortunate, since each was blighted for a quite individual reason, although financial problems played a significant part in the downfall of all of them.

The first of this latter group was American in origin, being an idea for a comprehensive express trans-Atlantic service which called for the construction of six (initially ten) liners to operate a high-speed shuttle schedule specifically to meet the requirements of American businessmen and travellers. Based on the principles of high productivity and intense equipment usage, the scheme was germinated in 1924 as a result of a meeting between Dr. Walter Boveri, of Brown Boveri & Co. Ltd. of Baden, Switzerland, and Mr. Lawrence R. Wilder, who was the Chairman of the New York Shipbuilding Corporation at Camden, N.J., which was the shipbuilding division of Brown Boveri's American subsidiary, the American Brown Boveri Electric Corporation. By 1926 the detailed design work on the proposed ships was well under way and, in this context, it is interesting to note that technicians at the New York Shipbuilding Corporation had been model-testing and studying the feasibility of designs for 1,000-foot Atlantic liners ever since 1914.

At this juncture, with the project destined for realization as a viable business proposition, Lawrence Wilder sought the financial participation of interested parties, and herein lay the apparent strength of the scheme, since it was one which had gained the confidence of certain established shipping men who were prepared to invest their own money in its success. Amongst those who joined Lawrence Wilder in promoting the project were Joseph E. Sheedy, former European Vice-President of the U.S. Merchant Marine's Emergency Fleet Corporation, and Mr. H. B. Walker, President of the American Steamship Owners Association. Besides this, the venture owed much of its credibility and impetus to the convictions of its founder, Lawrence Wilder himself.

In the summer of 1927 the Transoceanic Corporation of the United States was formed with a capital of $50 million to manage the project and to administer the construction of the six ships. Concurrently, the Blue Ribbon Line, registered as The New York–London–Paris Steamship Company, was established as the North Atlantic operating company. It was proposed to run the ships, one of which would sail every other day from either side of the Atlantic between Montauk Point, Long Island, and Southampton or Plymouth and Le Havre, the aim being to provide an electric railway connection between New York and Montauk Point for the passengers, and that this would also be built by the American Brown Boveri Electric Corporation. The choice of Montauk Point as the home terminal was the same as that chosen by W. F. Gibbs for his twin American Line super-liners and for much the same reasons. Montauk Point would permit quicker turn-rounds and it would be possible to deliver westbound passengers to their destinations hours sooner.

The American public came to hear of the Blue Ribbon Line project for the first time on 14 September 1927, when the *New York Herald Tribune* carried an exclusive story on the scheme by their shipping correspondent, John Kelly. From his 'scoop', details of the ships began to emerge but, as subsequent announcements revealed, much of the dimensional and statistical information had to be viewed with some caution, since the specifications for the ships continued to change for some time and were obviously still under development. One thing that was evident, however, was that the liners were of a very novel design. They were to be four day 'clipper'* vessels capable of a continuous sea-speed of 31 to 33 knots and a maximum speed of 35 knots. According to Kelly's article, there were to

*In the mistaken jargon of the day.

51. An artist's impression of one of the Blue Ribbon liners – the first to be named FLYING CLOUD.

be ten 20,000-ton liners, 800 feet* in length with a beam of 80 feet and a 24-foot draught, but this was soon to be revised to six ships of 35,000 tons, each with an overall length of 900 feet† and a beam of 90 feet, maintaining the high length/beam ratio of 10:1 which was apparently fundamental to their design. 'Departure' displacement would have been around 50,000 tons, which included bunker capacity for the round trip.

Accommodation numbers also tended to fluctuate, varying from 400 to 800 per ship in first-class only. There was to be space for 1,000 tons of express cargo and mail. The cabins were to be a little larger than Pullman drawing rooms, which measured some 15 × 10 feet, and there would be a total absence of extravagant public rooms, swimming pools and similar passenger amenities of like nature. If this description sounds to be somewhat spartan, the explanation given seemed to be justified, for it appeared that the need to devote a disproportionate amount of space to engines of massive size, which were essential to the high speeds required for the service, overrode all other considerations. As if to allay any doubts passengers may have had about crossing in these ships, Wilder himself pointed out that there would nevertheless be a fair degree of comfort aboard. The dining rooms would be positioned in the after part of the vessels, as would the promenade space also.

This latter situation was necessitated by what was the most striking and

*243.84 metres.
†274.32 metres.

revolutionary feature of the ships, since they had been designed as aeroplane-carrying auxiliaries and, as a result, the funnels and masts were to be set to one side of a long, uncluttered upper deck in order to leave a large, clear area on which the aircraft could land and take off. Twenty-four 'planes were to be carried by each vessel in commercial service to expedite rapid delivery of mail and passengers in a hurry, but the number would be increased to a hundred machines in war time. These aeroplanes were to be housed in a hangar under the runway deck, and a number of aircraft mechanics were to be included as part of the regular crew.

The concept of ships carrying aircraft was very much in vogue in the late 1920s as a result of the experiments with the *Ile de France* and after Clarence Chamberlin's successful flight off the *Leviathan* in August 1927, but the Wilder suggestions had little in common with these catapult-launched single 'plane trials. His ideas, instead, reflected a strong naval influence. The New York Shipbuilding Corporation had, after all, just completed the U.S. Navy's giant aircraft-carrier *Saratoga*.

It was proposed to give the first ship in the fleet the very appropriate name of *Flying Cloud,* since it was taken from one of the most celebrated of the American-built clipper ships and, more tenuously, it was held to have a certain connotation with her possible function as an aircraft-carrier. At this time, it was estimated that each of the six units would cost around $21 million* to build.

Tests on 20-foot models of the liners were conducted on 17 October 1927 at the Experimental Model Basin at the Washington Navy Yard and, from the findings which stemmed from them, it was estimated that the high-pressure, super-heat turbine engines intended for the *Flying Cloud* ships would need to generate 130,000 s.h.p. for a service speed of 33 knots and 160,000 s.h.p. for a maximum speed of 35 knots.

When considered individually, the liners under contemplation for the Blue Ribbon Line were not particularly large, especially when compared with others being forecast at that time or already under construction for other lines, but the project as a whole was both colossal and expensive. The Blue Ribbon Line's backers were putting up $50 million of private capital but, naturally enough, a request for a loan from the United States Government, under the provisions of the 1920 Merchant Marine Act,† was a key point of the proposals, and an outline submission for a

*Say – £4,375,000.
† See Appendix 2.

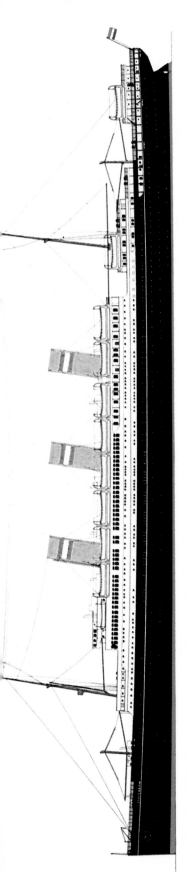

52. *The STATENDAM, as originally conceived. (p.61 et seq.)*

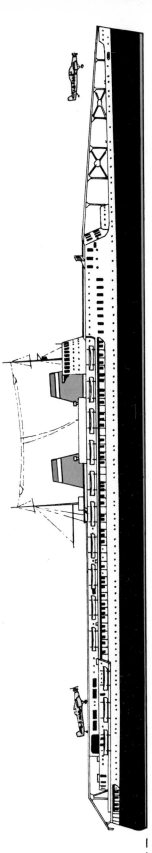

53. *A profile view of the FLYING CLOUD aircraft carrier/passenger liner design. The aircraft depicted on the flight deck and taking off are themselves based on an ill-fated concept dating from the 1920s.*

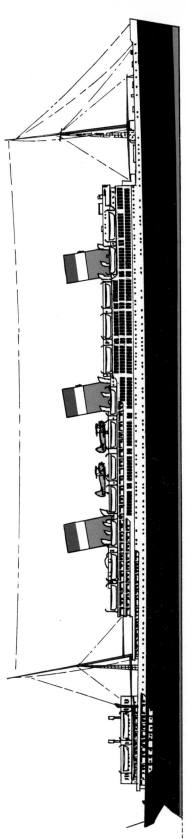

54. *Theodore Ferris' design for the U.S. Lines, which preceded the two LEVIATHANS project.*

55. *The White Star Line's OCEANIC making an imaginary departure from New York.*

Shipping Board Construction Fund loan was made on 21 November 1927. Further hearings were scheduled for early 1928.

Wilder and his associates were well aware of the great need for such a subsidy in order to get their project off the ground and, realizing that Congress had to be more than convinced of the economic viability of the scheme before committing so large a sum as the $94½ million* that was required, they had the entire concept examined by a series of committees of so-called 'disinterested experts'. These covered such aspects of the enterprise as design, marine engineering and propulsion, operation and economics, and they were assisted very ably by some extremely influential consultants. Included amongst these were Theodore E. Ferris, the noted American naval architect, Elmer A. Sperry, of the Sperry Gyroscope Company and Sir Charles Parsons of the Parsons Marine Steam Turbine Company. A great deal of publicity was given to this exercise in the American press and, in the light of subsequent events, it became misconstrued as an attempt to acquire business endorsement and technical approval for the scheme as an influencing factor in applying for Federal aid.

Detailed statements on the Blue Ribbon Line proposal were presented to the U.S. Shipping Board during hearings on 10 and 24 January 1928. In his submissions, Wilder aimed to sell the idea of six auxiliary aircraft-carriers for use in a national emergency – six potential warships which were not affected by the restrictions and limitations of the 1921 Washington Naval Conference – and also the freedom of dependence on vessels under foreign flags for the carriage of trans-Atlantic passengers and freight as an added inducement. To add weight to his arguments, he pointed out that over 60% of the traffic then being carried was of U.S. nationality or manufacture.

In exchange, Wilder sought, in the first place, a 75% construction costs loan and, in the second, a revision of the Mail-carrying Act to the advantage of fast ships. Finally, because insurance was limited on any one ship, he requested protection in the event of total loss in the form of cancellation of the loans against the ships to the extent not covered by amortization and insurance.

In spite of the strong representations made by the scheme's originator, the Shipping Board was apparently not impressed by the carefully

*Almost £20 million.

82

compiled proposals, and expressed an unwillingness to assist the project financially. In a complete rejection of the construction loan application, Chairman T. V. O'Connor, speaking on behalf of the Board on 27 April 1928, described the plan as *'technically open to criticism, economically unsound and financially nebulous.'*

As a result of this pronouncement, many of Lawrence Wilder's supporters, including Dr. Walter Boveri, then decided to dissociate themselves from the Blue Ribbon Line and certain of them, in marked contrast to their earlier standpoint, became critical of the whole venture and of its prospects. Such overt scepticism from persons previously so closely connected with the scheme did little to enhance the now slender chances of success for the *Flying Cloud* and her sisters.

Much to his credit, Lawrence Wilder remained undeterred in spite of this setback. He severed his connections with his Swiss employers and, in so doing, purchased from them the shipbuilding division of the American Brown Boveri Electric Corporation – the now defunct New York Shipbuilding Corporation. His intentions were to proceed alone with the Blue Ribbon Line project if necessary.

As events turned out, this necessity did not arise because, although voices of uncertainty were being raised from certain quarters, other people were impressed very favourably both by the potential of the scheme and by the sincerity of the Blue Ribbon Line's promoter. Outstanding among those whose careers became involved with the efforts of this company and the Transoceanic Corporation was Captain Herbert Hartley, master of the *Leviathan* and Commodore of the United States Lines. Disillusioned with the prospects for the revitalization of the United States Lines' fleet, Captain Hartley resigned his position to become Director of Operations for the new enterprise, in which his aspirations for a strong U.S. Merchant Marine appeared to have a rewarding outlet.

One aspect which may have had a particular appeal to Hartley was Wilder's interest in purchasing the United States Lines' ships, including the *Leviathan,* as part of the Blue Ribbon operation. As a result of the failure to gain a Shipping Board loan, Wilder did not expect to have any of the new ships in service before 1931, so he wished to acquire the United States Lines' fleet as an interim measure, in order to gain experience and goodwill in readiness for the express ship service.

* See Appendix 2.

56. Captain Herbert Hartley.

Within a month, Herbert Hartley was accompanying Lawrence Wilder on visits to the White House to lobby President Coolidge for support for both the Blue Ribbon Line and the purchase of the United States Lines. They were busy months, and the former Commodore was involved in many other activities, including giving radio talks on the express ship proposition and making visits to Montauk Point to clarify the berthing and passenger handling requirements. During May and June he assisted with the preparation of a revised submission to the United States Navy for approval of the planned ships under the loan provisions of the recently implemented Jones–White Act of 1928.*

That the Blue Ribbon Line scheme made no further progress, in spite of all these efforts, was mainly due to doubts about the strength of Wilder's financial backing at this point. Doomed to failure, the decline of the enterprise was rapid and, by late November 1928, after less than a year with the company, a disenchanted and disappointed Captain Herbert Hartley was suing the Transoceanic Corporation for $75,000 – the unpaid amount due to him under the terms of his contract.

Ironically, it could be said that Hartley's association with the Blue Ribbon Line project was in itself partly instrumental in bringing about its downfall. After he had decided to resign as Commodore of the United States Lines on 24 January 1928, he had called in at the offices of the U.S. Shipping Board to discuss his decision with friends on the Board who were sympathetic to his sense of frustration. As it turned out, the Board was engaged in discussions on the Transoceanic Corporation's loan application at the time of his arrival, and he was invited to sit in on their deliberations, which he duly did. Later, it was claimed that less than a quarter of an hour elapsed from the time that the news of Hartley's resignation from the U.S. Lines was received to the Board giving tentative approval to the express ship application. However, within three days, and largely as a result of unfavourable statements in the press, the United States Senate ordered the Shipping Board to investigate the financial status of the Transoceanic Corporation and the way it was proposing to use Government funds in the construction of new ships. Without any question, this investigation had a significant bearing on the subsequent judgement relating to the Company's loan request.

Still worse was to follow because, before the year was out, the activities of Lawrence Wilder and Herbert Hartley in pursuance of their Blue Ribbon project had quite unwittingly provoked yet another investigation by the Senate into Marine lobbying practices, and it was this which led to Hartley terminating his employment with the Transoceanic Corporation in October 1928. He had, in fact, been under considerable attack in the press, particularly from the Hearst Newspaper Group, in which it was alleged that he had influenced the Shipping Board over the *Flying Cloud* issue when he had visited them on 24 January 1928. Much stress was

*See Appendix 2.

57. The LEVIATHAN was Capt. Hartley's last command and was the pride of the United States' mercantile marine. When her crew came ashore at Southampton, the police and the public houses needed no shipping intelligence to tell them that the ship was in, particularly in the days of prohibition!

placed on the fact that the scheme was one which was in line with the sentiments he had expressed previously in his desire for a better U.S. Merchant Marine and that, within twenty-four hours of his resignation from the U.S. Lines, his new position with the Blue Ribbon Line was announced.

There is little doubt that his visit to the U.S. Shipping Board at the very crucial moment when it was in session on that fateful day was pure coincidence – but it proved to be a very unfortunate and costly one. Moreover, Hartley undoubtedly had his enemies in the press and was not entirely popular in all quarters, although this had stemmed from his time as captain of the *Leviathan,* since he was a ship-master who tended to maintain a certain dignity and aloofness aboard, and not to associate with the passengers to the degree that had become expected of masters of the big passenger ships. In another age and in other circumstances this was common enough practice, but, where the *Leviathan* was concerned, it was not an attitude which everyone understood and of those who took offence at it, one may be sure that some journalists were numbered amongst them.

At all events, whatever their motives, the American press made a great deal of all this and, as a result of their columns on the subject, the title 'fast ship project' was given an unfortunate new meaning by playing on the colloquial connotation of the word 'fast',* which carried the implication that the Blue Ribbon Line project was a fraudulent attempt to swindle money out of the United States Government, while unfortunate individuals, such as Captain Herbert Hartley, were regarded as the victims of the proponents' deceit. In short, the press wanted it all ways, but the latter suggestions were no more true or fair than the first ones had been.

Lawrence Wilder's plans were undoubtedly rather ambitious, even though they were based on the successful American concept of mass-marketing, but there is no question that he himself had real faith in the principles of the scheme. This was clearly evident when he addressed the Propeller Club of New York on the subject of his projected ships on 18 October 1928. Considering the moribund state of the project at that time, nobody in his audience could have doubted his enthusiasm or sincerity and, indeed, he campaigned alone for nine more, long years to win support for the 'clipper' liners and, at the time of his death in 1937, he was

*i.e. 'sharp' – perhaps not completely honest and straightforward.

in the process of putting the plan before the United States Shipping Board for the second time.

While Lawrence Wilder may have lacked an appreciation of some of the costs and problems involved in managing and operating six such ships so far as his own personal experience was concerned, he had availed himself of the best expertise available and, despite the judgement of T. V. O'Connor and his Board, it would be difficult to fault him on that score. Granted that there was already stiff competition on the North Atlantic seaway, but this was known. It is easy to say that he failed to take account of the imminence of the leaner years which lay ahead, but less easy to justify that contention, since his scheme was not grandiose in the sense that he was advocating out-size vessels, though its grandeur lay rather in the number of them. The fact was that other owners were building ships for the route in the period in which Wilder was involved, and these proved to be successful.

One aspect of his scheme which cannot be questioned was his far-sighted faith in the integral relationship between ships and aircraft and, for this reason, the aeroplane auxiliary element in the *Flying Cloud's* design was, perhaps, the greatest legacy to posterity of the Blue Ribbon project, for it triggered off the concept of building passenger liners with a basic structure expressly suited for conversion to full aircraft-carriers in wartime. It undoubtedly influenced both the Japanese Government with its aircraft-carrier/liner programme, in which many vessels were completed, and the U.S. Maritime Commission's own P-4-P design, both described in detail in later chapters. In fact, many well-known passenger liners were considered for adaptation to aircraft-carrying roles in the Second World War, including the Norddeutscher Lloyd's famous record-breaker *Europa*.

Thus the *Flying Cloud* and her stillborn sisters faded into history, to become yet another sad chapter in the review of unrealized ventures in the realm of the passenger liner. Meanwhile, there were other developments on the other side of the Atlantic.

58. *It was a gamble to instal steam turbines on the LUSITANIA and the MAURETANIA (above) in 1907, though it was shown to be more than justified in the event.*

IX THE *OCEANIC*

The next project precipitated by the sudden domination of the Atlantic passenger trade by the Germans and Italians had been on the cards in Great Britain for almost fifty years, but it was only considered seriously at this time when prestige and a truly competitive reply to these foreign liners was demanded. This was, in fact, the 1,000-foot long White Star liner basically designed as far back as 1880 by Sir Edward Harland.* Now brought to life again as the *Oceanic,* the ship's design was improved radically to match and exceed the best foreign ships afloat. The White Star Line had returned to British ownership in 1926 as the International Mercantile Marine began to shed its foreign flag subsidiaries, the buyer being the Royal Mail Steam Packet Company. Lord Kylsant, the Chairman of the Royal Mail Group, was a champion of the motor ship and, due to his influence, the new express liner was planned to be propelled by diesel-electric engines – a revolutionary innovation for the adoption of which there was no proven precedent.

For this reason, the installation of these marine engines in the *Oceanic* would have been a greater gamble than the installation of steam turbines in the *Lusitania* and *Mauretania* had been in 1907, since the liner *Carmania,* built two years earlier, had acted as something of an engine test-bed for the two Cunard record-breakers. Quite obviously, her future owners and her builders were fully aware of the immensity of the decision to install such engines, but their caution and protracted hesitation in deciding firmly whether the generating machinery for the liner's electric drive should be diesel instead of turbine only contributed to her eventual cancellation.

*Page 16.

In the end, the question of the *Oceanic's* engines was finally resolved in favour of a diesel-electric power unit but, before any substantial progress could be made with her construction, the effects of the great Depression began to be felt. Due to the severity of the economic crisis, abandonment of the project at such an early stage was the only logical course of action open to the White Star Line in their endeavours to try to remain in business. Had the debate over the engines not taken so long, until financial pressures had become even more severe, it is conceivable that the ship would have been so advanced that a decision would have been made to complete her. As it was, only the keel had been laid.

Before reflecting on the fate of the *Oceanic,* it is first necessary to take a look at the unfortunate ship to see how much more progress towards the eventual realization of a 1,000-foot liner had been made on this occasion. In fact, the stage reached with the *Oceanic* was the furthest of any of the pre-*Normandie* 1,000-foot liner projects,* for her construction was actually started.

Knowledge of the *Oceanic* project first came to the Maritime world in August 1926, when an announcement indicated that a giant 25-knot liner to replace the *Homeric,* whose service speed was inadequate, was under consideration by the White Star Line. The press statement also suggested that the new vessel would bear a 'family resemblance' to the old *Olympic.* This was somewhat misleading, because the final design showed a liner with three squat motorship-type funnels and the now more familiar cruiser stern. Her appearance, in fact, had far more in common with the smaller *Britannic* of 1930 and with the Royal Mail liner *Asturias* which entered service in March 1927: the first of a long line of Harland and Wolff-built motor vessels propelled by double-acting 4-stroke diesel machinery.

Work on the new ship's design took two years and reached its climax when the contract for her construction was placed on 18 June 1928. In their historic announcement, the White Star Line declared that their new liner, to be named *Oceanic* after the Company's pioneer ship, was to be built as expected by Harland and Wolff Limited at Belfast. The building was expected to take about three and a half years, and the final cost to be in the region of £3½ million. The *Oceanic* was to measure 60,000 gross tons with an overall length of 1,010 feet,† a beam of 120 feet and a

*The *Normandie* was 1,029 feet (313.64 metres) overall: 981 feet (299.01 metres) between perpendiculars.
†307.85 metres.

draught of 38 feet. The details of her engines were only released many years later by Mr. Cuthbert Coulson Pounder, Director and Chief Technical Engineer of Harland and Wolff, after the Second World War. These showed that the quadruple screw *Oceanic* would have had 47 six-cylinder, exhaust turbo-charged, four-stroke single-acting diesel engines producing a total of 275,000 i.h.p. and coupled in pairs to electric generators. The total weight of the installation would have been some 17,000 tons, equal to the displacement tonnage of a smaller liner of the day! She was to have been Great Britain's answer to the *Bremen* and, with a speed in the region of 30 knots, might well have rivalled the latter for the Atlantic Blue Riband honours.

The first keel plates of the *Oceanic,* yard number 844, were laid down ten days after the memorable order for her construction was announced. She was to be built in the famous Musgrave yard on Queen's Island, a massive shipbuilding complex built during World War I for the construction of wartime standard vessels, but which became the future birthplace of many other celebrated ships. With all due pomp and ceremony, the building of yet another revolutionary White Star liner was begun, but it was not long before it became apparent that all was not well with the new ship. The slow pace of the work was a clear indication that something was amiss.

The fears were eventually substantiated on 23 July 1929 when all work was stopped on the *Oceanic's* almost complete keel structure, and a formal announcement the same September confirmed that further work was to be deferred temporarily pending final decisions on her propulsive machinery. Meanwhile the keel section was to remain undisturbed on the slipway but, in spite of this reassuring statement, the vessel was to be mentioned for what was probably the last time at the White Star Line's Annual General Meeting the following May, when Lord Kylsant, in his Chairman's report, repeated, in so many words, the formal announcement of the previous September, and then . . . there was silence. . . .

The question remained posed whether the problem with the *Oceanic* was simply one of an engineering nature. Undoubtedly the advent of the turbine-driven record-breaker *Bremen* in 1929 must have given rise to plenty of cause for doubt over the *Oceanic's* engines, but perhaps the real reason for her abandonment was an economic one. The world financial

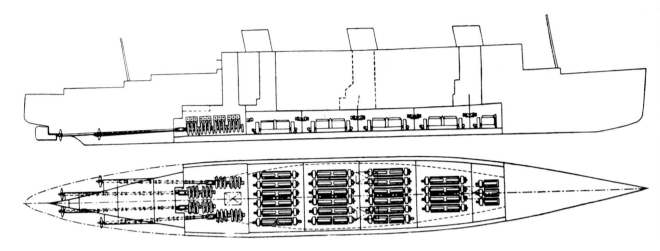

59. *The engine arrangement of the OCEANIC.*

crisis was worsening rapidly in late 1929, and the Royal Mail Group was known to be having money difficulties. It had become like a monster that had outgrown itself, and was encountering increasing difficulties in maintaining its position as a leading shipping concern.* The Government was not prepared to stake a loan to help to build the new liner on such a shaky foundation, particularly when it also had the problem of being expected to provide similar aid to the rival Cunard Line; the other major British company with a predominant North Atlantic interest, which was also about to embark on the construction of a new express ship for its premier service. Such national rivalry was impractical during the unfavourable economic circumstances then prevailing, and could not be encouraged at the expense of the tax-payer.

Undoubtedly the ailing White Star Line could not finance the project on its own, and so the giant *Oceanic* was discarded and priority given to a more economic sister-ship of the *Britannic* – the *Georgic* of 1932.† Meanwhile, the *Oceanic's* keel structure was broken up discreetly and the giant liner was gradually forgotten, denying Harland and Wolff the honour of building the first liner of over 1,000 feet in length.

It seemed slightly ironical that, soon afterwards in the very depths of

*The crash of the company a couple of years later is outside the scope of this book.
†27,759 gross tons.

60. Lord Kylsant.

the Depression, rumours began to circulate to the effect that the White Star Line, as if with the bravado of a condemned man, was contemplating another giant of over 70,000 gross tons. Or was this an example of journalistic clairvoyancy? Perhaps a premonition of a combined Cunard-White Star Line and of the birth of number 534, the *Queen Mary,* of 1,020 feet* overall length? In 1934, when Cunard were also struggling, amalgamation was the principal condition laid down by the British Government for a loan to enable work to resume on this vessel.

*310.9 metres.

61. *In the event, the OCEANIC was replaced in some sort by building a sister ship to the BRITANNIC (above) named the GEORGIC*
The ships were similar in appearance, except that the latter vessel had a rounded facing to the fore end of her superstructure. Thes
were the only two British motor ships built for the trans-Atlantic run. It will be noted that the BRITANNIC had three double-banke
sets of boats per side under Welin davits with falls, and the GEORGIC had four. The reader may form his own opinions about this
With her typically stumpy funnels and her overall appearance, the BRITANNIC was clearly influenced by the design of the gia
liner OCEANIC.

X THE UNITED STATES LINES
SISTER SHIPS – THE TWO
LEVIATHANS

Another equally ill-fated American project, the fifth major scheme to be announced in the late 1920s, now appeared on the scene. This was a far more viable proposition than that of the 'Clipper' liners, being requested initially by the United States Department of Commerce in the terms of the sale of the United States Lines to Paul Wadsworth Chapman and his associates in 1929. Plans for a pair of 31-knot super-liners for a weekly service, to compete directly with the *Bremen, Europa, Rex* and *Conte di Savoia,* had to be ready by 13 February 1930 at the latest.

The contract for the United States Lines, of which this stipulation formed an essential part, was won by Paul Wadsworth Chapman after a very competitive struggle, and this is quite an interesting story on its own.

From August 1921, after the financial collapse of the United States Mail Line, the various ships of its fleet had remained under the control of the Shipping Board of the Department of Commerce. The vessels were operated on a bare-boat charter basis* for the Shipping Board under the collective name of United States Lines, the management being performed by a consortium composed of the Moore McCormack Company, the Roosevelt Steamship Company and the United American Lines. The Department of Commerce was anxious, however, to shed its responsibility for the United States Lines on to total private ownership and, to be

*See Glossary.

sure that the fleet did not return to them again, they sought a group of business men who were financially sound to take control of it.

One person who was very keen to steer the future course of the *Leviathan* and her companions was William Francis Gibbs, who made several bids for the United States Lines fleet in association with Mr. J. H. Winchester, the head of a charter firm of long standing. The first offer by Gibbs and Winchester came in 1926, and it was to buy the fleet outright. This was rejected, but they soon followed it with two other modified bids in the same year. The second of these was a proposal to buy the American Merchant Lines freighter service as well as the United States Lines with a down payment of $200,000 – a very low figure which later formed part and parcel of newspaper allegations – and it carried with it an offer to build two companion ships to the *Leviathan* with an investment of $30 million. This was the first mention of prospective consorts for the *Leviathan,* but this bid was said to have been blocked by political and press activities and no progress was made.

As their next move, the Gibbs-Winchester team proposed to recondition the *Mount Vernon* and *Agamemnon,* as previously mentioned,* as part of an offer to purchase the United States Lines fleet, but this also failed. In fact, 1928 saw a great deal of interest in this company when the U.S. Shipping Board opened bids for the purchase of the ships on 15 January. There was, for instance, a bid of $6 million by P. A. S. Franklin of the American Line S.S. Corporation on behalf of the I.M.M., which had faded as a force in the shipping world since commencing to dispose of its foreign assets. Though regarded as a rather low offer at the time, compared with others that were tabled, the I.M.M.'s bid was probably the most financially sound as later events were to demonstrate. Against this, the Gibbs and Winchester partnership were now offering $10 million, but this was exceeded by a bid of $16,300,000 from a syndicate headed by Paul Wadsworth Chapman, a wealthy Chicago financier. Lawrence R. Wilder, bidding in the name of the Blue Ribbon Line, entered the field later in the year, but the real fight for ownership of the line was between the Gibbs-Winchester team and the Chapman group.

Although Gibbs and Winchester had the greatest experience of shipping behind them, Chapman's group had strong financial support and its bid finally won the day, with the provision that two ships comparable with

*Page 72.

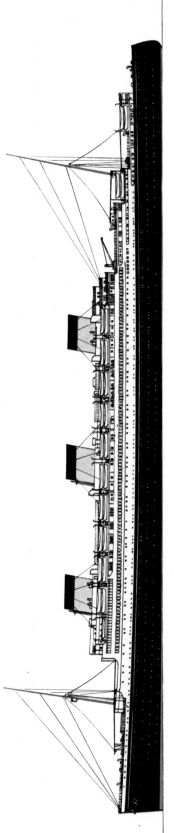

62. *A drawing of the proposed OCEANIC. (See p.89 et seq.)*

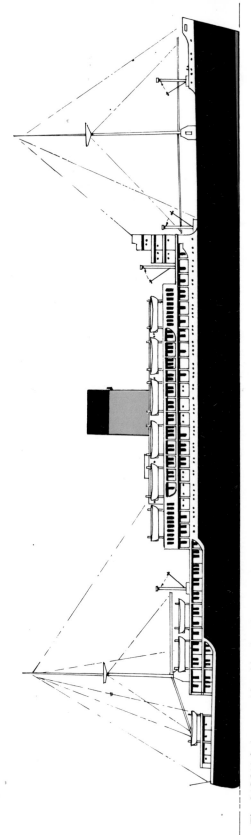

63. *The JASON design, considered by the Blue Funnel Line. (See p.120)*

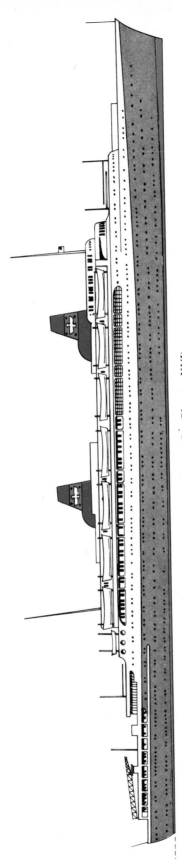

64. *The P-4-P passenger liner/aircraft carrier in American President Lines' colours. (See Chapter XVI)*

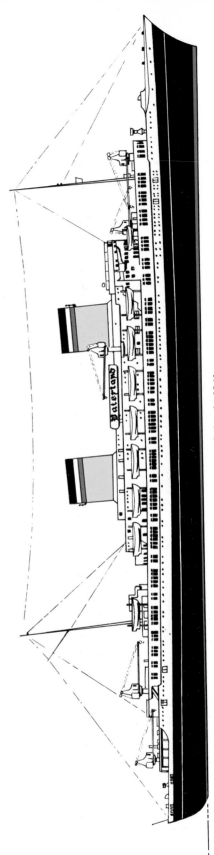

65. *The Hamburg Amerika Line's turbo-electric liner VATERLAND, due for completion in 1941.*

the *Leviathan,* costing not less than $25 million each, should be built by them within two years of the purchase of the fleet. Other smaller ships were also planned as part of this deal.

Little was known in shipping circles of P. W. Chapman, the leading character in the purchase of the ailing United States Lines. He had been born in Jerseyville, Illinois, into a family of lawyers and bankers, and his own business background had been in finance and public utilities (service industries), where he had had considerable success. Now, his emergence as President of the United States Lines was to precipitate an equally keen interest in passenger shipping and its co-ordination with air travel.

While Chapman may have lacked shipping experience himself, he made up for this deficiency in his board appointments. Among those selected was Joseph E. Sheedy, who had been active with the Blue Ribbon project until its Federal rebuff in April 1928, to become Vice-President, and William Perrott, the former Operations Manager of the United States Lines while it was under Government control. Perrott was to be responsible for managing the construction programmes of the new company.

In order to comply with the stipulations of the contract with the U.S. Shipping Board, one of America's most distinguished naval architects, Mr. Theodore E. Ferris, was commissioned to design the two giant liners of at least 45,000 tons which were required. Simultaneously, Mr. Ernest H. Rigg, Chief Naval Architect at the New York Shipbuilding Corporation, was engaged to design two ships for the secondary mail service to Hamburg. Both men had played a prominent part on the Blue Ribbon Line technical committees, and Theodore Ferris was particularly well-known for his design work on the Ward Line coastwise steamers *Morro Castle* and *Oriente.*

The initial proposals for the express liners for the Channel ports service, which were released in mid-1929, were for two more-or-less updated versions of the *Leviathan,* with which they were intended to run. Each was to have a capacity for 3,000 passengers and 1,000 crew, and each was to carry two catapult-launched mail seaplanes. In appearance, they were rather disappointing, having a close resemblance to the earlier, fifteen-year-old ship, with three tall funnels and a counter stern. Unlike the *Leviathan,* however, they would have had a slightly raked bow and all

66. *Theodore Ferris' second design for the super-liners covered by Paul W. Chapman's project –
the two LEVIATHANS.*

the lifeboats would have been carried on the boat deck. They were also considerably larger, with a gross tonnage in excess of 60,000 and an overall length of over 1,000 feet. A service speed of 26 knots was envisaged.

It was anticipated that construction of the two liners would begin early in 1930, with the building costs put at $28 million per ship. However, in February of that year, Theodore Ferris put forward vastly amended designs for the United States Lines' new super-liners.

In size, these modified ships were somewhat smaller than the previous pair, but they were much faster and they featured a profile design more in keeping with the styles of the time. Although they resembled the contemporary *Bremen* in many respects, they also bore a close similarity with the much later *Queen Elizabeth* and would have pioneered features first introduced in the latter vessel. In spite of the Depression and the rock-bottom value of shipping shares, over $440,000 was spent in testing and proving the design, and in preparing the proposal for submission to the United States Shipping Board for approval under the terms of the contract, in order that the vessels would qualify for Government construction loans as approved ships under the terms of the Jones-White Act of 1928.*

Twenty-two scale models were made for testing in the United States

*See Appendix 2.

Model Basin at Washington, D.C. with the assistance of sixty naval architects. The designs that were selected for further appraisal as a result of these tests were approved by the American Bureau of Shipping and Lloyds of London. Concurrently with this research, a 57-page bound booklet was published covering the economic aspects and the mail subsidy possibilities of the proposals, while Theodore Ferris addressed the Society of Naval Architects and Marine Engineers in New York from a 32-page paper on the subject of his super-liners on 20 November 1931.

The design specification finally agreed had two versions: one for geared-turbine propulsion and the other for turbo-electric propulsion. Both versions were basically identical in appearance, but their dimensions varied slightly. The turbo-electric design was slightly bigger with a gross tonnage of 60,000 on an overall length of 985 feet,* compared with 56,000 gross tons and 963 feet † for the geared-turbine version, but both vessels were narrow enough to pass through the Panama Canal locks. The two liners were to be quadruple screw, with a maximum speed of 32 knots and a service speed of 29.5 knots. Designed maximum shaft horsepower was 180,000 at 174 r.p.m. for the geared turbine version, and 200,000 at 180 r.p.m. for the turbo-electric ship. The propelling units in the geared-turbine vessel consisted of four-pinion, single-reduction engine types arranged on the four shafts with the inboard propellers turning outward and the outboard ones turning inward. In the electric-drive ship there would have been a single motor on each shaft, screw rotation being the same as for the other version.

On the design aspect, they had a cruiser stern similar to the later *Queen Elizabeth,* two widely-spaced funnels with squashed-hat cowls, a curved and raked stem with a bulbous forefoot,‡ and a rounded fore end to their superstructure. Watertight sub-division was in accordance with the United States Navy standards in anticipation of their use as auxiliaries. The Ferris liners were to be built of a high-elastic nickel steel which would save weight while increasing structural strength, and aluminium was to be used extensively for the deck houses to reduce weight still further.

Among the features incorporated into the two liners were a novel solarium on the upper deck with a living garden, a shopping arcade to be called 'Fifth Avenue', and the inevitable aircraft catapult and seaplane to dispatch the mail one day early. Passenger accommodation was provided

*300.23 metres.
†293.52 metres.
‡See Glossary, under 'Bulbous Bow'.

for 2,800 passengers in three classes, the largest percentage being in First Class. It was estimated that the cost of these modified liners would be approximately $30 million each. With Government approval and with Federal aid, in the shape of a promised $31 million construction loan, Mr. Chapman hoped to have one ship in service by 1936 and the second by 1940.

These two ships were to be named the *Leviathan 2* and the *Leviathan 3*. Whilst the object was obvious, such nomenclature was rather out of keeping with that normally used for Atlantic liners and, perhaps, was rather more reminiscent of a string of barges. However, due to the repetition involved and to avoid possible confusion with the existing *Leviathan* (ex-*Vaterland*), these two names will not be used within this text.

All seemed to be set fair for this latest American enterprise, but time was fast running out for P. W. Chapman. As a result of the economic slump, the returns for the first two years were disappointing, to understate the case. The total number of passengers carried by the Company had fallen from 80,161 in 1929 to only 65,408 in 1930. By the end of 1931 the number had dropped to a mere 43,310. By then unable to fulfil their commitments, the Chapman team defaulted in its payments to the Shipping Board and the Government was, therefore, compelled to foreclose in October 1931. The Company was thereupon offered for sale again, and this time it was bought by what remained of the old International Mercantile Marine.

The new owners inherited the twenty-year-old *Leviathan* and the two Ernest Rigg-designed cabin ships, *Manhattan* and *Washington,* that Mr. Chapman had ordered on 24 May 1930. They were not, however, bound to a contract which insisted on the construction of two new giant express liners, and, in view of the prevailing economic climate, the new owners reappraised completely the proposal for the Ferris sisters from a much more critical standpoint. The viability of the scheme depended to a great extent on the United States mail subsidies, as there was expected to be much competition for passenger traffic from other express luxury liners on the North Atlantic route, and these subsidies seemed, unfortunately, to be calculated to the disadvantage of the express ship. The mail rate over 20-knots did not increase in the same proportion for speeds in excess of this figure as it did below it. Under 20 knots, an extra $1 per mile was

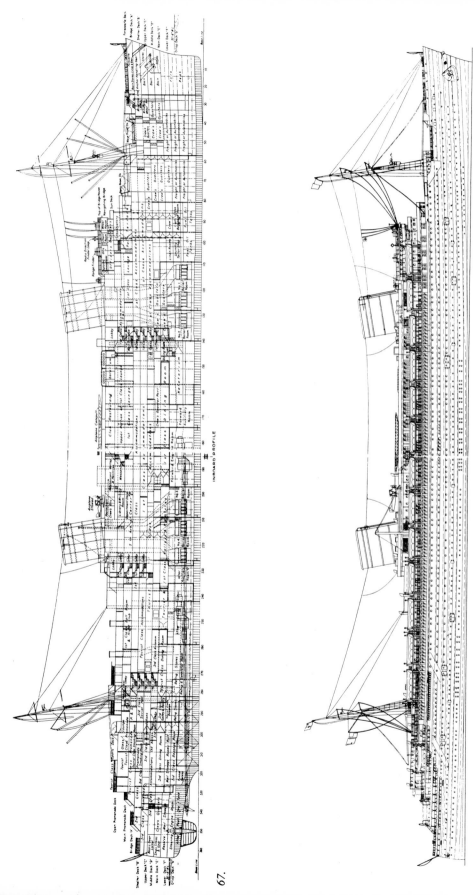

67.

68. Line drawings of the second Ferris design which appeared in 'Marine Engineering' in December, 1931.

paid for each additional knot in speed, yet over 20 knots the rate was increased by only 50 cents for each additional knot. Consequently, a 20-knot vessel, with its smaller engines, could earn more net profit carrying mail than a 30-knot ship whose larger engines made her very much less economical to run and reduced her earnings from passengers due to the loss of cabin accommodation to the increased space required by the machinery.

This seemed to decide the issue for the new owners of the United States Lines, and little more was heard of the two giant sisters. However, they reappeared briefly when, in 1936, the Merchant Marine Act amended the differential on the mail subsidies to operate to the advantage of the faster vessels, and a new proposal to build the two Ferris passenger liners was included in the Act while it was in Bill form. With the repeal of the 18th Amendment also militating in their favour,* the outlook seemed to be brighter once more, but this fresh proposal was voted out before the Bill became an Act of Law, and that concluded the matter.

As for Paul Wadsworth Chapman, one might suppose that his somewhat retrograde experiences with the United States Lines had dampened his embryonic enthusiasm for passenger shipping, but this was far from being the case! Despite this initial setback, in which he had lost control of the United States Lines, his belief in the monster passenger liner had been confirmed and he was to become one of the greatest campaigners for such vessels of immense proportions. Over the next twenty years he maintained his association with Theodore Ferris and, together, they produced plans for colossal liners in which they demonstrated great ingenuity and their unswerving belief in such vessels. Although the commercial value of these ships was open to question, one could only marvel at their very size and magnificence.

The foregoing account concludes the situation in the United States during this inclement period. Meanwhile, in Europe, shipping was also in a steep downward spiral, but new plans, aimed partly to cope with these difficult circumstances, were nevertheless still being devised. Yet, as was so often the case, willing investors were hard to find, and many otherwise good schemes never had an opportunity to prove themselves for this reason.

Since the end of the First World War, the Hamburg Amerika Line,

*See Appendix 2.

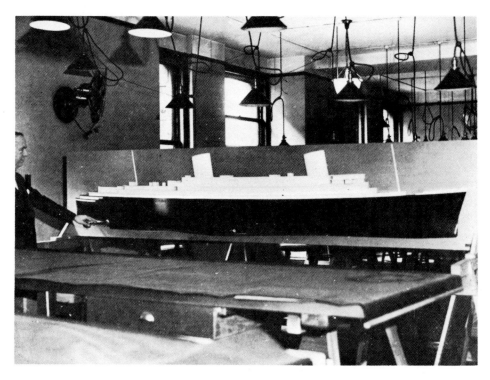

69. *Half-model of Ferris' second design in his New York office in 1930. Theodore Ferris himself is just visible on the left of the picture.*

having re-established most of its passenger services, had contented itself with rather small and not particularly attractive liners to carry out its schedules. However, in the early 1930s, it seemed that they might be ready to return to their former splendour in the days of Imperial Germany. The company announced that it intended to build the first of a number of 30-knot super-liners, whose size and standard of luxury would exceed anything else then afloat or projected. About the same time the Canadian Pacific Line reported that it proposed to build a sister to the *Empress of Britain,* a successful ship which had been earning a good income for her owners, while the Italia Line were said to be planning a third vessel to complement the *Rex* and *Conte di Savoia.* None of these ships materialized, however, and the blame for this probably lay in the continued effects of the Depression.

70. The MAURETANIA, of immortal fame, was perhaps the most charismatic of all passenger ships and was the fastest in the world for no less than 22 years.

71. The EMPRESS OF BRITAIN of 1931 was 42,348 gross tons and the largest and fastest vessel running on the northern trans-Atlantic route to the St. Lawrence, often meeting her mail contract in conditions of thick fog and ice. There was no highly developed radar available to her, and no major advance in the navigation of ice-fields had been made since the loss of the TITANIC. In the event, she was lost in the second World War by enemy action. A sister ship, mooted in the 1930s, failed to materialize.

XI THE ATLANTIC STEAM
NAVIGATION COMPANY DESIGN

Another ambitious proposition was being fostered in Great Britain at this time. With the dissolution of the White Star Line in 1934, one of the company's executives, Major Frank Bustard, attempted to establish a good, second-grade trans-Atlantic service to supplement the express mail schedules provided by the Cunard-White Star Line. Cunard later placed the motorships *Britannic* and *Georgic* in a somewhat similar service based on London, which proved to be very successful, but Major Bustard regarded Liverpool, at one time the Mecca of Britain's passenger shipping trade, as being a more suitable terminus port, especially if a good train service to the capital could be arranged.

His first step was to form a new company, the Atlantic Steam Navigation Company (The Atlantic Line) in late 1934 with offices in Cockspur Street in London, and then he negotiated a suitable rail link between Euston* and Liverpool with the London, Midland and Scottish Railway Company. With this accomplished, his next move was to acquire the necessary ships with which to operate the service. Initially, Major Bustard tendered to purchase the vessels of the Red Star Line which had been put up for sale as part of the I.M.M.'s budgetary measures implemented during the Depression. The ships included in the sale were the *Belgenland, Pennland* and *Westernland,* in addition to the former Atlantic Transport Line cargo-passenger steamers *Minnetonka* and *Minnewaska* which the Red Star Line had operated since 1930.

The plan was to carry tourist passengers only on the five ships at a one-

*One of the main London termini.

108

72. A late photograph of Lt. Col. Frank Bustard, taken in 1966.

way fare of £10, with *à la carte* menus as an extra. The British Government, however, would not support the purchase financially because the proposed vessels would have been competing with the Cunard-White Star Line which had already received Treasury assistance, and the Red Star Line was sold instead to Arnold Bernstein, the Hamburg shipowner. This sale only covered the *Pennland* and *Westernland,* which made substantial profits for their new German owners, while the *Belgenland* was transferred within the I.M.M. to the Panama Pacific Line and re-named *Columbia.* The *Minnetonka* and the *Minnewaska* were sold for scrapping only ten years after being completed.

73. The BELGENLAND, of 27,132 gross tons, passing down Gravesend Reach. She was the largest ship to use the Port of London at that time.

In view of this outcome to his first moves, it was necessary to have designs prepared for two new liners suitable to operate the Atlantic Line service, and for this Major Bustard approached Vickers Armstrong, who presumably would have eventually built the two sister ships.

Vickers Armstrong conceived two very attractive three-funnelled ships of about 33,000 gross tons with an overall length of 685 feet* and a beam of 90 feet. The two liners were to carry 1,500 passengers in two classes, Cabin and Tourist, with a service speed of 22 knots from geared turbine engines. There was speculation in the American press during late 1936 that the two vessels were to be named *Silverswift* and *Silverfalcon,* though no real evidence can be discovered to support this assertion.

These ships were pleasing in every respect, commercially sound vehicles, and there was more than a hint of the White Star's planned *Oceanic* of seven years earlier in the shipbuilder's profile. Perhaps this is not so surprising, since Major Bustard held an executive position with the White Star at the time of the brief *Oceanic* episode.

A service which provided for a sailing from either side of the Atlantic every ten days was proposed, operating from Liverpool, Dublin (Dun Laoghaire) and New York. The Dublin call was included to exploit the strong family links between the Irish people there and in the U.S.A.

With shipyard prices negotiated at £2¼ million per vessel and tentative delivery dates agreed, the ingredients for the project were complete. This

*208.79 metres.

was a viable and sensible scheme which was not intended to compete with other U.K.-based liners in any way for passengers travelling by the premier express services. Instead, it was directed at winning for Great Britain a further handsome chunk of that lucrative part of the trade which catered for the passenger who was not so wealthy – the traveller who really did not care so much about the speed of the crossing, especially if it meant paying a lower fare for the pleasure. At the time, this trade was dominated by the Continental and American lines.

Having catered for all possible contingencies, on 4 October 1938 Major Bustard approached the Bank of England for financial assistance but, due to a negative attitude by the Government of the day, which did not appear to appreciate the value of having a comprehensive secondary trans-Atlantic service, a loan of £2½ million spread over two years was opposed, and no other help was forthcoming for the construction of these two well-conceived liners.

This was not only a great disappointment to Major Bustard, but a most unfortunate loss for Great Britain, for a valuable section of the North Atlantic traffic was abandoned almost entirely, while two potential hospital ships, which would have been invaluable in the World War which was looming, were also forfeited. One of the features of the design of these ships was their suitability for conversion to this role during war-time – a conversion for which Major Bustard had made it clear that they would be available immediately.

Nevertheless, Bustard pursued his project with undaunted deter-mination, and he then approached other established shipping companies, including the Orient and Anchor Lines, for consideration of his plans in the hope that they would subsidize his enterprise. For various reasons, however, these concerns were unable to involve themselves in the project and, with the outbreak of war – the final and inevitable confrontation with the Third Reich – he reluctantly conceded defeat and finally aban-doned his scheme. Right up to his death Major Bustard (later Lieutenant-Colonel Bustard, and the last surviving ex-White Star Line Director) felt that the lack of positive support for his constructive and practical sugges-tions was a great pity. The fact that his ships were never realized can only be regarded as an unnecessarily blank page in the history of Great Britain's maritime trade.

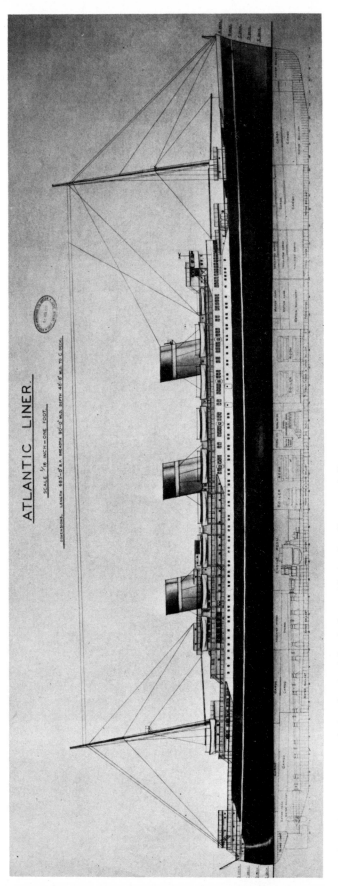

ATLANTIC LINER.

SCALE 1/16 INCH = ONE FOOT.

DIMENSIONS. LENGTH 685'-0" B.P. BREADTH 90'-0" MLD. DEPTH 45'-6" MLD. TO C. DECK.

74. *The Vickers Armstrong design for the Atlantic Steam Navigation Company's liners.*

Before closing this chapter, a few brief biographical notes about the man must surely be in order, for the personal vitality which this dynamic individual displayed in his business affairs was equally evident in his private and social acitivities. Frank Bustard was born in Liverpool in February 1886 and, following a distinguished career in the army, he was equally successful in the passenger shipping business, and was also well-known for his extrovert involvement in sports activities, being a member of the so-called 'Champion Eight' of the Liverpool gymnasium and a contestant for the Liverpool and Merseyside Amateur Wrestling Championship. He died in January 1974, aged 87, but his memory lives on in the present-day European Ferries Company, the offspring of his Atlantic Steam Navigation Company which turned to coastal activities after the rebuff to its North Atlantic aspirations.

75. *The BREMEN (51,656 gross tons) and the EUROPA (49,746 gross tons) captured the Atlantic Blue Riband from the MAURETANIA and their success was, in some measure, a spur to other grandiose schemes. The EUROPA is seen above.*

XII THE "YANKEE CLIPPERS"

While Frank Bustard's Atlantic Line episode was unfolding, Paul Wadsworth Chapman, in collaboration with his colleague, Theodore Ernest Ferris, had evolved his latest, most elaborate and most gigantic proposal for two passenger liners to wear the United States ensign. This effort, developed from the earlier plans for the United States Lines, not only confirmed Chapman's enthusiastic belief in the giant passenger liners, but also indicated his genius as a prophet of maritime trends, for the outstanding characteristic of his two new liners was that they were to be one-class cabin ships aimed specifically at the tourist class traveller. (Such tourist liners did not become commonplace features of the passenger shipping scene until the 1960s.) Credit for the scheme was entirely due to P. W. Chapman, the entrepreneur, but praise for the design of the ships deservedly belongs to Theodore Ferris.

Projected at a time when sheer size was so important, these two ships would have been monsters – phenomenal, colossal ocean wonders! They were the largest passenger liners ever conceived, yet their sleek proportions concealed their immense size, for their displacement would have been about 105,000 tons each, with a gross tonnage slightly less at 100,000. (In comparison, the *Normandie,* originally quoted as 86,495 gross tons in 1938, would have constituted the biggest of the giant liners ever completed, but this figure was subsequently considered to be unreliable and that she was in reality 83,423 tons – this surprising variation possibly being due to differences in measurement – putting the *Queen Elizabeth* at the top of the league at 83,673 gross tons.) Their other main dimensions were an overall length of 1,250 feet* and a beam of 144 feet. The crews

*381 metres.

76. Projected cabin layout for the Yankee Clipper scheme.

would have numbered between 1,500 and 1,750.

Five thousand cabins were to be provided on each of these super-liners for a total of 10,000 passengers, and each cabin was to have a private bath. Fares across the Atlantic were to be $50* per passenger each way, meals costing extra, and with the 'run of the ship' for all. Private single occupancy of cabins was an optional extra at an increased price, and meals were to be served in three popular and distinct types of restaurants at appropriate prices.

The design of the two liners envisaged them as completely enclosed ships with air-conditioning throughout. As for the interior decorations of these mammoth vessels, their commodious spaces would, without doubt, have given rise to great ingenuity and creativity within the limitations of

*Approx. £10!

77. A model of the Yankee Clipper design.

the fare and the class of passenger to be carried. Both Chapman and Ferris had a strong inclination towards adopting new ideas and inventions, and it is certain that, in addition to the luxurious décor and furnishings that were characteristic of all the great liners of the period, there would have been all manner of modern shipboard facilities and new-fangled contrivances in the two liners.

It was intended to operate the two 'Yankee Clippers', as they were dubbed with total disregard for the real meaning of the term,* at 34 knots, with a reserve maximum of 38 knots. This was to be achieved with a geared turbine installation producing 380,000 s.h.p. and driving four propellers.

A contingency feature of the design, for auxiliary deployment during national emergencies, was their use as troop transports, with a capacity for 40,000 men each. Additionally, they featured Lawrence Wilder's innovation of an aircraft-carrying capability, for their two masts were to be telescopic and the funnels could be retracted below the level of the upper deck, leaving a clear flight deck 800 feet long and the full width of the ship. Aeroplane storage space was provided beneath the flight deck and, in order to keep the upper superstructure levels clear for flying operations, the lifeboats were placed on the main deck.

However these fine ships, the very epitome of the giant liner concept, never came to be built. The year was 1937, and the *Normandie* and *Queen Mary* were already in service and gaining for France and Great Britain the distinction of being the only countries to place passenger liners of over 1,000 feet in length into service. The Chapman/Ferris project should

*The word 'clipper' normally signified a sailing ship of exceptionally fine lines, beauty and speed.

78. Paul Wadsworth Chapman.

have been America's answer to them and, in its scale, it would have far surpassed the two European giants and placed the United States at the top of the league amongst the maritime nations operating the North Atlantic route. Almost coincidentally with the release of the Chapman/Ferris scheme, the United States Maritime Commission was set up, replacing the previous Shipping Board, and one of its first major tasks was to establish some sort of order into the heterogeneous merchant fleet then owned by the United States, since it comprised out-dated war-prize vessels of foreign origin and a variety of 'one-off' ships. Their approach to the problem was, basically, the introduction of standard ship types, and these received priority over mammoth express liners in the national expenditure. This policy was not only very unfortunate for Messrs. Chapman and Ferris, but its very wisdom might be called into question, especially when one considers just how heavily America had to depend on her allies for troop-carriers under the Lease-Lend scheme in the ensuing World War.

Even though it was their second major set-back, this was by no means the end of the road for Chapman and Ferris. In 1949, after the war was over, the construction of their two 'class-distinction-less' cabin ships was advocated once again, with a third ship for operation in the Pacific also suggested. This, however, is jumping ahead of our chronology, and we must first return to pre-War days.

The 'Yankee Clippers' scheme was not the only unsuccessful liner project in the United States at this time. In the mid-1930s, the Dollar Line, which operated from the U.S. West Coast to Japan, ambitiously planned to build two 'super-liners' close in size and speed to the *Bremen* and *Europa,* which operated on the North Atlantic route. The two ships were intended to complement the *President Coolidge* and the *President Hoover,* and they were said to be of 'conventional appearance'. The two older *Presidents,* handsome turbo-electric liners built in 1931, provided only a relatively small representation on this route compared with the many modern vessels owned by the Nippon Yusen Kaisha and the Canadian Pacific Lines, and so it was intended that these huge new liners should also challenge this foreign domination of the trans-Pacific run. The project, however, was short-lived.

With the majority of Congressmen being naturally from land-locked and land-orientated states, and with the financial losses of the *Leviathan* on the North Atlantic being ever present in their minds, these factors combined to put a federal subsidy out of the question. With no other financial support available, the Dollar giants were doomed from the outset. It seemed that, at about this time, many Americans shared the belief that they could not operate a super-liner profitably or successfully and, as it turned out, their doubts appeared to be substantiated when, in 1938, the United States Maritime Commission was compelled to intervene in the affairs of the Dollar Line, which had been slipping deeper and deeper into financial trouble, in order to protect the Federal loans already made to the Company. The result of this action was the formation of the American President Lines, which was soon to have new ideas of its own.

79. *The LEVIATHAN in Southampton's Ocean Dock, with the HOMERIC ahead of her and the MAJESTIC to the left in the floating dock. The word 'successful' is frequently used of ships, though its meaning is not always clear. A vessel which performs well but is run at a loss may still be a success if she engenders the national prestige intended for her. Two similar vessels on the same route, but under different flags, may produce quite different financial results if the one is hedged by onerous regulations and/or union demands and restrictive practices, and the other is not. (Hence the recent flight to 'flags of convenience'). U.S. Congressmen judged the LEVIATHAN by her losses, and thus killed the proposed ships for the Dollar Line which might well have been successful on a quite different route and in quite different circumstances. This is not to say that Congress was right or wrong in the matter, but it does demonstrate that the destiny of these two superlative, modern ships which never came into existence was damned by the continuing presence of another, ageing one. Had the LEVIATHAN never existed, or had she been sunk by a German U-boat (p.64), the Dollar liners might have reached the water!*

XIII THE *JASON*

The mid-1930s saw the beginning of an upsurge in the construction of new passenger liners: a fact which reflected the vast improvement in international commerce following the Depression and the particularly auspicious situation in the shipping world as a whole, which was a direct result of this upturn in international trade. Not all of these new passenger ship projects were successful, however, and one scheme which failed was that proposed by the Shaw Savill and Blue Funnel Lines, which operated a joint service on the U.K.-Australian route. In the late 1920s, Shaw Savill had already lost two tentatively-planned 20,000 gross ton 17-knot passenger liners as a result of being taken over by the Royal Mail organization. Now, their new plan involved the construction of a series of 900-foot long motor vessels as an extension of their famous Empire Food ships. In the event, the unjustifiably high cost of liners of this calibre for a route which did not warrant them proved to be a fatal ingredient. From this point, further discussions on the question of constructing new ships for the Dominion trade centered around a design for somewhat smaller quadruple screw motor ships, and the outcome of them was the placing of an order by the Shaw Savill Line for the 682-foot* *Dominion Monarch* in 1937. Lord Essendon, the Chairman of Shaw Savill and Albion, who was a committed advocate of the large passenger/cargo type of vessel, urged his Blue Funnel counterparts to follow suit, and it was generally expected that they, too, would follow with a similar vessel.

In fact, a decision in principle was made to this effect in the summer of 1939. Although Alfred Holt & Company, owners of the Blue Funnel

*207.87 metres.

80. The DOMINION MONARCH.

Line, were basically opposed to the large liner concept, the directors agreed somewhat reluctantly to the construction of a similar vessel to the *Dominion Monarch* in order to provide this vessel with a suitable consort and as a replacement for the ageing *Nestor* and *Ulysses*. However, certain detailed preferences in the design of the Blue Funnel ship would have made her substantially, as well as visually, different from the *Dominion Monarch*. Given the name *Jason* for discussion purposes, she would have had similar dimensions and tonnage to the *Dominion Monarch* but, instead of the exclusive first-class accommodation of 500 in the Shaw Savill ship, the *Jason* would have had cabin space for 1,000 tourist passengers only, at the expense of some of the refrigerated cargo capacity.

The Blue Funnel also chose a different propulsion arrangement, preferring a simpler twin-propeller drive system. There would have been two

Burmeister and Wain engines instead of the *Dominion Monarch's* four Doxford diesels. One of the reasons behind their preference for this simpler engine arrangement may have been the vast maintenance problems associated with the latter ship's quadruple engine installation – a disadvantage which almost resulted in her capture by the Japanese in Singapore in 1942. Externally, the two liners would have had a very similar appearance except that the *Jason* would have had one funnel and two masts, whereas the *Dominion Monarch* had two funnels and one mast.

The order for the *Jason* was forecast for 1940, but the outbreak of war interfered with this and the plan was then abandoned. It is probably safe to say that the Blue Funnel directors greeted this enforced abandonment of the scheme with some relief, since they had never given their full support to the building of such a ship in the first place. As for Shaw Savill, in the absence of a firm commitment to the *Jason,* they had been compelled to terminate the joint service arrangement with the Blue Funnel Line. In February 1939, when the *Dominion Monarch* (27,155 tons) went into service, a new Australian route from Southampton was inaugurated, calling at Teneriffe, Cape Town, Durban, Fremantle, Melbourne, Sydney, Wellington and Lyttleton. Thereafter, Shaw Savill reorganized its Australian services completely and, in spite of a tacit agreement to the provision of a consort to the *Dominion Monarch,* Blue Funnel displayed no great urgency in trying to reinstate the close working arrangement they had enjoyed on the Empire run hitherto.

As things turned out, with the services of the two companies no longer closely linked, when the Blue Funnel Lines did proceed with new vessels after the war, they opted for a completely different solution to their new ship requirements, and this took the form of the much smaller cargo- of the *Patroclus* type, and the second of these ships was given the name *Jason.*

It is interesting to note that, despite the fact that they originated from distinctly different approaches, both the *Dominion Monarch* and the *Helenus*-class ships were highly successful.

81. The launch of the first STOCKHOLM.

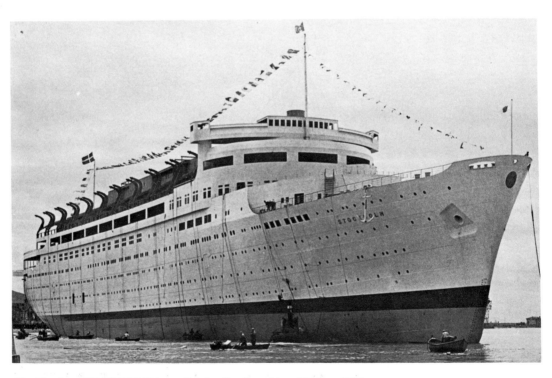

82. The first STOCKHOLM immediately after launching, 29 May, 1938.

XIV THE TWO *STOCKHOLMS*

During this period, the liner projects which fell by the wayside were very much the minority of all those begun. Most of the plans bore fruit and many big passenger ships, which have since become famous, proceeded without obstacle from the drawing board to the slipway, and from the slipway to the water to begin the ships' first and life-long association in their own element. In due course the maiden voyages completed this perfect maritime metamorphosis. Amongst the many success stories of the period were the later P. & O. *Straths,* the German trio *Gneisenau, Potsdam* and *Scharnhorst* for the Far East service, and the Union Castle Line's *Athlone* and *Stirling Castle.* Other new liners were the Orient Line's *Orion* and *Orcades,* the *Pretoria* and *Windhuk* of the Deutsche-Öst Afrika Line, while the Gdynia America Line took delivery of the smaller *Batory* and *Pilsudski.* However, the crowning event of the mid-1930s was the entry into service of the *Normandie* and *Queen Mary* and, viewed with hindsight, what greater proof could there have been that the ocean passenger liner had reached a glorious and most spectacular peak at that time?

This great shipbuilding boom did not end with these ships for, as the barometer of world trade rose ever upwards, so even more ships began to take shape on the drawing boards and in shipyard berths. The list of new buildings was impressive, to say the very least, and it included a new *Mauretania* and a second *Nieuw Amsterdam.* In addition there was the *Capetown Castle,* the *Pasteur,* the *America,* the previously mentioned *Dominion Monarch* and finally, of course, the greatest of them all – the *Queen Elizabeth,* due for completion in 1940. In fact, these years were so favourable for passenger ships of all categories that it is hard to believe that any scheme could have fallen the victim of bad luck. Nevertheless, ill-fortune comes in many forms, and no ship could have had a greater meed of it than the liner whose story is now related.

It began in 1935 when the relatively youthful Swedish America Line, just twenty years old, embarked upon its most ambitious project to that time. Preliminary design work was started on a large liner for the North Atlantic route: a vessel which would place Sweden on a level with the more established maritime nations on the world's prestige sea route. Planned to be of around 28,500 gross tons on completion, the new ship, given the name *Stockholm,* was ordered from the Monfalcone yard of the Cantieri Riuniti dell' Adriatico in 1936 and laid down on 10 March the following year. The *Stockholm* was an unusual liner and a quite unique experiment. Designed by the Swedish America Line's Technical Director, Mr. E. Th. Christiansson,* she was to be a purpose-built, dual-role, regular service vessel and an 'off-peak' cruise ship − a trend more commonplace three and a half decades later, but not at that time.

With her smaller consorts, the *Gripsholm* of 1925 and the *Kungsholm* of 1928, the *Stockholm* was intended to make pleasure cruises to North Cape, the Caribbean and the Baltic when not employed on the North Atlantic service. Her passenger accommodation was, therefore, styled with her twin-purpose career in mind, and it differed vastly from the accommodation in other great trans-Atlantic liners of the period.

The usual system of two corridors was abandoned in favour of a single broad, centre one along the whole length of the stateroom decks. As a result, all cabins would have been very large, and practically all cruising passengers would have had outside cabins. This was reflected in her passenger numbers for, while on the North Atlantic, the *Stockholm* would have carried 1,350 in four classes − de-luxe, cabin, tourist and third − whereas on cruises she would have carried only 620 passengers in one class.

In addition to her unconventional accommodation layout, the equipment and fittings of the *Stockholm* included many novel features. The most interesting of the installations to be fitted in the vessel was her air-conditioning plant. This treated and controlled the air temperature and humidity to all her saloons and passenger cabins, and it made her the first

*Mr. E. Th. Christiansson died in 1981 at the age of 80. He went to sea as a boy of 14 in the barquentine *Jonstorp* and sailed in various ships, on deck and in the engine room, until he came ashore and took a job as a ships' plater while he studied for his engineering examinations. After this somewhat unorthodox start, he had a most successful career as a ship designer.

passenger liner to be so fitted. Even more thought was given to the passengers' comfort with regard to stability and vibration, and a number of features were incorporated into the design to improve these factors. First, the *Stockholm* had big, stream-lined bilge keels: second, anti-rolling tanks,* capable of reducing roll from 15° to 5°, were fitted and, finally, in the most fundamental approach to the stability of the ship, she had a very carefully thought out length/beam ratio. The proportions which resulted were an overall length of 678 feet† and a beam measurement of 83 feet, giving a ratio of 8:1. Her draught would have been 28 feet when fully loaded.

The *Stockholm* was designed as a triple-screw motor ship, and was the largest vessel of her time with this machinery/propeller combination. Her engines consisted of three 10-cylinder C.R.A.-Sulzer SD72 single-acting main units giving a total of 22,000 i.h.p. It had been suggested originally that she should be fitted with twelve 10-cylinder medium-speed engines geared in fours to the three propeller shafts. These would have been manufactured by the Atlas Diesel Company of Stockholm, but the Swedish America Line preferred the direct drive arrangement of the C.R.A.-Sulzer design. The *Stockholm's* service speed was to be 18½ knots with a maximum speed of 20 knots.

With her construction financed on a barter arrangement in exchange for coal, the *Stockholm* was the first and, with the exception of the Clyde-built *Kungsholm* of 1966, the only really large liner ordered by Sweden. Unfortunately, however, as already indicated, she was a very unlucky ship.

The building of the vessel proceeded through 1937 and 1938 and was distinguished at that time by the extensive use of electric arc welding in the hull structure. The new liner was launched by H.R.H. Princess Ingeborg, mother of Queen Astrid of Sweden, on 29 May 1938. She was nearing completion by the end of that year, with her sea trials scheduled for March 1939, but on 19 December 1938 the vessel was gutted by fire. The blaze spread through the ship rapidly, being fanned by strong gusts of the wind that was blowing, and fire-fighting was made particularly difficult by the toxic fumes containing acetic acid which developed from the burning insulation material fitted on board. On account of the vast quantities of water pumped into her, the unlucky liner gradually lost stability and finally sank at her fitting out berth.

*See Glossary, under Anti-Rolling Tanks.
† 206.65 metres.

83. An artist's impression of the first STOCKHOLM.

After the fire had been extinguished, the charred hulk was examined in an attempt to establish its cause, but the findings were inconclusive, although the inspection did reveal quite clearly that the ship and most of her fittings were beyond salvage. Almost immediately it was decided to construct another almost identical liner, also to bear the name *Stockholm,* using the undamaged parts of the wreck, including the original oil engines, wherever possible. Work was consequently resumed on the vacant slip-way and the second hull, yard number 1203, was launched on 10 March 1940.

This new *Stockholm* was completed in 1941 and in appearance she was already a hint of the post-war Swedish America Line ships *Kungsholm* of 1953 and the *Gripsholm* of 1958. The new *Stockholm* measured 29,305 gross tons, but this was later increased to 30,390. She had ten decks, six of which extended the full length of the ship. All the features and appoint-ments of the original vessel were present in the replacement and she was a

84. The first STOCKHOLM ablaze and listing to port at her fitting out berth.

very luxurious and beautiful liner in every respect.

The *Stockholm* carried out her sea trials in the Spring of 1941, but the outbreak of the Second World War in September 1939 had led to the immediate blockade of the Skaggerak and thus, due to the long delay since the first ship had been laid down, it was impossible for the fine new liner to be delivered to her owners. The President of the Swedish America Line was said to have wept when he saw his splendid ship and knew that he could not have her in his fleet.

Later in the same year the vessel was sold back to the Italians, who at once set about converting her to a troopship. This work was finished in 1942, and she reappeared as the *Sabaudia,* to be managed for the Italian Government by the Italia Line. Perhaps surprisingly, in view of her recent conversion, she was immediately laid up at Monfalcone. Contrary to popular belief, neither this vessel, nor the *Rex* nor the *Conte di Savoia,* were used for trooping in the end, because of their large size and obvious

85. *Unlike her predecessor, the second STOCKHOLM was launched with masts and funnels in position.*

86. *The second STOCKHOLM undergoing her sea trials.*

87. *Another view of the second STOCKHOLM – a luckless liner whose fate was sealed by a war in which her country had no part.*

88. First-class gallery.

89. First-class lounge.

In a spirit of competition, most large liners had generally provided not only luxury in the first-class accommodation, but also a magnificence of décor and standards vastly in excess of the experience and expectations of their passengers, invariably causing admiration but, sometimes, criticism. The Orient Company had broken with this tradition in their ORION and ORCADES . . .

91. The first-class bar.

. . . in 1935 and 1937, but these were for the Australian run. The STOCKHOLM (2) provided luxury with greater simplicity and, had she gone into service on the North Atlantic, her accommodation would have produced a sensation. Her designers were, in fact, some years ahead of their times, since these trends only appeared on the route after the 2nd, World War.

92. *The SABAUDIA, ex-STOCKHOLM, alongside at the Cantieri Riuniti dell'Adriatico yard at Monfalcone. The change of paint and angle of view belies her size.*

vulnerability to air attack in the Mediterranean – a vulnerability demonstrated graphically by the attack on the Taranto naval base by 'planes of the Fleet Air Arm in November 1940. For a while she was used as a German accommodation ship in Trieste following the Italian capitulation, and then she was towed to the supposed safety of Vallone de Zaule, south of Sabba and fairly near Trieste.

It seemed that Fate was still banked against the luckless liner. On 6 July 1944 the *Sabaudia* was spotted at her anchorage by British aircraft, bombed and set on fire. The conflagration could not be controlled and the blazing ship drifted helplessly until she finally went aground. Later, the half-sunken, burnt-out hulk was bombed again for the second time in May 1945 and became a total loss, lying near the wrecks of the *Duilio* and *Giulio Cesare*.

When the war ended, the *Sabaudia* was refloated by Messrs. D. & C. Tripcovich, who sold the wreck to Messrs. Goriup. They dismantled it at the San Rocco Repair Yard at Muggia, not far from Trieste, from 1947 to

93. The SABAUDIA being towed to Vallone di Zaule, near Trieste, c.1944. She had never received her full complement of boats.

1950. This was a tragically ignominious end for such a fine ship, which had never been put to any good use at all. Miraculously, the main engines were once again recovered practically intact and these were sold: one to be fitted to the m.v. *Trieste,* which was a new cargo liner, yard number 1780, at the Cantieri Riuniti dell' Adriatico's San Marco shipyard.

The name *Stockholm* can, perhaps, be considered to have been an unlucky one from the point of view of the Swedish America Line for, apart from the two giant liners of that name lost in 1938 and 1944 as described above, the next *Stockholm,* built in 1947, was involved in the tragic collision with the *Andrea Doria* on 26 July 1956: a disaster which resulted in the loss of 53 lives and the sinking of the Italian liner.

94. *A graveyard of liners. View at Vallone di Zaule on 16 October, 1947, showing the wreck of the SABAUDIA (left background); the GIULIO CESARE (foreground) and the DUILIO.*

95. *A close-up view of the wreck of the SABAUDIA, ex-STOCKHOLM — a sad and sorry spectacle. Note her buckled plates and the scale of the ship shown by the men on the hull.*

XV THE *KASHIWARA MARU* AND *IZUMO MARU*

At this point we should return to 1936 to witness the commencement of another ship project which became disrupted by Destiny. Early in that year a statement had been issued that the next Olympiad, to follow the games in Berlin, would be held at Tokyo in 1940. This venue was subsequently transferred to Helsinki before being finally abandoned altogether, but the immediate result of this decision was that Japan realized very quickly that vast numbers of people might be expected to attend so spectacular an event of such international importance. Both the Canadian Pacific and Dollar Lines would benefit from the consequent upsurge in passenger traffic, but the Japanese had no intention of allowing their foreign competitors to dominate the battle for profits which this increased influx of people would bring to their country. This consideration, therefore, prompted a decision to build Japan's first giant passenger liners, and two luxury vessels were consequently evolved for the Nippon Yusen Kaisha's Pacific service. These ships were expected to elevate Japan's status as a passenger-carrying maritime nation but, as things turned out, they were destined instead to be among the first doomed liners ordered for a route other than the North Atlantic.

From the very outset the design work was influenced very strongly by the requirements of the Japanese Government's Naval rearmament policy, and the two liners were immediately earmarked for conversion into aircraft carriers if necessary. The reasons for this went back to 1927, when the Japanese Government resolved to implement a naval building programme which would provide their country with a naval force strong enough to challenge the combined strengths of the American and British Pacific Fleets, but which would not contravene the strength limitations laid down by the Washington Naval Conference of 1921. With the reinforcement of the naval air arm particularly in mind, this was to be achieved by the construction of a number of passenger ships which would serve commercial purposes during peacetime, but which would be so designed that, in the event of a national emergency, they could be transformed into aircraft carriers very rapidly.

The first group of liners to be completed within the concepts of this new strategy were the 17,000 gross ton N.Y.K. motor ships *Asama Maru, Tatsuta Maru* and *Chichibu Maru,* built for the San Francisco run, but never actually requisitioned by the Japanese navy in the event. A second group of three similar ships planned for the N.Y.K.'s European service were cancelled in 1935 on economic grounds. With the expiry of the first London Naval Treaty on 31 December 1936, Japan moved into a treaty-free era and unwisely aggravated the political scene by both proliferating her rearmament scheme and by blatantly exposing its intentions for, in an appendix to the *Imperial Japanese Navy Fleet Register,* all the liners concerned were listed as reserve aircraft carriers.

From 1938 onwards another five passenger vessels were built and were also intended for conversion to aircraft carriers. These were the N.Y.K. 17,000 gross ton motor ships *Nitta Maru, Kasuga Maru* and *Yawata Maru,* which became the *Chuyo, Taiyo* and *Unyo* respectively, and the smaller Osaka Shosen Kaisha motor ships *Argentina Maru* and *Brazil Maru,* of which only the former was requisitioned to become the auxiliary carrier *Kaiyo.*

Meanwhile the negotiations over the design and building costs of the two larger ships planned from 1936 proceeded rather discordantly, with neither the size, speed nor the question of cost-sharing being resolved. Eventually, however, agreement was reached on ships of 27,700 gross tons and 25 knots speed, with 60% of the building costs being met by the Ministry of Trade. This amounted to 8½ million yen over five years. The design of the two ships was to be shared between the Ministry of Trade, the Admiralty and the Central Planning Department of the Japanese Imperial Fleet.

96. *The original conception of the KASHIWARA MARU, to which her final form bore not the slightest resemblance.*

The Nippon Yusen Kaisha gave the names *Kashiwara Maru* and *Izumo Maru* to the two liners which emerged from the final design. The former was ordered from Mitsubishi Heavy Industries at Nagasaki, and the latter from Kawasaki Heavy Industries at Kobe. Unlike the other new N.Y.K. liners, these two vessels were to be twin-screw turbine steamers with a passenger capacity of 890 in three classes. The *Kashiwara Maru* was laid down on 20 March 1939, but there was a delay on her sister ship and work on her did not begin until November of that year.

In August 1940, barely one year after construction had started (and more than a year before Pearl Harbour), it was decided to take advantage of their suitability for conversion and they were purchased by the Imperial Japanese Navy while still on the stocks. Strictly speaking, they did not become full naval vessels until after the Battle of Midway in July 1942, as all ex-merchant aircraft carriers were listed under their mercantile names until that time, although they were actually christened with their new names on launching, the *Kashiwara Maru* becoming the *Junyo,* and the *Izumo Maru* the *Hiyo.* Conversion to 'flat-tops' began immediately and the *Izumo Maru* soon reached a stage of construction as advanced as that of her sister. In fact, she was launched two days before the *Kashiwara Maru* on 24 June 1941, although the latter ship was the first of the pair to be completed, being commissioned on 5 May 1942.

She displaced 28,300 tons when fully loaded and her overall length was 722 feet.* Her geared turbines supplied by destroyer-type boilers, which produced 56,630 s.h.p., gave her an operational speed of 22½ knots maximum, which was somewhat poorer than the 25½ knots for which she was designed. Aircraft capacity was 48, with a reserve maximum of 53 'planes.

In many respects the *Junyo* and her sister were test beds, for their design incorporated many features which were under trial for the later Japanese aircraft carriers *Taiho* and *Shinano.* Notable amongst these was an island bridge superstructure situated on the starboard side and surmounted by a funnel which inclined outboard at 26°. The *Junyo* and *Hiyo* were the first Japanese carriers to be completed in this way. In addition, they were given a light overall armour of two layers of 25mm Ducol steel, and the inflammable supplies and munition storerooms were similarly protected. The 690 × 89½-foot flight-deck was constructed entirely of steel plate – a distinct improvement on the earlier wooden decks. Compared with normal passenger ships, their number of water-tight bulkheads was greatly increased to such a degree that no-one seeing the hull under construction would have gained any impression that they were looking at a passenger vessel at all. In fact, the conversion of the *Kashiwara Maru* and *Izumo Maru* was much more extensive than on any of the other former passenger liners and, on its conclusion, they were more correctly rated as light fleet carriers. Only the *Aquila,* rebuilt from the passenger liner *Roma* for the Italian Navy, underwent a more extensive conversion.

The *Junyo* and *Hiyo* differed in appearance considerably from other Japanese aircraft carriers, being shorter and higher out of the water than those ships which had been designed for the purpose from the start. They also lacked the characteristic lipped bow of other Japanese warships.

Both vessels participated in many of the naval battles in the Pacific, the

*220.07 metres.

97.

98. *No-one seeing the KASHIWARA MARU on the stocks, and observing her scantlings and the degree of her sub-division, would have supposed her to be a passenger liner. The top picture was taken on 31st January and the lower on 20 May, 1940.*

Junyo's baptism of fire coming only a month after her completion in the Aleutian Islands campaign. The Aleutians are a chain of volcanic islands owned by the United States which are strung out from Alaska to about 450 miles east of the Kamchatka Peninsula in Soviet Asia. Partly as a diversionary tactic from the main Japanese offensive on Midway Island, the *Junyo*, with the smaller *Ryujo*, was sent to attack Dutch Harbour and support a planned occupation of the islands of Kiska and Attu, under the command of Rear-Admiral Kakuta.

En passant, it might be remarked that Admiral Kakuta was proved to be something of a Jonah to the Japanese for, two years later, during the Battle of the Philippine Sea, he was to distinguish himself in a somewhat ignominious fashion when, as Base Air Force Commander on the island of Tinian in the Marianas group, he misled his fleet commander into believing that his aircraft had inflicted crippling damage on the American Task Forces. On the basis of this erroneous information, Vice-Admiral Ozawa led his fleet carriers into a battle which cost him two of his major units, the *Shokaku* and the *Taiho*, within 24 hours. He (Ozawa) had, incidentally, taken over the command of the fast carrier strike force from another officer who had fallen out of favour — Vice-Admiral Nagumo, whose successes at Pearl Harbour and in the Coral Sea had paled before the disasters of Midway* and Santa Cruz.

However, the task force under Rear-Admiral Kakuta arrived off Dutch Harbour on the morning of 4 June 1942, but its impact as a decoy group was minimal and, if the whole operation was not actually a tactical blunder, it had a very disastrous result in that it provided the Americans with the means to establish eventual air superiority over the Japanese. Of the few 'planes to actually attack shore installations — for most turned back because of the extremely adverse weather conditions — one Zeke fighter was critically damaged and forced to crash land at the eastern end of Unalaska Island. Subsequently discovered relatively intact, and put through exhaustive test flights, it provided the vital information regarding the few design weaknesses in this superb plane which, at that time, out-matched every comparable Allied machine.

After this abortive sortie, on 31 July 1942, the *Junyo* was joined by the *Hiyo* which, on completion, was slightly lighter, displacing 27,500 tons fully loaded. Together, they formed the Second Aircraft Carrier Division,

---

*The Battle of Midway was the first decisive defeat suffered by the Japanese navy in 450 years — since, in fact. Admiral Hideyoshi was routed by the Korean admiral Yi-sun in 1592 off the Korean coast.

100. The JUNYO and HIYO seen at sea from a Japanese destroyer — in a very different role from the passenger trade.

99. The JUNYO's deck, bridge and funnel during the Pacific War.

101. A poor, but rare, view of the HIYO in action during the Battle of the Phillipine Sea, enlarged from the frame of a film. She blew up and sank shortly after this picture was taken.

which was a part of Vice-Admiral Nobutake Kondo's newly created Vanguard Force, and they were engaged actively in the Battle of the Eastern Solomons in August 1942 and then in the Battle of the Santa Cruz Islands in the following October. The *Hiyo* was withdrawn from the latter engagement at an early stage due to engine trouble but, while she limped away rather ignominiously, the *Junyo* distinguished herself by the part she played in the battle. Her planes made a significant contribution by damaging the American carrier *USS Enterprise,* and they dealt the death blow to another *Yorktown*-class vessel, the *USS Hornet.*

The next month, in November, the two ex-liners were in action again, first providing fighter protection to the surface ships attacking Henderson Field on Guadalcanal, and later in the Battle of Tassafaronga but, when the Guadalcanal campaign came to a close, they were virtually inactive for the next two years.

During this period they were used briefly in the action round Attu, in the Aleutian Islands, after which they went into operation as aircraft ferries in May 1943, but both ships fell foul of torpedoes that summer while performing this duty. The *Hiyo* was hit first on 11 June, south of Tokyo Bay, by the United States submarine *Trigger,* but she remained afloat and was towed into Yokosuka for repairs by the light cruiser *Isuzu*. The *Junyo* was struck soon afterwards, while on passage through the Bungo Suido (the channel between Shikoku and Honshu) although she also succeeded in reaching port – in her case Kure, where her damage was repaired.

By June 1944 the two vessels were back in action in the Battle of the Philippine Sea and, together with the *Ryuho,* they formed the Japanese Aircraft Carrier Force B under Rear-Admiral Takaji Joshima, this being a unit of Vice-Admiral Jisaburo Ozawa's First Task Fleet. Late in the afternoon of the 20th, when north-west of Luzon, Force B was attacked by American dive- and torpedo-bombers from the aircraft carrier *Bellau Wood,* and the *Hiyo* was hit by both bombs and torpedoes. Apart from other more obvious damage, her tanks had sustained critical fractures and, two hours after the attack, she was racked by a massive explosion when the vapour from the leaking tanks was ignited. She was promptly engulfed by uncontrollable fires and rolled over and sank in a position approximately 300 miles west of Saipan. The *Junyo* was also damaged, being bombed in the funnel, but she managed to escape to Japan with the other ships the following day.

After completing her repairs, the *Junyo* was restricted to training and transport duties in Japan's home waters but, while thus employed, she was torpedoed for a second time while off Cape Nomo-zaki, south of Nagasaki on 9 December 1944 by the United States submarines *Redfish* and *Sea Devil.* She was partly repaired at Sasebo this time but, due to incompletion of repairs, was relegated to reserve status and laid up in the port. In this situation the *Junyo* sustained further hits by bombs from American aircraft attacking Japan during 1945, and was eventually found damaged and de-commissioned at Sasebo by the Allied occupation forces that August. She was not used, like other captured carriers, to repatriate Japanese troops from Indo-China under the supervision of the Americans, but instead was sent for scrap locally on 28 May 1946, the work being completed in late 1947.

During the war, it was reported that the *Junyo* and *Hiyo* were also known by the names *Hayataka* and *Hitaka* respectively. In fact, for a while, they were identified as being four different ships. It appears that the words *Hayataka* and *Hitaka* are, in fact, alternatives for the more

102. The JUNYO's midship structure and funnel, after the war.

familiar names *Junyo* and *Hiyo*. (Familiar, that is, to those with some understanding of Japanese!) This mistaken identity resulted partly from the introduction of the Nihon Shiki, or Kokutai Shiki, system of transliteration in 1937. Principally, however, the confusion was due to the potential ambiguity of the 'kana' (see Glossary), whereby it can be read in more than one way. Consequently 'Junyo' means 'falcon', or 'swift hawk', while 'Hayataka' means 'Fast or swift bird (or hawk)'. Similarly, 'Hiyo' means 'Flying hawk', while 'Hitaka' means 'flying (or soaring) bird (or hawk)'. It can be said with certainty that four separate aircraft carriers with these names never existed, but there is ample evidence that the U.S. Naval records, together with Lloyds Casualty reports and other sources of the same calibre, were still confused up to and after 1959. There were other Japanese carriers besides the *Junyo* and *Hiyo* which were subject to this incorrect identification, among them being the three

103. The JUNYO laid up at Sasebo, as she was found by the American occupation forces. Note the submarine alongside.

that were re-built from the small N.Y.K. motor ships *Nitta Maru, Kasuga Maru* and *Yawata Maru.* Although officially renamed *Chuyo, Taiyo* and *Unyo,* they were also identified as *Okitaka, Otaka* and *Kumotaka* respectively. It was all rather confusing.

An interesting postcript to the story of the *Kashiwara Maru* and *Izumo Maru* concerns the only remaining relic of these vessels, of which very few people are now aware. This is the *Junyo's* eighteen-inch ship's bell which was presented as a war-prize to Fordham College, New York. The bell was sent to Fordham by Admiral Chester Nimitz in answer to a request for a trophy which could be retained as a memorial to the Fordham students killed during the war. Flown from Japan to Pearl Harbour, the bell was collected there by the light cruiser *Detroit* and transported to Philadelphia. It was finally dedicated at Fordham in December 1945, and remains there to this day. According to the Rev. Edward S. Dunn of the

104. Looking aft from close alongside the JUNYO's starboard side, she gives the impression of being a complete 'flat-top', with no superstructure.

University Library, the bell is tolled on all festive occasions, but its primary function is to signal the start of Fordham's annual Academic Procession of Graduation!

Had the Second World War not intervened and had they been completed as intended, there is no doubt that these two ships would have been a great credit to the Japanese Mercantile Marine. As events proved, they joined the ranks of those vessels doomed by destiny not to enter the service for which they had been intended but, unlike the majority of the big ships which are included in this unhappy roster, they crowded a great deal into their relatively short lives, contributing to the history of sea warfare; seeing a variety of action by no means unmixed with success, and suffering damage only to come back and fight another day until their respective fates were finally sealed. Taking account of their actual sea time, few passenger liners can have had so concentrated an experience of excitement and action in so short a time – whatever the roles in which they found themselves cast.

105. *Looking aft and down on to the JUNYO's flight deck after the Japanese surrender, with American officers surveying the carrier. Note the positions of the (removed) deck-edge guns.*

106. Conceived as the passenger liner *KASHIWARA MARU*, the ship lived a violent life as the aircraft carrier *JUNYO*, and was survived only by her bell in an American University – thus did Destiny cast her dice. Here, far removed from the war zones of the Aleutians, New Guinea, the Solomons and the Philippine Sea, Harry S. Truman tolls her bell for the first time in its new site at Fordham University for its charter centenary on 11 May, 1946. Admiral E. King, the President's naval aide, stands beside him.

XVI THE MARITIME COMMISSION'S
P–4–P DESIGN

Almost concurrently, and in reply to the design and construction of the *Kashiwara Maru* and *Izumo Maru,* the newly formed American President Lines(APL) planned competitors for these rumoured Japanese vessels. A report in the *New York Times* of 28 April 1939 stated that three sister ships to the *President Coolidge* were envisaged, but this plan was dropped following a close inspection of this vessel and her turbo-electric machinery by Commander (later Admiral) H. L. Vickery, Director of the Technical Division of the United States Maritime Commission, and this Government organization then submitted its own alternative proposal for the American President Lines' Pacific route.

Established in June 1936, the Maritime Commission had not wasted any time in producing its designs for standard ship types to replace the many ageing units in the American merchant fleet. These designs were classified with a letter and number code which indicated the type of ship, length of hull, engine type, number of propellers, etc. The letters C and T referred to cargo ships and tankers respectively and, just as predictably, P was used to indicate passenger vessels.* Although she was created by W. F. Gibbs before the inception of the Maritime Commission, the United States Line's *America* was given a P4 designation, the number 4 indicating a length between 700 and 800 feet † – in her case 723 feet overall‡.

Early in 1939 a further P4 design, that for the trans-Pacific passenger liners, appeared on the Commission's drawing boards. Known as the P–4–P,§ this design was in many ways a resurrection of the *Flying*

*See Appendix 3.
†213.36–243.84 metres.
‡220.37 metres.
§See page 313.

150

Cloud passenger liner/aircraft carrier, although somewhat smaller. The vessels' dimensions would have been 35,500 gross tons with an overall length of 759 feet* and a beam of 98 feet. Draught would have been 32 feet and her displacement approximately 41,000 tons.

This early Maritime Commission design was distinctive – even revolutionary – in its approach to the hull specification, which featured a combination of high strength and low weight. This was to be achieved in a number of ways. It was intended to weld the hulls of the P–4–P ships wherever possible, while they had also been designed in such a way as to obviate the necessity for expansion joints. Further weight reductions would have been achieved through the layout and design of the propulsion machinery. Additionally, the P–4–P ships would have had no fresh water tanks, the proposed installation of a large evaporating plant making this unnecessary. As a result of this and of the increased efficiency of the main propelling plant, it was stated that in this particular design it would be possible to make a complete voyage without utilizing ballast tanks. For protection in the event of collision, the ships were to be given subdivision of an extraordinarily high standard, perhaps reflecting the National Defence needs. The hull was to contain 14 main watertight transverse bulkheads with numerous other additional watertight and oiltight ones.

Apart from the safety features incorporated in the hull structure, the P–4–P design was also noteworthy for the elaborate security arrangements for the prevention of fire. A highly efficient fire detection system was to be installed in each ship and incombustible materials were specified for all bulkheads, deckheads,† linings and partitions.

Regarding the propulsion machinery, there were to be two triple expansion steam turbines, each driving its own propeller through double reduction gears from an entirely independent engine room. The machinery in the forward engine room would have driven the port propeller, while that in the after engine room would have driven the starboard one. The two turbines would have operated on a re-heat regenerative cycle producing a total normal output of 58,000 shaft horse-power and a maximum total output of 88,000 shaft horse-power. This would have sustained a sea-speed of 25 knots.

Accommodation would have been provided for between 800 and 1,000

*231.34 metres.
† To a landsman, 'ceilings'. (This word has a quite different nautical connotation.)

107. A model of the P-4-P design.

passengers in three classes, with a crew of 500. An ultra-modern air-conditioning installation was proposed, supplying every cabin and state-room with heating in the winter and with cooling and dehumidification in the summer. All lighting aboard the ships would have been of the fluorescent type, which would have saved generator capacity – an additional weight reduction – while it was also regarded as lending itself more readily to artistic innovation in lighting effects. Passenger liners on the Orient routes were noted for their high standards of comfort and roominess, passenger complements invariably being lower than those aboard ships of equivalent size on the Atlantic run. The P–4–P vessels would have been no exception to this rule, with more than adequate provision of all the usual passenger amenities.

The planned decoration for the lounges, dining rooms and other public centres were distinguished by the use of light, relaxing pastel shades. Separate swimming pools were to be provided for each of the Cabin, Tourist and Third classes of passengers, while the games and promenade deck spaces were to be unusually large and unobstructed in consequence of the auxiliary (war-time) features of the P–4–P design.

The cargo space for each ship was to be 535,000 cubic feet, of which some 7% would have been refrigerated. Large holds were to be fitted forward and aft, with ample facilities for handling cargo through conventional hatches, as well as through side ports. Special provision was also made for the carriage of a number of automobiles in an enclosed space at the forward end of the promenade deck.

The P−4−Ps were specifically designed as passenger ships suitable for rapid modification into aircraft carriers in times of national emergency. Like the *Flying Cloud,* their twin funnels would have been situated to one side of the upper deck, but it was not planned to fit a permanent flight deck aboard these ships as would have been the case with that vessel, since there was no aeroplane-carrying application intended for them during their commercial service. In fact, apart from the offset funnels, the auxiliary characteristics of the ships would not have been readily apparent. This approach had the benefit of providing, in addition to the four decks in the hull proper, promenade, boat and sun decks in the superstructure for increased passenger space. In comparing the P−4−P conception with the *Flying Cloud,* the emphasis had been switched from adaptability to convertibility, the former being primarily a passenger liner, while the latter had been first and foremost an auxiliary aircraft carrier.

Since the successful utilization of the P−4−P's auxiliary capability depended on a fast and economic conversion, this was to be made possible through the incorporation of special features in the design and construction stages. Beneath the light superstructure, which was to be fitted as a pre-fabricated unit, and therefore readily removable, the main deck was to be strengthened in readiness for the construction of a flight deck. All decks were to be flush throughout the ships in order to facilitate the installation of hangars, workshops and stores for armaments and aircraft spares and, in addition, the passenger accommodation was to be laid out in such a way that it would suit adaptation to officers' and crews' quarters during military employment.

The Maritime Commission's comprehensive design plans were disclosed to naval architects and marine engineers in New York in January 1940, for their consideration. They were received with enthusiastic approval and W. F. Gibbs was among the many famous names who endorsed them. At the same time, details were released about the Commission's proposed construction programme for the P−4−P liners and it was announced that, initially, there would only be two such vessels, and not three as originally intended. These two would be built (it was thought) on the East Coast for the Commission's own account and chartered by them to the American President Lines for service on the California−Orient route: San Francisco—Los Angeles—Yokohama—Kobe—Shanghai—Manila and calling at Hawaii both ways. The ships were to be ready for service in 1943. Furthermore, it was stated that additional vessels of the P—4—P type would be built later for the San Francisco—Australasian run.

A slight interruption, which threatened to endanger the P—4—P's prospects, occurred in February 1940 when the House of Representatives substantially reduced the amount of money in the Ship Construction Appropriations Bill. Subsequently the Senate Appropriations Committee reviewed the pruned bill and favoured the restoration of an amount to the original appropriation which would be specifically earmarked for the liners destined for the Pacific trade. These wishes were endorsed by the rest of Congress, and it was now expected that tenders would be invited for the construction of the two liners.

There was, however, a further delay in May 1940 when the Maritime Commission postponed the opening of tendering until 18 June to permit shipbuilders further opportunity to study the design specifications. The *New York Times* had reported that at least one interested party had expressed anxiety about the strength of the hull, considering that, in view of the horse-power and speed requirements, the hull structure was too light in weight. In spite of the apparent disquiet on this score, no alterations were made to the P—4—P hull details and, perhaps significantly, only one tender for construction was received.

This came from the Seattle—Tacoma Shipbuilding Corporation of Seattle, Washington, on the west coast, and there was nothing from the east coast. On 10 September 1940 they offered to build the two vessels for $28,458,000 per ship on a fixed price contract, or $23,715,000 on an adjusted price basis, the delivery of the first one to be late in 1943 and the second in the summer of 1944. In spite of this, the two liners were never built.

The press blamed the shipyards, alleging that they were not interested in building Maritime Commission designs, completely disregarding the fact that Seattle—Tacoma had made a bid — if a lone one. As for the Commission itself, they made no apparent response to the single tender they did receive, though whether they regarded the price as being too high or had some other reason was never disclosed. Whatever the cause, the projected P–4–Ps were dropped in August 1941, in order that all ship-yards could concentrate their efforts totally on designs specifically required to prepare the country to be on a proper war footing. These included P2-type transports, later adapted for civilian work, and the highly successful *Essex* class of fast attack carriers.

After the war, the American President Lines proceeded to pursue their new building policies and, throughout the subsequent fifteen years, were involved in a number of ambitious and exciting projects.

108. The Hapag liner HAMBURG, after she had been lengthened and given a bulbous bow in 1934 and her speed had been increased from 15½ to 19½ knots. This vessel was mined off Sassnitz in 1945, but was later salvaged to become re-built as the Russian YURY DOLGORUKI.

XVII HAPAG'S SECOND *VATERLAND*

Just as the loom of impending war in the Pacific had changed the destinies of the *Izumo Maru, Kashiwara Maru* and the P-4-P ships, so the actual outbreak of hostilities in Europe interfered with the futures of a number of newly planned ocean liners.

Under the control of Hitler's National Socialists, Germany had once again become a powerful and assertive industrial nation. Once more, efforts were being made to elevate the prestige of her merchant fleet to a position befitting her political and military status. One objective was to regain the premier rank on the North Atlantic route which had been held briefly by the *Bremen* and *Europa,* but the resurgence of the German passenger fleet had wider goals. Indeed, the aim was to have the best ships with the highest standards on every sea route, to compete directly with every foreign company.

The Hamburg Sud-Amerika Line had announced plans to refit and complement the *Cap Arcona* on the River Plate service while the Deutsche Öst-Afrika Line was proposing the construction of two 25,000 gross ton vessels (or bigger), for a fast South and East Africa service to challenge the new Union Castle motor ships, but the War interrupted both schemes while they were still in the preliminary planning stages. Yet another project which proceeded much further involved the Hamburg Amerika Line (Hapag) which had not owned a first-rate giant passenger liner since the pre-World War I *Bismarck* trio.

Hapag's North Atlantic presence since the early 1920s had been in the form of the *New York, Hansa* ex *Albert Ballin, Hamburg* and *Deutschland,* a quartet which, in spite of some excellent public rooms, were

109. This waterline model of the new VATERLAND . . .

commonly regarded as being somewhat slow and spartan. Certainly they had few of the luxurious appurtenances and little of the aura of extravagance and gracious living normally associated with this prestigious route.

In a bid to improve their standards on the Western Ocean, the Hamburg Amerika Line began to consider replacements for their four, older and smaller liners around 1935. Two years later the first of a class of three turbo-electric passenger ships was ordered from Blohm and Voss at Hamburg, as yard Number 523. The builders' models revealed a magnificent two-funnelled vessel with a turtle-back forecastle similar to that on the *Normandie*. Although never christened officially, the name *Vaterland* was definitely intended for the new liner and she was referred to as such in official Hapag documents. Laid down in 1938, one of the most interesting features of the 41,000 gross ton ship was the proposal that her engines should consist of a turbo-electric machinery installation.

Designed to produce 62,000 total shaft horse-power for a maximum speed of 25½ knots, the propulsion consisted of eight Benson forced

110. . . . showed her to be a vessel of great individuality.

circulation boilers. These would generate steam at 950 p.s.i. and a super-heat temperature of 877° Fahrenheit to drive the steam turbine ends of the A.C. generator sets which, in turn, would drive the motors on the twin screw shafts.

The *Vaterland's* principal dimensions were 827 feet* in length overall and 98½ feet beam with a designed displacement of 36,000 tons, making her comparable in size to the present day *Oriana* and *Canberra*. She was intended to have carried 1,322 passengers on the North Atlantic run, divided into 354 First class, 435 Tourist class and 533 Third class. In the winter months she would have cruised with a smaller passenger complement.

Welding was used extensively in the construction of the *Vaterland*. The shell butts of her hull were welded but the seams were riveted, while on the upper decks both the seams and butts were welded. The decks themselves were riveted to the hull shell by an angle bar.

Work on the ship proceeded regardless of the outbreak of war, as there was a foreseeable possibility that her berth would be required for one of

*252.07 metres.

111. The launch of the VATERLAND on 24th August, 1940, – a bow view and . . .

the diesel super-battleships of the *Gross Deutschland* class that were planned. Conceived under the 'Z' Plan – the blueprint of the renascent Kriegsmarine – there were to be six of these monster battleships with a displacement of 65,000 tons, an overall length of 912 feet* and a main armament of eight 16-inch guns. Their proposed diesel propulsion arrangement, comprising three engines producing 165,000 shaft horse-power, was chosen for the increased range it would give the ships, whose operations would, of necessity, have to be independent of bases.

The anticipated need for the *Vaterland's* slipway was realized in 1940, so she was launched without ceremony on 24 August of that year. The super-battleship that was laid down on the vacated slip was herself cancelled soon after being begun and broken up on the stocks. As for the *Vaterland,* all work on her construction was halted following her launch owing to lack of raw materials, and the incomplete liner was chained to the wharf in the Kuhwerder Harbour where she was used as a store-ship for furniture wood.

* 277.98 metres.

112. . . . a quarter view, with the almost-completed battleship BISMARCK beyond.

On 25 July 1943 she was badly damaged during a particularly heavy air-raid on Hamburg. Bombs penetrated the steel of her decks, and exploded below, blowing out some of her decks while the wood, stored aboard her, was set alight and the resulting blaze caused further extensive damage to both the steel decks and the hull itself. It is interesting to note that, in spite of the explosions and of the intense heat, none of the welded seams of the shell or decks opened up; a testimony to the good workmanship which had gone into the vessel.

The *Vaterland* was abandoned in her damaged and sorry state until the end of the War when, once again, Germany was made to forfeit her merchant fleet as reparations to the Allies, to whom it was left to decide the future of the scarred wreck. Although much of the damage was superficial and could have been restored fairly easily, it was considered to be too expensive to replace all the annealed steelwork. Consequently the half-completed *Vaterland* was broken up locally in 1948. During this period, much of the Blohm and Voss shipyard was demolished under the

160

113. The wreck of the bomb-damaged VATERLAND in Hamburg in 1945.

supervision of the British Control Commission and the confiscated material, which included machine-tools, medical instruments, theodolites and quantities of scrap metal, was shipped back to England from the 'Backloading Depot' at the Togo Quay, Hamburg. Amongst this was the scrap metal from the *Vaterland,* which was destined to reappear in post-war Britain as part of the materials for one reconstruction project or another, perhaps demonstrating that some fortune comes from every adversity.

Had the *Vaterland* and her sisters been completed and survived the war, the inference is that they would have been confiscated and would have passed to some other flag, but they would certainly have made their mark and enhanced the prestige of whatever country had operated them.

114. With her fore-deck blasted upwards by exploding bombs, the VATERLAND gave the impression of a voracious sperm whale, before she was broken up.

XVIII NORDDEUTSCHER LLOYD'S
AMERIKA/VIKTORIA

While the Hamburg Amerika Line was occupied with the *Vaterland* project, the Norddeutscher Lloyd was involved with plans to supersede their record-breaking sisters *Bremen* and *Europa*. This particular project was evolved entirely with a view to the re-acquisition of the Atlantic Blue Riband for Germany, to be exploited as a symbol of Nazi achievement. Two ships were contemplated, although only one was actually designed, and the involvement of the German Government was evident from the start by the collaboration of their naval experts with both the architects from the Deschimag A. G. Weser shipyard at Bremen and with technical representatives from the Norddeutscher Lloyd itself.

Work commenced in 1937 under the supervision of Dr.-Ing. Gustav Bauer, the Chief Engineer of the project, who was well-known for his Bauer-Wach exhaust steam turbine. Some years before, in the mid-1920s, he had also been responsible for the machinery design of the *Bremen* and *Europa*.

Designed as a four-day ship for the North Atlantic, the new liner would have been a prodigious vessel, vying only with the *Queen Mary* and *Normandie,* for, with an overall length of 1,070 feet,* her registered tonnage would have been well in excess of 80,000 gross tons. Her length between perpendiculars would have been exactly 1,000 feet,† the moulded beam 112 feet and her draught 35 feet with a displacement of 65,000 tons. Initially christened *Amerika,* the new liner was planned as a

*326.15 metres.
*304.8 metres.

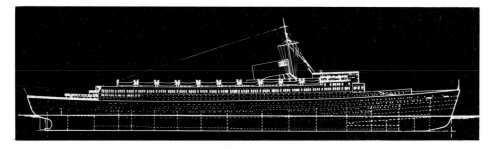

115. A line drawing of the projected Norddeutscher Lloyd giant VIKTORIA.

replacement for the slow and ageing *Columbus* and, in addition to her trans-Atlantic employment, she would have been used for off-peak cruises for the Deutsche Arbeitsfront's *'Kraft durch Freude'* (Strength through Joy) movement in conjunction with the *Wilhelm Gustloff* and *Robert Ley.*

As the prime task of the new vessel was to wrest the Atlantic Blue Riband from the *Queen Mary,* she would have had turbo-electric engines producing a maximum shaft horse-power of 300,000 to give her the formidable speed of 36 to 38 knots! In order to attain these speeds the fuel oil consumption would have been approximately 100 tons per hour! In comparison, the fuel consumption of the contemporary and similar-sized *Queen Elizabeth* was only 45 tons per hour. Thus the indication is that the *Amerika* would hardly have been an economical proposition and that such a high designed speed could only have been justified to satisfy the rather nebulous matter of national prestige. The normal output of each of the five main turbines would have been 49,700 shaft horse-power which, after power conversion from the turbines to the propulsion motors and after some transmission losses, would have given a total delivered service rating of 246,000 shaft horse-power. Driving five screws, one to each propulsion motor and turbine set, the resulting service speed would have been of the order of 34 knots. This arrangement of five propeller shafts in the design of the *Amerika* was determined because the maximum shaft horse-power to any one screw was limited to 60,000 and this was consequently the only approach by which the required total power output could be achieved. Steam to her five turbines

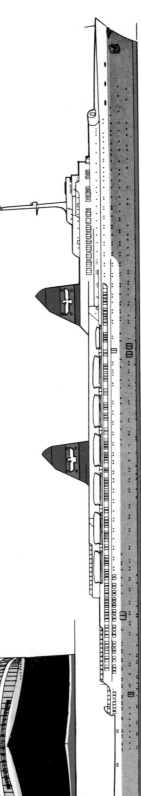

116. *Vladimir Yourkevitch's concept of the BRETAGNE, the French Line's projected consort for the NORMANDIE, in contrast to the VIKTORIA (lower plate) revealed an almost total abandonment of aesthetic values in favour of purely functional characteristics. Her twin, athwartships funnels and high, long superstructure give her an unattractive profile, while her bow view (Pl.117) is no better. The blue sections of her upperworks represent glass. (See Chapter XIX)*

117.

118. *The P5-S2-E1 design, drawn in profile from U.S. Maritime Commission plans dated 21 May, 1946.*

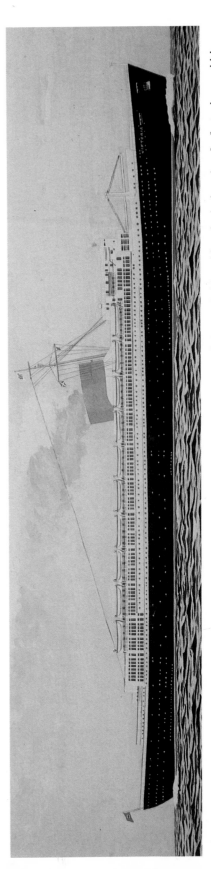

119. *An artist's impression of the AMERIKA/VIKTORIA, giving force to the axim that a really well-designed ship seldom looks her size. In fact, she would have exceeded 80,000 tons and, had she gone into commission, would have been extremely extravagant in her fuel consumption.*

120. *Although the smallest of the four liners of over 1,000 feet in length actually completed, the QUEEN MARY nevertheless had vast proportions, as may be seen in this impressive photograph of her anchored of Gillkicker Point, in the Solent, but, by comparison, N.D.L.'s AMERIKA would have been 10,000 tons larger and a little longer: the C.G.T.'s BRETAGNE would have been 150 feet longer; the 'Yankee Clippers' would have been a quarter as long again, and the UNITED NATIONS class would have been half as big again as the famous Cunarder.*

121. One of the 'Strength through Joy' liners was the WILHELM GUSTLOFF, seen here in Hamburg. Her loss, due to Russian submarine action, when she was evacuating personnel and refugees from East Germany in the 1939/45 war, resulted in the greatest loss of life ever known in a single ship disaster.

122. Dr. Ing. Gustav Bauer, who was in charge of the VIKTORIA Project.

would have been supplied at a pressure of 867 p.s.i. from 24 boilers with a total heating surface of 720 square metres.*

The *Amerika* would have been built to the highest standards according to the instructions of Germanischer Lloyd, with watertight subdivision to the requirements of international agreements. The usual high standard of interior appointments were to be incorporated, while her approximate complement would have been 2,000 passengers in three classes — 400 Cabin, 700 Tourist and 900 Third. The total crew number was estimated at 1,000.

During 1938 a propeller-less model of the *Amerika* was built by the Deschimag shipyard and put through tank tests in Hamburg by the Hamburgische Schiffbau-Versuchsanstalt (Research Institute for Ship Construction). These were very successful, and the keel-laying ceremony for the new ship was duly prepared for the Autumn of 1939, when it would have taken place formally in Adolf Hitler's presence. However, before this was possible, the outbreak of the Second World War occurred

*7,750 ft².

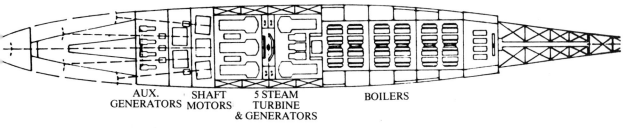

AUX.   SHAFT   5 STEAM   BOILERS
GENERATORS MOTORS   TURBINE
               & GENERATORS

123. The engine layout of the AMERIKA/VIKTORIA. Note the five propeller shafts.

and the project was deferred temporarily due to more important war work, but the Führer did not allow this German wonder ship, supervised under his decree by the Reichverkehrsministeriums, to be neglected. During the war it was announced that the Hamburg Amerika Line (Hapag) and the Norddeutscher Lloyd would be merged into one organization, the Deutsche Amerika Line, and that when the war was concluded victoriously, the first ship to be built for the new company would be the giant express liner, now appropriately (as was thought) re-named *Viktoria*. There was even talk of making the vessel even larger with a gross tonnage in excess of 90,000.

The planned amalgamation never came about (although in July 1970 the Hapag and N.D.L. concerns did merge voluntarily to become the Hapag-Lloyd A.G.), while the construction of the *Viktoria* was never even started. On Germany's defeat, the entire project was abandoned, although the Norddeutscher Lloyd officials were said to have been still actively interested in a liner of the *Viktoria* type as late as 1947. All the same, nothing resulted and reports over the subsequent twenty five years that new liners were under construction for either the Hamburg Amerika or Norddeutscher Lloyd lines proved to be totally erroneous. Certainly new German liners were subjects for discussion, although little more transpired beyond this. Indeed, West German Government officials had more to say on the subject than any of the operating companies!

In 1956, the *New York Herald Tribune* correspondent, Walter Hamshar, reported that the West German Transport Minister, Dr. Hans-Cristoph Seebohm, had announced the imminence of two new 25,000 to 30,000-ton vessels, one for each of two companies, for North Atlantic operation. These medium-sized liners would have carried large amounts of cargo, but fewer than 900 passengers and would have featured nuclear power drive. While no companies were named specifically, Hamshar felt sure that the Norddeutscher Lloyd and Hapag were the operators concerned. Looking back with hindsight, it is perhaps more probable that the other line involved, apart from the Norddeutscher Lloyd, was the newly established Hamburg Atlantik Line. The Norddeutscher Lloyd had just recommenced its North Atlantic services with the *Berlin,* formerly the Swedish America Line's *Gripsholm* and, while Hapag concentrated on cargo services, the Hamburg Atlantik's aim was specifically the passenger market.

As events proved, neither of these companies proceeded with new tonnage, either then or for some time afterwards. Instead they opted for drastic 'face-lifts' on older, second-hand vessels. In the N.D.L.'s case, this was the *Pasteur,* former flagship of the Compagnie Sud-Atlantique, noted more for her enormous funnel than for anything else, which eventually emerged as the fifth *Bremen* in July 1959.

The Hamburg Atlantik Line, for its part, rebuilt completely the laid-up *Empress of Scotland,* ex *Empress of Japan,* as the two-funnelled *Hanseatic.* When her new career was brought to an abrupt end by fire in September 1966, she was replaced by another *Hanseatic* – the ex-*Shalom,* of Zim Israel Lines. Then, in February 1969, the Hamburg Atlantik Line, by now called the German Atlantik Line, complemented the second *Hanseatic* with the 25,000 gross ton *Hamburg* and, in so doing, became the first German passenger company to complete a new liner after the Second World War. A new *Europa,* of approximately 30,000 gross tons, which was ordered by Hapag-Lloyd in 1978 and completed in 1981, was only the second new major German passenger liner in 41 years.

Viewing the economic miracle achieved by West Germany in the years subsequent to her defeat, this might seem to be odd on the face of it, but it is probably fair to say that the reasons lie in the changed face of the whole North Atlantic liner scenario as a result of the advance of air travel which, to a great extent, has killed the whole former concept of the passenger liner running on regular routes to pre-determined schedules.

XIX THE *BRETAGNE*

T he Norddeutscher Lloyd were not the only company interested in new tonnage for the North Atlantic run in the years immediately prior to the Second World War. The Italia Line had two 'very fast' liners of 60,000 gross tons under consideration which were to be built more or less concurrently, but these never got beyond the 'talking' stage. In France, the Compagnie Générale Transatlantique (C.G.T.) were well aware of the German plans for high-speed super-liners, and they knew that good progress was being made with the *Queen Elizabeth* across the Channel. The fact that the *Normandie* might, in these circumstances, remain a lone ship on their service (since the *Ile de France* was too slow to provide a balanced schedule with her) clearly affected her chances of success, and this had not escaped their notice. Thus they wanted running mates desperately for their famed record-breaker and, of course, an equally important ambition was to regain the prestigious Atlantic Blue Riband.

In April 1939 the problem assumed a new urgency when their passenger liner *Paris* was destroyed by fire at Le Havre, and the French Government then authorized the expediting of plans for a new liner. Consequently the C.G.T. turned to the design drawings of the *Normandie* which already existed, in order to save both time and expense. From these they proposed to develop a suitable consort: a liner in the classic French style perpetuating the character of its illustrious predecessor.

Eventually the new building specification emerged. This indicated that the projected second ship, to be named *Bretagne,* would be modelled directly on the successful lines of the *Normandie,* as had been expected,

124. Although the VIKTORIA was still forecast after the war, the new HAMBURG was the only liner to be constructed in Germany for her own flag in 25 years.

but would incorporate minor alterations influenced by the operational experience gained from the earlier ship, as well as the benefits of technical progress made since the *Normandie's* conception. The gross tonnage of the new vessel was expected to be approximately 85,000, while her linear dimensions would have been virtually identical to the previous vessel.

The C.G.T. required a service speed of at least 32 knots for the *Bretagne* which could have been achieved, at a price, as a result of the engineering advances made since the *Normandie's* power plant had been constructed in the early 1930s. However, details of the size and type of the propulsion machinery planned to enable the new ship to attempt the Atlantic record were not released, and one can only speculate whether or not the *Bretagne* would have had a turbo-electric arrangement such as that installed in the *Normandie*. The fact that the hull strength and layout had been designed around machinery of this type and weight suggests that this would have been most probable.

Additionally, in the absence of drawings and sketches, it is only possible to guess at the new liner's likely appearance, and whether engineering improvements would have influenced her externally. Undoubtedly she would have borne a general resemblance to the

Normandie, particularly with the unmistakeable Yourkevitch hull shape, but technical officials of the C.G.T. (now part of the Compagnie Générale Maritime) are quite positive that she would have had only two funnels, compared with three in the former ship.

The French Minister of Merchant Marine, Louis de Chappedelaine, announced in late May 1939 that the Compagnie Générale Transatlantique was expected to order the *Bretagne* from the Penhoët shipyard of Chantiers et Ateliers de St. Nazaire within a few months. The keel-laying was planned for early 1940, with the launching by Autumn 1942 and completion in the Spring of 1944. There was also speculation on a second similar vessel later, for which the name *Provence* was mooted.

Meanwhile, Vladimir Yourkevitch, the famed designer of the *Normandie,* entered the scene himself by submitting his own new ideas for the design of the proposed super-liner *Bretagne.* Formerly a naval architect in Imperial Russia, he had emigrated from France to the United States of America in 1937, sailing, naturally enough, in the *Normandie.* He established offices in New York and commenced to evolve his own design specifications for the next generation of ocean liners: liners which could compete favourably with passenger aircraft, whose impending threat Yourkevitch could see looming on the horizon. It was the plans which resulted from this exercise which he now offered to the C.G.T.

These revealed another truly prodigious vessel, much larger than the *Normandie,* with a registered tonnage in excess of 100,000 tons. The dimensions of the Yourkevitch design were 1,148 feet* overall length and 138 feet beam, in comparison with the *Normandie's* figures of 1,029 feet† and 118 feet respectively.

As in the case of the enlarged version of the *Normandie,* no revelations were forthcoming as to the intended prime-mover in the machinery of the Yourkevitch concept, although a service speed of 34 knots was confidently forecast for this massive liner. Much of this extra speed would have been achieved as a result of the extreme streamlining of the hull and superstructure.

In consequence of these hydro-dynamic refinements, the Yourkevitch design had a quite unusual profile. The hull exhibited much less of the flare that typified the *Normandie,* being long and slab-sided, although the Yourkevitch bow form was retained. A cruiser stern contrasted with the

*349.91 metres.
†313.64 metres.

elliptical counter of the earlier liner. The superstructure was long, quite uncluttered and with rounded steps between decks forward and aft. There were no visible projections from either the hull or the superstructure – not even bridge or docking wings – and the concealment of deck gear was taken a stage further from the *Normandie* with the lifeboats enclosed under sliding glass panels on the upper-deck. Two modernistic funnels were situated athwartships of each side of this upper deck and, with the absence of masts, these would have contained the radio aerials and look-out posts. Between the funnels a broad platform, inclining slightly to the stern, was suggested for the operation of aeroplanes carrying express mail and, presumably, for impatient or unpunctual members of the passenger list. It was intended that, when not employed for this purpose, this open deck area would be available for passenger recreation, although in practice it might well have proved to be unsuitable, for such an exposed deck, subject to strong sea winds, apart from the apparent wind created by the speed of the ship herself, might have presented a serious hazard to passengers.

Yourkevitch's proposals for the *Bretagne* represented a considerable departure from his earlier thoughts on passenger liners but, if the exterior design was radical, then the suggested interior arrangements were revolutionary, especially where a company like the C.G.T. was concerned.

Even though Yourkevitch proposed a high grade of luxurious appointments for his ship in keeping with the customary standards aboard existing vessels of the C.G.T. fleet, accommodation was nevertheless provided for only a single class of passengers, totalling an incredible 5,000. The approximate fare level for this one-class complement was Tourist, and one thing that Yourkevitch had in mind particularly for this type of ship was the provision of cheap passages for the growing mass of travel-hungry tourists – America's so-called 'two-week vacationists'. Consequently shipboard facilities were geared to the requirements of such passengers.

Cabin space would have been entirely in two-berth units, each of them with a private bathroom with a shower and toilet, indicating a conversion to the Ferris/Chapman philosophy of mass-handling in trans-Atlantic travel. Applying the principle further, Yourkevitch suggested for his liner what he described as 'Pleasure-Planning' facilities, which consisted primarily of inexpensive restaurants and other forms of low-cost catering service which would enable passengers to decide their own meal expenses

125. *Vladimir Yourkevitch's masterpiece, the NORMANDIE, leaving her builder's yard in April, 1935. On her trials she achieved 31.9 knots over several miles and, on her maiden voyage, crossed from Cowes to the Ambrose Light at an average speed of 29.94 knots, capturing for herself the Atlantic Blue Riband.*

separately from their ticket price. With regard to entertainment, a similar approach was intimated, with a wide variety of different recreational and leisure centres instead of an extravagant concentration of effort on the traditional ocean liner public rooms. Certainly a ship of the type drafted by Vladimir Yourkevitch would have been completely different from anything that the C.G.T. either were, or had been, operating.

With an eye to military adaptation, a more than usually important consideration at that particular time, as well as the influence that this might have had on Government funding, Yourkevitch had designed the ship so that it could be converted into a troopship readily, with a capacity for 13,000 fully equipped soldiers.

The Compagnie Générale Transatlantique, although apparently impressed with Yourkevitch's proposals, nevertheless rejected them. They were still quite definitely in the 'luxury liner' business, and there would be no place for such a ship in the fleet of a company whose name was synonymous with unsurpassable standards of shipboard comfort, spaciousness and service.

This may have been a short-sighted decision, although no liner company would have conceded at that time that passenger aircraft would one day be regarded as a serious threat to the livelihood of their ships. Indeed, even twenty years later when the menace was fully appreciated, no established trans-Atlantic passenger company opted for such a drastically different type of vessel and, in any case, in the summer of 1939 the C.G.T. were still anxious to promote the image of exclusive luxury and old world culture and sophistication which was associated with their name.

Quite apart from this, there were time and cost factors to consider. It would have taken some appreciable time to have worked up detailed construction plans for a completely new design, whereas the *Normandie's* plans already existed. Against this, Yourkevitch claimed that a vessel of the type that he was proposing would cost less to build than the 800 million francs* that the *Normandie* had cost.

Whilst disputing Yourkevitch's figures, Marcel Olivier, a C.G.T. director speaking in June 1939, confirmed that the Company 's preference was to abide by the super-*Normandie* concept and, by way of comparison based on this approach, he revealed that the *Bretagne* was expected to cost his firm no more than 1,000 million francs.

*Say £4,166,166, or $20 million, at August 1939 rates of exchange.

Understandably, Vladimir Yourkevitch was disappointed at the outcome, but his frustration was diminished by the knowledge that it would have been impossible to have proceeded immediately with his ship anyway, as no dry-dock or building berth of sufficient capacity was then in existence.

The C.G.T. proceeded with their new liner as forecast but, by this time, war had broken out in Europe. Nevertheless, in spite of this outbreak of hostilities, in September 1939 there were no intentions to abandon the scheme, although close adherence to the original building programme as outlined was prevented by one obstacle. The only suitable slipway at the Penhoët yard large enough to accommodate the giant *Bretagne* was already occupied by the 35,000 ton aircraft carrier *Joffre,* one of a pair which were being built for the French Navy. This was regarded as causing no more than a minor delay, and it was intended that the construction of the *Bretagne* would go ahead once the carrier was launched in late 1940.

However, in the winter of 1939/40, while these problems were being ironed out, no one even remotely considered the possibility of a threat to the *Bretagne* of far greater significance, namely: the French nation being overrun and occupied by the German army. Such a notion seemed to be beyond credibility but, as it turned out within six months, that was precisely what happened. In occupied France, those shipbuilding facilities which had not been prudently sabotaged in time found themselves in the service of their German overlords. Consequently the incomplete *Joffre* was broken up on the slipway and, once vacated, this was used for quite different purposes far removed from the halcyon affairs of trans-Atlantic travel.

So it came about that, in May 1945, the Compagnie Générale Transatlantique not only lacked their super-liner *Bretagne,* but they had also lost the beautiful *Normandie* which had been gutted by fire so unfortunately during the war − a loss which was only partly remedied by the advent of the *France* in 1962, despite the acquisition of the *Liberté,* ex *Europa.*

As for Vladimir Yourkevitch, on the completion of his work on his *Bretagne* concept, he became involved once more with the *Normandie,* his first-born. Sadly, in February 1942, he witnessed the needless devastation of his great liner in New York, and the stories of his frustrated

attempts to save her from capsizing and of her total loss are well known.*
Throughout 1942 and 1943 he was closely involved in the preparations to
raise the great ship from the mud and slime of her Manhattan cradle and,
after this had been accomplished, he worked on elaborate and comprehensive plans for her complete reconstruction. When these were rejected,
he prepared new suggestions and, even as the *Normandie's* hull was being
dismantled at the Lipsett breakers' yard across the harbour at Port
Newark, New Jersey, he was finalizing yet another proposal to re-build
her as a medium-sized liner.

Yourkevitch continued to promote his ambitious plans for massive
'cafeteria-type' ships like his *Bretagne* design after the war, in parallel
with Paul Chapman, Theodore Ferris and A. C. Hardy. In 1946, his
Bretagne plans were further streamlined, resulting in the elimination of
one of the funnels, whilst the one which remained was given an even more
modern look and was still situated on the extreme edge of the hull on the
starboard side. Although nothing resulted from Yourkevitch's campaign
for revolutionary trans-Atlantic tonnage, it influenced his approach
when he was engaged as consultant to Hyman Cantor in 1956 for the Sea
Coach Line project. The design for the *Peace* and the *Goodwill,*
described in detail later, was a direct development from the *Bretagne*
concept, with a close similarity in both overall dimensions and general
layout, but when this scheme failed in the early 1960s, it dashed the last
hope of putting Yourkevitch's mass-transportation ideas into practice.

A visionary Vladimir Yourkevitch may have been but, if he be
described thus, it must be as a visionary of genius, as evidenced by his
achievements with the *Normandie,* and it is certain that his name will
remain recorded on the rolls of fame so long as maritime history con-
tinues to be read. He himself died on 16 December 1964, aged 79, and, as
events proved, his most grandiose and inspired conceptions died with
him. It is almost two millennia since Christ said *'A prophet is not without
honour, save in his own country . . .'* and that saw is not only as true today
as it was then, but all too often he never receives the full honours that he
merits anywhere at all in his lifetime. This is an unpalatable truth of which
this book provides a number of examples.

*While being converted to a troopship for the U.S. Government, welders accidentally ignited a pile of
mattresses which started a massive conflagration which got completely out of control. The gutted ship, now
full of water, sank at her berth.

126. *Vladimir Yourkevitch in his office on Broadway, New York, in 1943, when he was hoping to raise the NORMANDIE.*

127. *Designed by Antoine Barthelmy, the FRANCE of 1961 was conceived to satisfy quite different commercial objectives, but was quite possibly the BRETAGNE in a post-war version, which was the largest that the C.G.T. could produce within the limitations of the financial help that the French Government was prepared to offer.*

XX THE TRANS-ATLANTIC LINER OF THE FUTURE

Simultaneously with the development of the *Bretagne,* Pierre de Malglaive, a close colleague of Vladimir Yourkevitch and the design co-ordinator for the *Normandie,* was himself studying express super-liners for the North Atlantic in collaboration with the noted British naval architect, A. C. Hardy.

Bearing in mind the anticipated need to compete with the impending challenge of air transportation, they evolved a ship which would be able to cross the Atlantic in 3½ days, with disembarkation on the 'States-side' at Montauk Bay. Exploiting a principal point of many earlier schemes, a fast boat-train service down Long Island to New York would have saved a further ten hours by eliminating 170 miles of the ship's journey as well as the slow process of docking in New York harbour. Similar provisions were proposed for the European side, between Plymouth and London and between St. Malo and Paris.

Described as 'The Trans-Atlantic Liner of the Future', the detailed design study was presented to the Institute of Marine Engineers on 14 December 1937. The liner so conceived was massive and far larger than any ship suggested previously, with a length of 1,350 feet* between perpendiculars, and the proposed engine room arrangement, intended to drive six screws, parallelled the vast scale of every other aspect of the ship.

This consisted of six electric main propulsion units of 396,000 total horse-power. Current to these motors would have been supplied by six Velox turbo-generators, each with a capacity of 51,000 kilowatts and

*411.48 metres.

128. *A group photograph taken c.1959 on the occasion of the first blasting of the Götaverken Arendal Shipyard, which includes persons known to readers of various interests. Front row, L to R: Ture Rinman (Editor 'Svensk Sjöfar Tidning'); the British vice-consul, Hilding Nielsen (Managing Director of A. B. Götaverken), Charles Bircha (Proprietor of the 'The Journal of Commerce', 'Sea Breezes', etc.), and A. C. Hardy (the eminent naval architect wh propounded the 'Trans-Atlantic Liner of the Future' – on this occasion neglecting the principle mentioned und Pl.5!). Second Row, L to R: Carl-Erik Bostrom (Publicity Manager, A. B. Götaverken), Jack Prince (Editor of 'Lloy List'), Bill Watson (Editor of 'Motorship'), Michael Bailey (Shipping Editor of 'The Times'), Peter Duff (Editor 'Shipping World'), and Nils Svensson (Technical Director of A. B. Götaverken and responsible for the Arend project). Back row, L to R: Dr. Lars Collin (Head of thermo-dynamics, A. B. Götaverken engine works), David Aicke (Editor of 'Shipping and Shipbuilding Record'), John MacDonald (Shipping Editor of 'The Financial Times'), Georg Stuart (Deputy Editor of 'Fairplay') and Graeme MacLennan (Editorial Director of 'Shipbuilding and Shippir Record').*

129. *The abortive schemes detailed in these pages were, with few exceptions, potentially viable and propounded by men of daring and imagination. That they failed was rather a matter of destiny than of their practicability. We say: 'Remember the GREAT EASTERN', for she was a vessel against all the odds; doubted from her inception and one which, at one time, seemed to be fated — the failure to launch her initially; the explosion off Hastings; her damage in the great gale, her stranding and so on but, if her career was not crowned with glory and success, that was rather because she was not utilized to her best advantage. Certainly her achievements were enough to confound the contemporary pundits and, by the standards of her day, she was much more than a mere 'monster ship'.*

130. The Q3 design, as envisaged (See Chapter XXVI)

131. The QUEEN ELIZABETH 2 – the Q4 – which finally emerged after the Q3 project had foundered.

complete with its own 'fuel-valve' type boiler. Such a power plant would have consumed 2,150 tons of fuel oil a day and necessitated the design of immense storage tanks and a unique ballasting system to maintain trim as the oil was consumed. Pierre de Malglaive and A. C. Hardy calculated that such an arrangement could provide a comfortable service speed of 37 knots.

The exterior of 'the Liner of the Future' was equally spectacular, being stream-lined to the finest degree. Like the 'Yankee Clippers', it also featured telescopic masts and retractable funnels, albeit for different reasons, and it is difficult to say who was influenced by whom. Without doubt, many prominent naval architects and designers in this period were propounding similar radical design innovations simultaneously.

During a voyage, flue gases and smoke would have been exhausted through vents at the stern. The two conventional funnels placed amid-ships, which normally were to be withdrawn through flaps in the upper deck, would have been used in harbour or when there was a strong following wind.

As for the superstructure, an alloy inverted hull over the main deck was suggested to provide the least air resistance, with the elimination of as much external gear as possible, and the lifeboats stowed under cover. The top (sports) deck would have been covered by a glass reinforced roof, to specifications prepared by the Pilkington Glass Company, and this was capable of resisting the battering of the heaviest Atlantic gales. Another innovation would have been retractable docking wings on the bridge, which would have laid flush with the ship's sides at sea and merely extended for harbour manoeuvring.

Interior features of the 'Liner of the Future' included gyro-stabilizers, even though the only previous experience with these in a large vessel – the Conte di Savoia – had only been successful to a partial degree but, from economic considerations, they had taken up an unconscionable amount of space. As for the passengers, escalators and travellators* were planned to facilitate more rapid movement from deck to deck.

The harbour installations and shore requirements, which were an integral part of Pierre de Malglaive and A. C. Hardy's study, were not overlooked either. The boat train connections mentioned were no mere simple rail-track affairs but, on the contrary, the designers envisaged

*Powered horizontal conveyors.

132. A poster illustrating the Bennie mono-rail near Glasgow, at Milngavie.

railplane type overhanging mono-rails which could travel at speeds up to 200 m.p.h. A test line for one of these propeller-driven vehicles was constructed by Mr. G. Bennie at Milngavie, near Glasgow, over the London and North-Eastern Railway.

Nothing ever came of the 'Liner of the Future'. Messrs. Bassett-Lowke, the celebrated model-making firm, built a display model, while most of the shipping and engineering journals carried features on the design but, as Pierre de Malglaive and A. C. Hardy explained, it had been no more than a design investigation: a prediction of the most likely future trends as they saw them, and not a specific design contract from a ship-owner.

Soon the world was plunged into hostilities and, when it emerged from

133. *A sketch of the Hardy/de Malglaive 'Liner of the Future', showing her funnels retracted.*

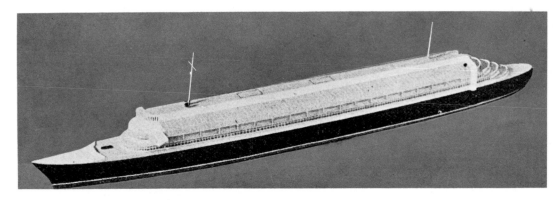

134. A model of 'The Liner of the Future' by Messrs. Bassett-Lowke.

the shadow of total conflict for the second time in thirty years, the various shipping companies once again took stock of their various situations.

The Second World War had been as much a struggle of science and technology as of military strategy and might. Sustained by a massive war effort, both sides had sought to maintain their offensives with more and more sophisticated and ingenious weaponry. A new and unparalleled importance was placed on scientific ingenuity and technical advancement and, through the perpetuation of this research as well as its commercial 'spin-offs', the immediate post-war period came to symbolize the dawning of a new technological age.

Many of the inventions which resulted from this had a direct influence on the passenger shipping business and, bearing this in mind, the different passenger lines began to reassemble their fleets, as far as possible devising applications or answers to these modern contrivances in the replacements they required.

Great Britain had fared best in the war with both her *Queens* coming through it unscathed, and this enabled the Cunard Line to resume sailings with little difficulty, and then to see how things developed. In France, the veteran *Ile de France* had survived, while that country was also awarded the *Europa,* which was renamed *Liberté.* Reconstruction of both these ships also allowed the Compagnie Générale Transatlantique time to consider their future plans, although it was rumoured that, for a while, consideration

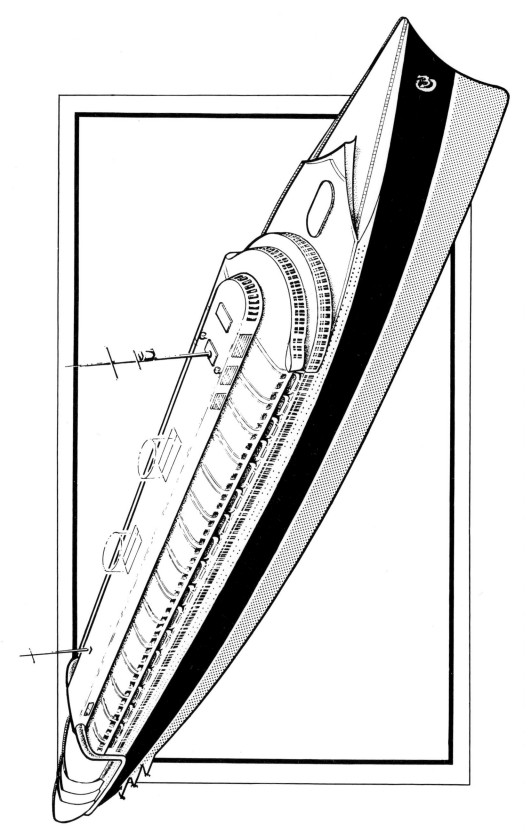

135. *Another rendering of this futuristic design, showing how the funnels would have looked when raised.*

188

was given to building three new 40,000 ton liners immediately. As stated previously, Germany made no attempt to rebuild her pre-war passenger ships at that time, although Italy made enormous strides in expanding her fleet beyond its previous magnitude and splendour. Only the United States stood conspicuously deficient on the side-lines.

One consequence of her desperation to build a respectable passenger fleet for the first time was that the majority of the giant liner projects over the next fifteen years were of American origin although, in the event, the only success stories were those of the *United States, Constitution* and *Independence*. The first major campaign for such new ships emanated from the United States Government's own official body – the Maritime Commission.

136. The INDEPENDENCE.

XXI THE PLANNED RENAISSANCE
OF THE
UNITED STATES MERCHANT MARINE

ollowing the Second World War, it was realized in the United States that the country could not become a first-class maritime power without making a significant contribution towards future passenger-carrying seaborne trade. The U.S.A. had been particularly adversely affected in this direction by the war, having had its entire fleet of passenger ships utilized for Government service as troopships. The facts were plain to see: a five-year break in any planned additions to an ageing fleet, and only one large liner, the *America,* having been added to the mercantile marine since the early nineteen-thirties.

The United States Maritime Commission (U.S.M.C.), established prior to the war, set its prime objective towards the planning of the rehabilitation of the United States' Merchant Marine. Following the end of hostilities, the requirement to establish large passenger liners on the key routes of the world was realized very clearly when the U.S.M.C. released a directive dated 25 October 1944 in which the then President, Franklin D. Roosevelt (himself a keen ship enthusiast), had requested that the U.S.M.C. prepare a plan for improving the American Merchant Marine and maintaining its future position. Moreover, he had stressed that no time should be lost in the preparations of designs for the construction of vessels for this purpose, and that the building of any new types should be scheduled to prevent interference with ships and materials required for war, whilst contracts should only be awarded on the basis of competitive tenders. The President had insisted that the plan should be implemented as an immediate priority, since both the employment situation and the conversion from a war- to a peace-time economy had to be considered.

To clarify these proposals, on which the U.S.M.C. were already actively engaged as a result of President Roosevelt's edict, it is necessary to refer to a paper presented to the Society of Naval Architects and Marine Engineers (SNAME) in 1945. Entitled *Large Passenger-Carrying Ships for Certain Essential Trade Routes,* it was read by James L. Bates, then Director of the Technical Division of the United States Maritime Commission.

In his paper, the author touched on some of the lessons learnt from the war and on possible future consequences of them that should be taken into consideration and applied to the proposed liners already under review, or to those which had already been accepted.

The Second World War had revealed that the large passenger liner was not generally suited for use as an aircraft carrier. Neither the *Queens* nor the *America* would have been ideal for such a purpose, either with or without elaborate and expensive conversion. It also seemed that neither such vessels nor their smaller sisters were well suited for the auxiliary cruiser role. However, liners such as the *America* and the *Mariposa* class had proved to be extremely valuable for troop transportation, and it would be for this purpose that they – or their future successors – should be viewed when plans were made for future national emergencies.

In considering some of these post-war effects, it was felt that, as a direct result of the enormous destruction of available labour and property abroad, many Western European ports would require the expenditure of much time and money for reconstruction. Even after this was done, it was felt (at that time, in 1945) that they might not attain their pre-war importance as commercial centres. The potential of the United States' interests in the Pacific had been affected favourably, while very attractive possibilities existed for trade with South America.

However, one development had emerged from the war which was feared to be about to present itself as a serious competitor, even as far back as 1945, and that was the passenger-carrying aircraft. At that time

137. The AMERICA had proved to be invaluable for troop transportation during the war.

Mr. Bates pointed out how the increase in speed and the multiplication of air routes was becoming phenomenal.

With the above factors in mind, he considered that all types of passenger transport would be utilized to capacity in the immediate post-war years, but he foresaw that air travel would later attract more and more of the available first-class passengers, mainly because of its superior speed. The future of water transportation would then tend towards the cruise for relaxation and comfort. (How very correct his predictions proved to be!)

The leading questions to be considered by the Government, ship operators and by naval architects were: *'Where shall the passenger ships of tomorrow operate and what shall be their outstanding characteristics?'* Apart from these, it also had to be asked: *'What future routes should be classed as essential?'*

The original intention was to develop high-speed passenger liners which would have had a minimum displacement and a minimum horse-power in order to keep first costs low, and which would consume a minimum amount of fuel. These ships were intended to be passenger-carriers only, but it was found that there would be a certain amount of unoccupied space in such vessels which could be utilized profitably for the stowage of high-earning cargoes (i.e. some 1,500–2,500 tons per ship). In these particular designs, speed would have been the major influence. Trends indicated that increases in speed above 20 knots should be accompanied by decreases in the amount of cargo carried, as well as in the time spent in port, in order to exploit this costly characteristic to the maximum.

Speed was to be given special consideration because, it was postulated, a smaller number of ships, given greater speed, might do the same work as a larger number at a lower speed. The very real possibilities of encroachment by air travel, with its much reduced journey times, would assuredly make low speeds intolerable anyway.

The radius of operation was to be fixed with the prime objective of completing the round voyage on one fuelling. However, sufficient tankage was to be provided where possible so that, in the event of being used on military service, a total radius of 12/15,000 miles could be achieved at the ship's designed speed.

Thus, in spite of the original intentions and in order that the ship's speed should be maintained in rough seas and that passenger comfort should be a prime consideration in these conditions, liners of great length and of large displacement were favoured. In other words, weather experienced on certain routes would exercise a positive influence on the design of the ship to operate on that route.

A number of trade routes were discussed in Mr. Bates' paper, not because they were the most important which might have been selected, but because passengers had been carried on them in the past and they looked to be promising for large, fast vessels of the future. Those under consideration were as follows:

(a) The trans-Atlantic service between New York, the British Isles and Western Europe and return. Total distance some 8,000 nautical miles.

(b) The eastern seaboard of the United States to the east coast of South

America, or New York, Rio de Janeiro, Santos, Montevideo, Buenos Aires and return, calling at Trinidad for bunkering facilities. Total distance involved approximately 12,000 nautical miles.

(c) The service between New York and the Mediterranean and return. Total distance about 9,000 nautical miles.

(d) The western seaboard of the United States to the Orient, or San Francisco, Honolulu, Yokohama, Shanghai, Hong Kong, Manila and return. Total distance about 14,500 nautical miles.

(e) The western seaboard of the United States to the Pacific Islands, Australia and New Zealand and return. Total distance some 16,000 nautical miles.

Each of the above-mentioned routes would have offered both cargo and passengers but, although the concept related primarily to the carriage of passengers (on which more will be said), this could not be considered independently of the cargo-carrying problem.

Route (a), whilst classed as 'essential' and a well-proven 'stamping ground', was at the time still highly competitive, and probably could not offer to American interests the same opportunities in future passenger transport development that were offered elsewhere.

Route (c) was thought to be of especial importance in developing closer relations between the United States and the Soviet Union, as well as the smaller nations located around the Mediterranean Basin.

Routes (b) and (d) offered exceptional opportunities for the development of mutually advantageous commercial and sociological relationships which suggested a promising future.

Finally, route (e), although offering fairly attractive prospects, also presented certain serious difficulties.

In order to meet the necessary requirements on the proposed essential routes, the U.S.M.C.'s studies investigated three schemes, namely: designs for routes (a) and (b) and (d) in consultation with prospective operators. The design for route (c), however, resulted from studies sponsored by the American Export Lines, which was the only private company, as such, which came forward with a design of its own for a large passenger ship and was ready to back it with its own money. (Prior to the war, the American Export Lines had also submitted its own designs and money in order to rejuvenate its own dry cargo fleet under the United States Merchant Marine Act of 1936.)

Route (e), apparently, could still be catered for by the Matson Line's passenger ships *Mariposa* and *Monterey* which had initially been built for, and operated under, subsidy contract between Pacific Coast ports and Australia.

The *Lurline,* built in 1932 for the domestic trade between California and Hawaii, still operated on that route in 1945. As no further vessels were proposed for the Australian route, which was well served at the time, this route does not come within the scope of this subject.

The proposed liners considered for routes (a) to (d) are dealt with in detail in the succeeding four sections. However, the reasons for the demise of some of the projects, or the factors which prevented them from proceeding to the building stage, were not always obvious or made manifest, as a result of which the authors can do no more than speculate about them. Nevertheless, the estimated cost of establishing passenger fleets on the particular routes cited at a total cost of $200–$225 million (£50 to £56 million) cannot be ruled out as a contributory factor for their failure to materialize. Today, when astronomical budgets, fanned by inflation, have become commonplace, it is easy to forget that such a sum seemed to be truly immense in the immediate post-war years, yet . . . it only represented an impost of roughly one dollar *per capita* of the U.S. population. . . !

XXIA DESIGN FOR THE NORTH ATLANTIC ROUTE – THE P4–S2–41

The P4–S2–41* design was determined in collaboration with the United States Lines who had operated a service on the North Atlantic route with the *Manhattan* and *Washington* prior to the war, when their ports of call had been Cobh, Plymouth, Le Havre and Hamburg, before returning via Le Havre, Southampton and Cobh. It was thought that post-war routing might have to be changed when trends were known better. At that time the United States Lines had never favoured, as had other operators, departures from New York on a fixed day of the week but, despite this, the Maritime Commission felt that this was important, and so weekly sailings from New York were accepted as a basic principle. With this in mind, it was assumed that, using three vessels, each would complete a round voyage every three weeks.

The success of the service operated by the *Manhattan* and *Washington* lent credence to the belief that this sort of service should be maintained. Furthermore, if there was to be an adherence to this sort of concept, direct competition could be avoided with the super-liners operated by the Cunard White Star at that time. Initially a fleet of four ships with a sustained sea-speed of 20-21 knots had been considered, but these vessels, operating on a 28-day schedule, would have had to provide an annual capacity for the transport of cargo and passengers equal to that furnished by the three faster ships finally considered. At first it was felt that their

*See page 315.

smaller size and lower speed would not have had disadvantageous effects on any future competition, but final economic studies indicated that a fleet based upon three 24-knot ships would be better than one based on four 20-knot vessels.

The proposed statistics of the P4−S2−41 were as follows:

Waterline length	745 feet
Beam	90 feet
Depth to strength deck	70.5 feet
Longitudinal co-efficient	0.598
Power plant	Steam turbines
Designed displacement	33,500 tons
Fuel oil capacity	4,000 tons
Fresh water	750 tons
Swimming pools	100 tons
Passengers, baggage, crew and provisions	800 tons
Dry cargo	6,220 tons
Reefer cargo	530 tons
Deadweight	12,400 tons
Designed speed	24 knots
Designed shaft horse-power	55,000
No. of screws	2
Designed steaming radius	8,000 miles
Number of passengers	1,200
Number of crew	669
Bale capacity	450,800 cu. ft.
Reefer capacity	53,000 cu. ft.

In order to develop the three-ship schedule, consideration was given to the problem of cargo handling at the various ports of call. The method favoured was arranged so as to have six open holds which could be served by a system of derricks and king posts. It was proposed that the ships' stores and refrigerated cargo could be handled through side ports by a newly developed type of gear, which would also be considered for the prospective South American liners.

Each ship was planned to accommodate about 1,200 passengers in two classes, and arrangements were to be provided for the alternative use of certain groups of state-rooms by either class, so as to ensure flexibility.

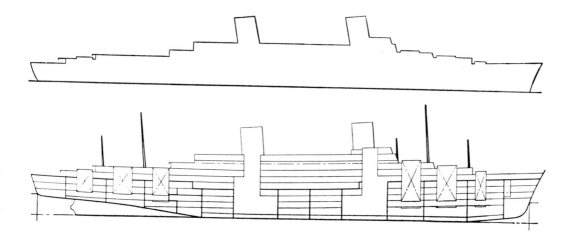

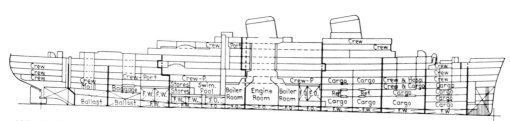

138. *Outboard and inboard profiles of the P4-S2-41 design, with that of the AMERICA (below)*
  for comparison.

The exact design speed of the P4–S2–41 proved to be a problem to
predict because, under favourable conditions of smooth water during the
Atlantic crossing, cargo and passengers would be handled at the various
ports to the desired schedule and, in this case, a sustained sea-speed of 24
knots would be sufficient.

However, if the crossing was made in rough or foggy conditions, or if
any emergencies occurred at the ports of call to disrupt their programme,
it would be desirable for the ships to be provided with a liberal margin of
power.

Comparison of the P4−S2−41 design with that of the *Manhattan* showed that the length had been increased by some 60 feet, and the depth from the promenade deck reduced from 75 to 70 feet, while the beam had been slightly increased. Taking account of existing practice in merchant ships, a novel design feature in the hull form of the P4−S2−41 was put forward, twin skegs being fitted underneath a relatively broad stern. Each skeg was to carry the propeller shaft and the propeller, abaft of which would be a rudder. The virtues of such a configuration were that a given metacentric height would be obtained on a decreased beam and also that the ships' mobility would be enhanced, because each rudder would operate in a propeller wake. It was feared, however, that, unless proposed model tests predicted a definite reduction in shaft horse-power, a more normal form of after-body would have to be adopted. Apparently the twin skeg form might have introduced certain variations in wake distribution which, if not properly controlled, would have led to objectionable vibration trouble.

The designed displacement of the P4−S2−41 also proved to be difficult to establish. It was thought to be theoretically possible to select a vessel with a smaller displacement than the one proposed. This was a prime example of the weather on a particular route affecting the design of the vessel intended to ply it. The storms and rough weather that would be encountered in the North Atlantic meant that any liner on that run would have to have heavy and carefully disposed scantlings. Quite apart from this, it was also obvious that, the greater the size of the vessel relative to the wave size that might be encountered, the more comfortable the passengers would be. The length selected, therefore, was considered to be conducive to passenger comfort, and the approximate displacement of 33,500 tons, whilst smaller in comparison to previous standards, was not decreased radically. In terms of displacement tonnage, the size would have fallen in the range determined by such pre-war liners as the *Rex* and *Conte di Savoia,* though comparatively less than that of the *Bremen* and of the first *Mauretania.*

With regard to the P4−S2−41's fore-body, two general types had been considered. The first of 'U' type cross-section as employed in the original design of the *America,* and the second a development of the 'V' section bow. It seemed that the latter would permit an increase in deck areas for

139. The WASHINGTON before the New York skyline.

passengers and crew forward, and also a positively smaller increase in cargo capacity. For speeds less than 20 knots, it was estimated that the 'V' section bow would require less horse-power than the 'U' section, but that at speeds in excess of 24 knots this power requirement would tend to increase. From the greater advantages gained by the 'V' section, it was decided to settle on this form.

It was considered that the chosen route for the P4−S2−41 would still be competitive, for in the immediate post-war era the flow of high-class freight was considerable. There was also a reasonable volume of passenger traffic to be attracted by the lower fares offered by the intermediate-speed liners. Even as far back as 1945, competition was anticipated from passenger-carrying aircraft and economic studies, conducted to forecast trends over the next twenty-year period, indicated a falling off in seaborne passenger traffic. The conclusions drawn from this study indicated that high-class freight business would be beneficial even if passenger volume during the second decade fell to one-eighth of normal ship capacity (which was assumed to be a 60% occupancy).

Around this period, when the P4–S2–41 design was being drawn up, the United States Lines (which had been the biggest operator on this route prior to the war) were aspiring to build two 35,000 gross ton consorts for the *America,* in spite of the fact that the P4–S2–41 was available to them and presumably could have fulfilled the same requirements. It was felt that this would be the best way of replacing the *Manhattan* and *Washington,* which remained the property of the U.S.M.C. but, after some deliberation, a decision was made against these intermediate ships which had been envisaged and in favour of two much larger liners of up to 50,000 tons, one of which emerged eventually as the *United States* in 1952.

This decision to opt for the bigger ships is comparable with that made later by the C.G.T. (French Line) in the mid-1950s. Under pressure from the French Government to construct two 35,000-ton sister ships to replace the *Ile de France* and the *Liberté,* they elected to build the single, giant *France* instead. The French Line justified this on the grounds that one super-liner would not only show the flag much more effectively on an international basis, but would be a bigger and better money-earner than the two more insignificant, medium-sized vessels. The big ship's prestige value alone should have been sufficient to convince the U.S. Government, as it did subsequently in the mid-1950s, that this philosophy was still important on the North Atlantic route.

Be this as it may, the U.S.M.C.'s P4–S2–41 design never did materialize in any form. The United States Lines re-introduced its Atlantic service in November 1946 when the re-furbished *America* made her first post-war voyage, and she was complemented in the same year by the *Washington,* which was chartered from the U.S.M.C.

XXIB DESIGN FOR THE NEW YORK TO EAST COAST OF SOUTH AMERICA ROUTE – THE P3–S2–DA1 (DA) DESIGN

This route had once included calls at Rio de Janeiro, Montevideo and Buenos Aires outward-bound, returning via Santos, Rio and bunkering at Trinidad. Based on their pre-war itineraries, Moore-McCormack, the principal operators on this trade, considered weekly sailings on the same day of the week from New York to be a major priority.

Before the Second World War they had operated the liners *Argentina, Brazil* and *Uruguay,* all with a service speed of 18 knots and dubbed the 'Good Neighbor Fleet'. These were then complemented on this run by a number of C-2 cargo vessels.* In this manner, the three liners were able to sail on a six-week round voyage basis, and left New York on alternate weeks.

A careful study predicted that a satisfactory programme of sailings could be maintained by five 22-knot cargo-passenger ships, sailing out of New York weekly with a 35-day round voyage schedule, but that, equally, the same target could be achieved by four 27-knot cargo-passenger liners sailing from New York on a 28-day cycle. However, from a profitability aspect, it was assumed that, if the service was operated without competition, it would be more lucrative to operate just two of the faster ships with sailings on *alternate* weeks.

One of the major requirements taken into consideration when drawing

*See page 312.

up the operating schedules was that a thorough examination should be made of the time necessary for the vessels to remain in port, both for cargo-handling and for passengers to go ashore for sight-seeing.

The proposed speed would have made it possible for the steaming time on the longest leg between New York and Rio to be reduced from about eleven days for the early 18-knot *Argentina* class to about seven and a half days. At the time, this was a significant improvement in the face of the emergence of air competition, as well as the fact that many of the prospective passengers would not be able to afford more time at sea and, in any case, might feel that more than a week afloat might become monotonous. The P3−S2−DA1,* otherwise known as the DA, would be operated on the basis that around 125 passengers per week out of New York could be expected, but she would have to provide for peak loads and expansion in travel. If a weekly sailing schedule was to be implemented, provision would have to be made for a passenger capacity of 250. Alternatively, if sailings were to be every other week, the capacity would have to be for around 550 passengers (470 first class and 80 third).

The proposed general particulars of the P3−S2−DA1 were as follows:

Overall length . . .	731.5 feet
Waterline length . . .	699 feet
Length between perpendiculars .	671 feet
Moulded beam . . .	70.5 feet
Depth to strength deck . .	56.5 feet
Longitudinal co-efficient . .	0.57
Designed displacement . .	22,750-23,500 tons
Fuel oil capacity . . .	5,200 tons
Fresh water	500 tons
Swimming pools . . .	100 tons
Passengers, baggage, crew and provisions	450 tons
Dry cargo	2,100 tons
Reefer cargo	400 tons
Deadweight	8,750 tons
Designed speed . . .	27 knots
Designed shaft horse-power .	60,500
No. of screws	2

* See page 315.

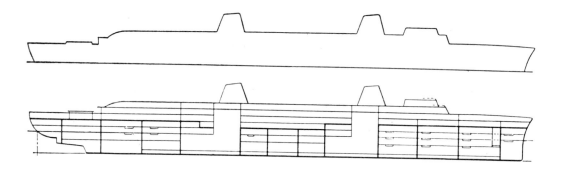

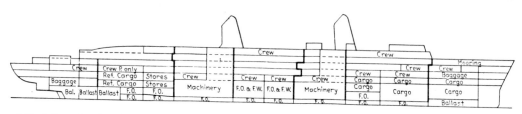

140. *Inboard and outboard profiles of the P3-S2-DA1 design, with that of the modified DA design (below) for purposes of comparison.*

Designed steaming radius . .	11,000 miles
Number of passengers . .	550-560
Number of crew . . .	449
Capacity for cargo . . .	235,000-250,000 cu. ft.

It was originally intended that the DA would carry a nominal cargo payload of about 1,000 tons, although Moore-McCormack Lines believed that provision would have to be made eventually for as much high-class freight as would be possible, with due regard to the time required for handling cargo in port, as well as its effect on shaft horsepower and on the fuel consumption brought about by the increased displacement. In the light of this more logical line of thought, provision was ultimately considered for approximately 2,100 tons of high class package goods in addition to 400 tons of refrigerated cargo.

A significant feature of the DA was that, although she was to have about 235,000 cubic feet of cargo space, she would carry no winches, since it was planned that the vessel's entire cargo would be handled through three side-ports. Each of these would be served by a side-port loader comprising hoisting, traversing and boom motions obtained with direct-current motors.

Several relevant factors influenced the choice of size and displacement of the DA: the first and most important of these was that the New York to east coast of South America route was considered to be definitely a fair weather run. Few severe storms had been encountered and, therefore, the structure of any contemplated ship would not be subjected to the constant buffeting experienced in the North Atlantic. This favoured a more moderate displacement tonnage, even when high speeds were considered. Secondly, if the power of the main engines and resulting fuel consumption were to be kept within acceptable and economical limits, a relatively greater length would be required for the high speed desired. The third influential factor was that, due to the shallow waters of the River Plate and the approaches to Buenos Aires, the proposed liner's draught would have to be restricted to 28 feet. The last item to have a bearing on the DA's proposed displacement would be the selection of a light but powerful propulsive plant as proven by the United States Navy. The displacement determined after consideration of the foregoing governing factors was moderate, if not actually rather small.

The justification for the dimensions and proportions selected were based on those relating to well-known English Channel steamers. It had been demonstrated after years of study and experience that this type of vessel exhibited very high speeds with unusually low displacements. This was in spite of the fact that the English Channel was notorious for its tempestuous and unpredictable waters.

In appearance, the DA's midship design showed a bulge of 2.25 feet which would have given an impression that the ship had an external shallow blister. The form of the DA had been selected carefully in every respect in order to provide sea-kindliness, easy manoeuvring and adequate stability throughout her operating range. The same hull form had been well proven in the Hamburg Sud Amerika Company's *Cap Polonio* of 1922, which had been built with a bulged midship section and

141. *The BRAZIL, one of the pre-war 'Good Neighbor' fleet, off Hamilton, Bermuda.*

which represented a prototype for this form of merchant ship. Further model-testing research experiments showed that the underwater cross-section of the DA, as with the P4−S2−41, should have a 'V' section bow, combined with a bulbous forefoot. With such a form, relatively low water resistance and the requisite stability on minimum dimensions, especially with regard to the beam, were predicted.

The safety requirements for the DA were all to comply with the rules advocated by the International Convention for Promoting Safety of Life at Sea of 1929, and by the United States Senate Report No. 184, covering watertight integrity. Under the recommendations laid down in these documents, the DA would have been a two-compartment class vessel: that is, the ship would be capable of surviving if any two of her adjacent compartments became flooded. She would have had eleven watertight bulkheads, the minimum watertight compartment length being 44 feet long.*

* 13.41 metres.

The fire detection system of the ship was to be of the zone type, whereby, if a fire occurred aboard, it could be identified in a certain zone or section of the ship, thus making it unnecessary to search all of the compartments within that zone in order to find its seat. In the DA's cargo spaces a carbon dioxide (CO_2) extinguishing system would have been employed.

At this stage of the development of the proposed design, the arrangement of passenger spaces was largely a matter of choice and any national influences or preferences would have had to be considered in the internal arrangement of the vessels.

The electrical power plant would have been four 1,250 kilowatt, 0.8 power factor, 60 Hz, A.C. generators and the main propulsion system was to be steam turbines. The proposed machinery for the P3–S2–DA1 was tabulated as follows:

Number of shafts .	2
Shaft horse-power .	60,500
Main boilers .	4×850 lbf/in^2 and 900°F
Auxiliary boilers .	none
Generators .	4 – Turbo-driven 1,250 KW
Emergency generators .	1 – Diesel-driven 150 KW
Circulators per condenser	Scoops – 29,000 g.p.m. pumps
Fire pumps .	4 – Motor-driven 400 g.p.m.
Flooding pumps	
Bilge .	2 – Submersible 1,050 g.p.m.
Ballast .	3 – Motor-driven 1,050 g.p.m.

Such was the design of the post-war DA that it was believed that she was the only vessel which would have had her machinery so arranged that, in the event of damage being sustained up to the limits of the safety factors in her sub-division (that is, if two adjacent compartments became flooded), her engines would still be operational. Other unique features of the design were that the use of auxiliary boilers had been considered, but had finally been abandoned, basically on economic grounds, while another significant departure from conventional marine engineering practice lay in the fact that the circulating water for the main condensers was to be supplied from 'scoops'.* The usual practice in European vessels at that time was the use of independent pumps.

*See Glossary, under 'Scoops'.

Although some people felt that the P3–S2–DA1 needed a 'face-lift' with her lack of sheer, pseudo-streamlining and widely-spaced trapezoidal funnels, it was still being considered to be a viable design a year later and was scheduled for construction in 1949. By this time, consideration was being given to establishing a route between Buenos Aires and New York of ten days duration, which would be continued on to Europe and, in these circumstances, a service speed of 27 knots would have been required for the same ship.

Moore-McCormack Lines had co-operated with the U.S.M.C. with regard to research into the operating trends on the South American route and, at the time, Mr. Emmet J. McCormack praised the design of the DA both from a speed and competitive aspect, stating that it should prove to be the most satisfactory for the trade. Nevertheless, in spite of this encomium, the DA was never built: perhaps due to its first costs, or perhaps because of the escalating air competition then being established to South America. A prime factor could have been that the original 'Good Neighbor' fleet, consisting of the *Brazil, Argentina* and *Uruguay,* was reconditioned after the war at a cost of $20 million (£5 million). These ships reached their peak in 1952 when they carried a record-breaking 25,000 passengers, but the volume steadily declined thereafter, which may account for the fact that replacements were not ordered until 1956, by which time the original trio had been reduced to two ships, both of them well past the statutory age limit so far as the terms of the U.S. Federal loan and mail contract were concerned.

The replacement vessels, the *Brasil* and the *Argentina,* which retained the old names,* were designed by the Bethlehem Steel Company, who do not appear to have made any reference to the DA concept. Completed by the Ingalls Shipbuilding Corporation of Pascagoula, Mississippi, these new 15,257 gross ton liners had only two features in common with the DA, namely: they each carried 557 passengers in luxurious style, and they were both specifically designed for the South American service. Apart from this, they could only carry 4,470 tons of cargo.

Sadly, from the date that they were built and throughout the time that they were owned by Moore-McCormack, the new *Brasil* and *Argentina* never operated profitably in any single year. This prompted the Chairman of the Company, when addressing a United States Congressional

---

*Except that the 'Brazil' was now the 'Brasil'.

142. *The new BRASIL looked well enough reflecting her white paint in the water, but her books of account reflected only 'red' balances.*

hearing shortly before the vessels were laid up, to make the statement: *'Why they were built in the first place remains a mystery of corporate decision-making'*.

Why indeed? Many very successful vessels have already been mentioned in the course of this book, in order to provide perspective or comparisons with those which form the burden of its theme, which is concerned with usually grandiose schemes for ships which either never came into existence at all, or which never fulfilled their designed functions. As to the former – the vessels which 'never were', even though the projects often left their mark on subsequent construction, it might be thought, if viewing these matters rather superficially, that their failure to reach fruition represented something rather negative and, besides, a great waste of money spent on all the origination charges before the projects were finally abandoned. In this context, it must be borne in mind that these charges represent a relatively miniscule amount when compared with the actual cost of constructing and equipping a large vessel but, in any case, they are a constant in the design of a new type of ship, whether she is built in the end or not. Whilst it must be granted that such charges are sheer loss to the promoters whenever a scheme falls by the wayside and, whilst it is only possible to consider the ultimate effects of constructing a ship in retrospect, it is undeniable that it is less unprofitable to scrap origination plans and to proceed no further, than to carry on building a ship which proves to run at a loss throughout her career, as in the case of the replacement *Brasil* and *Argentina*.

It is easy to pontificate, and to write with the benefit of hindsight. Few entrepreneurs have the ability to view the future in crystal balls and, even when the writing is writ clearly on the walls, it often occurs that it is not what they want to read. Sometimes, when conditions seemed to be set fair for the enterprise in hand, the promoters found themselves involved with Governments and, as is well known, no bodies can prove to be more fickle. Had the various schemes set forth in this book finally blossomed onto the passenger routes of the world, some would probably have produced vessels whose careers would have been attended with financial success and great fame, whilst others might have found themselves in precisely the opposite case. Who knows? The threads of Fate are often woven into imponderable weaves, and if the ships which form the subjects of the chapters of this book were doomed by the Norn of Destiny, it must be borne in mind that many of the great liners which became enshrined in the rolls of maritime history might equally well have suffered a like fate, depending on the circumstances prevailing when they were conceived. This statement represents no mere flight of fancy, and older readers may recall the manner in which the *Queen Mary,* not only one of the biggest, but one of the most successful and charismatic of all the great liners ever built, remained poised for long on the very horns of Fortune. Laid down as yard Number 534 on one of John Brown's slipways in August 1930 in all good faith, the serious economic situation led to all work being suspended on her when she was in a relatively advanced state of construction, and so she remained, a huge metaphorical question mark dominating the surrounding Clydebank, for nearly two and a half years. By that time, after insistence that the White Star and Cunard Lines be amalgamated (which *might* not have been agreed), the Government of the day had agreed to subsidize the vessel, and this, too, was something of a gamble, since all governments are notoriously capricious and, in any case, the political climate alters not only the view of the government in power, but can change it to one of widely different opinions and policies.

The gestation period of the *Queen Mary* was both long and difficult, but she emerged in the end to become a household word throughout the world — as it happened. Yet one cannot feel otherwise than that the Fates, if such there be, had no sense of unanimity about her future and that she could equally well have been the subject of a chapter in this book devoted to vessels Damned by Destiny. Everybody knows that there was nothing wrong with the ship, which was not only a record-breaker that captured the Blue Riband, but which gave a service, perhaps second to none, in peace and war yet, had she been abandoned on the stocks, there would always have been a doubt about her achievements had she not gone into commission.

So one must judge the vessels of which we have written. They did not fail on their potential merits as ships at sea, but for longshore considerations, most usually based on finance or the like but, when one considers the roster of those grandly conceived vessels which 'might have been', and tries to speculate on what they might have achieved, it may be that there are too many imponderables to reach clear-cut conclusions. In many cases, the answer is to remember how nearly the *Queen Mary* missed coming into being but, in considering the more immediate problem, it is certain that it was better to abandon a ship in her design stage than to proceed with her and to run her at a loss.

XXIC THE AMERICAN EXPORT LINES' DESIGN FOR THE MEDITERRANEAN RUN (THE *INDEPENDENCE* CLASS)

As previously stated (p. 193), the American Export Lines were the only company to come forward and to submit a design for a large passenger ship financed by themselves in response to the U.S.M.C.'s proposals for large liners on certain essential routes and, in the event, the design was not only accepted but some of the ships actually materialized. However, before studying the completed vessels, it is worth examining the background reasoning behind American Export's contemplated passenger liners.

Prior to the 1939-45 War, this company had operated a passenger trade with a quartet of cargo-passenger steamships, collectively styled as the 'Four Aces',* which offered a single class of accommodation for 125 passengers. These provided a service between New York and the Western Mediterranean and Levantine ports, and proved to be popular, even in the Depression. However, by June 1941, American Export had had blueprints drawn up for two much larger liners whose construction had to be postponed owing to the war.

When peace was finally established again, it was apparent that, with the big Italian liners *Rex* and *Conte di Savoia* no longer on the Mediterranean run, the passenger market for the surviving operators on that

*Four 9,359-ton vessels with accommodation for 100 first class passengers named the *Excalibur, Exochorda, Exeter* and the *Excambion* which entered service in 1931 and became known as 'The Four Aces'. They were superseded after the war by four new vessels, taken over from the U.S. Navy and with the same names, entering service in 1948 and also known as 'The Four Aces'.

143. Both the REX and the CONTE DI SAVOIA (above) had been sunk by Allied aircraft in Italian sheltered waters during the war and were no longer on the Mediterranean run, for . . .

service would be greatly enhanced in comparison with their pre-war conditions.

It was also appreciated that ships of the type and size of the 'Four Aces', while successful as cargo-carriers, did not earn an adequate return from their passenger trade. Accordingly, an investigation was instituted into the characteristics of ships of increased – but not excessive – size.

It was considered that provision should be made for the carriage of a large amount of cargo and, at the same time, it was recognized that the ability to offer high-speed transport for the available cargo would be a potent argument in favour of securing additional high-class freight. Also, since high speed and regularity of schedule would lend confidence to shippers and discourage competition from slower ships correspondingly, it was decided that a sea speed of 22 knots would ensure a satisfactory schedule and be sufficient to realize these requirements.

In normal circumstances it might have been expected that they would first develop a careful economic analysis of their chosen trade route, and would then have based the technical design upon the findings of such a

144.... *although both had been raised, they were in a sorry state, as in the case of the CONTE DI SAVOIA (above).*

study. However, so far as this particular case was concerned, American Export changed the usual order of priorities and, somewhat loosely, adopted the following procedure:

1. To accept a basic 22 knots speed and to assume three ships (to meet the desired schedule).

2. To give each ship adequate cargo capacity and adequate cargo-handling facilities.

3. To provide capacity for enough passengers to meet the anticipated demands and to ensure an acceptable return on the investment for passenger accommodation.

Further study along these lines indicated a ship of moderate size (650 feet* in length) and with a passenger capacity for about 600. The conclusion was that, with careful operation, such a vessel should be able to keep out of the 'red' financially.

The dimensions selected for the American Export liners were as follows:

*198.12 metres.

Length, waterline	. . . . .	650 feet
Beam	. . . .	89 feet
Depth to strength deck	. . . .	62 feet
Longitudinal co-efficient	. . . .	0.616
Power plant	. . . . . .	Geared steam turbines
Designed displacement	. . . .	30,000 tons
Fuel oil capacity	. . . . .	5,400 tons
Fresh water	. . . . . .	670 tons
Swimming pools	. . . . .	100 tons
Passengers, baggage, crew and provisions	.	650 tons
Dry cargo	. . . . . .	5,060 tons
Reefer cargo	. . . . . .	500 tons
Total deadweight	. . . . .	12,380 tons
Designed speed	. . . . .	22 knots
Designed shaft horse-power	. . .	37,000
Number of screws	. . . . .	2
Designed steaming radius	. . . .	12,500 miles
Number of passengers	. . . .	678
Number of crew	. . . . .	417
Bale capacity	. . . . . .	477,000 cubic feet
Reefer capacity	. . . . .	51,800 cubic feet

The American Export Lines introduced into these projected liners an innovation which departed from accepted practice quite radically, but which gave them the utmost satisfaction. They instructed a firm of industrial designers and interior decorators, led by Henry Dryfuss, to develop the passenger accommodation completely, subject only to the structural strength and sub-division determined by the naval architect. Their commission included the arrangements for public spaces, food service, the ships' services affecting passengers and stateroom accommodation and so forth. Throughout the studies the closest co-operation was maintained with the naval architect. So far as the public rooms and cabins were concerned, the number of de-luxe suites was limited and the type of staterooms in the tourist class as originally contemplated was slightly enlarged in size, being similar in layout and furnishings to the sleeper compartments on the North American trans-continental trains of those days. The proposed size of the lounge was decreased, whilst that of the smoking room was increased in comparison to the trend of the time.

One of the principal reasons for giving this firm of industrial designers and interior decorators a free hand in developing the designs for the ships' interiors in this way was the hope that something distinctly modern and aesthetically pleasing would result from it – an expectation which the Company considered to be fulfilled in the event.

One of the salient features of interest was the provision of an inside swimming pool in a ship intended to operate on a route which was generally considered to be a warm weather one. This may well have been due to the experience gained in the pre-war Italian liners which had shown that, even on this passage, the outdoor swimming pool was usable for only a relatively small proportion of the time during the crossing.

At this time, in 1945, it was thought that American Export Lines had all the potential for a ship of high efficiency from the ordinary technical standpoint, as well as one of unusual attractiveness, and many people thought that the design would probably mark the beginning of a new epoch in passenger comfort, interior decoration and exterior appearance. However, it was felt that this design was strangely out of place among the other U.S.M.C. proposals, for the midship section appeared to be high and wide, whereas the profile was considered by some to be a little 'dumpy' and that it could be improved by removing everything but the bridge, chart-house and so on from the navigation bridge deck and placing the structures so removed on the boat and sun decks. Another opinion advanced was that, when viewing the ships in profile, the small spaces abaft each funnel were not entirely in harmony with the rest of the design.

In spite of these minor constructive criticisms, American Export were prepared to back up their ideas with action, and placed an order with the Bethlehem Steel Company's Shipbuilding Division at Quincy, Mass. for two of the originally proposed trio.

Subsequently, on 19 March 1949, the keel of the *Independence* was laid at the Fore River yard at Quincy, followed on 12 July by that of the *Constitution*. Each liner cost $25 million* to build and was constructed to United States troopship specifications, with accommodation for 1,003 passengers in three classes. Both vessels had a load displacement of 30,100 tons. Following completion, the *Independence* achieved 26.105 knots during her trials, even though her predicted speed was to be only 22½ knots, and, following these, she entered service on her intended route to the Mediterranean on 11 February 1951. The *Constitution* followed suit four months later, on 21 June.

*Approx. £6¼ million.

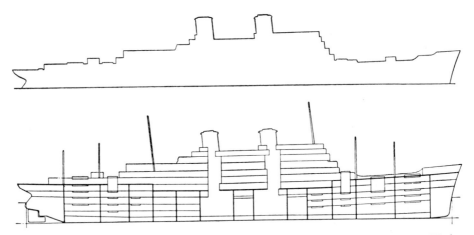

145. *Outboard and inboard profiles of the American Export Lines 1945 INDEPENDENCE class design.*

As the only ships actually to be completed from the massive U.S.M.C. programme, they were the first major American passenger liners to be built after the Second World War. With a gross tonnage of 29,496 (23,719 by U.S. measurement),* they were, with the exception of the *America,* the largest passenger ships under the U.S. flag and, prior to the advent of the *United States,* they were also the fastest American liners afloat. Normal service speed was maintained at 22½ knots, which enabled the New York to Naples crossing to be made in eight days, utilizing only 67% of the available shaft horse-power.

So far from being 'Damned by Destiny', these two vessels ran for many years under most auspicious circumstances, and the reader may well wonder how they come to be included in this book since, according to the terms of reference which we have set ourselves, they might seem to have no business in these pages and, indeed, to represent the exceptions which prove our rules. After a certain amount of soul-searching, it was deemed right to include them for several reasons.

In the first place, the intention was to build three such liners, and only two were actually built. Thus, although the original scheme was fulfilled, it was in an attenuated form, and the fact that the third sister never came

*See Glossary under 'Tonnage'.

into being may well have been due to the exceptionally fine performance of the first two, which were reported to be big money-makers in the booming steamship travel market of the 1950s, and to the fact that they were complemented on their run by the new 'Aces' class of passenger-carrying cargo ships, namely: the *Excalibur, Excambion, Exochorda* and *Exeter* (the old names having been resuscitated).

Next, it will have been observed that this chapter has been divided into five distinct sections, each of which is concerned, in one form or another, with projects under the aegis of the U.S. Maritime Commission, and in sum they represent its ambitions at the time in respect of the building of large passenger liners. Had we considered each of these projects in isolation, there would certainly have been no case for including the matter of the *Independence* and *Constitution,* but the fact is that the schemes were related to the degree that all came under the umbrella of the U.S.M.C. and, when viewed in their entirety, the efforts of this body at this time did not, apart from these two ships, ever get its projected liners down the slipways.

The interesting aspect of the building and subsequent success of the *Independence* and *Constitution* must surely lie in two distinct factors in which they differed and may have had much advantage over the other contemporary schemes in this chapter which proved to be abortive in the event. In the first place, unlike the other vessels which never came into being, they were not dependant on Government funding and, had the American Export Lines not come forward with their own cash, one is left wondering whether they would ever have been built at all. Moreover, now surviving – at the time of writing – for some thirty odd years, they may be said to substantiate the objections which many American shipping men had voiced regarding the U.S.M.C. designs and their beliefs that those produced by private enterprise tended to be superior to those produced by the Government body.

Perhaps this may be read as an indictment of the U.S. Maritime Commission. Certainly we have already discussed the P-4-P in Chapter XVI; we have dealt with the P4-S2-41 and the P3-S2-DA1 already in this chapter, and we shall describe the PXE project in the next section. Whilst bearing in mind that it is easy to over-simplify causes and effects, the difference in the outcomes of these various schemes to that of the

Independence and *Constitution* speaks for itself. The question of the designs is one matter: that of federal finance — or of subsidies from Governments at large — is another, and this book contains sufficient examples to demonstrate how so many other ships, often splendidly conceived, foundered on the treacherous shoals of central Government monetary assistance. The two concepts of National Prestige and of economic viability in connection with large liners sometimes ran in harness, but sometimes in opposition, and this was a situation which fluctuated over the years since the argument for National Prestige was, all too often, dictated or frustrated by political or economic considerations far removed from the seaways of the oceans. Thus the *Independence* and the *Constitution* have been included since, due to the initiatives of the American Export Lines, the omens for their future were not only improved immeasureably, but they serve to set the other U.S.M.C. schemes which failed to materialize into a proper perspective.

As for the two ships themselves, their accommodation was enlarged to take 1,119 passengers during their 'off-season' refit in 1959. In the same year, when two of the 'Aces' were withdrawn from service, American Export purchased the smaller *Badger Mariner* and renamed her *Atlantic* to act as a consort for the original pair. At that time, with all the benefit of hindsight, it seemed that the Company's original decision to build only two of the planned liners was a wise one and, indeed, at the time of writing, both vessels are still afloat and, after two changes of ownership, have only recently been rebuilt for cruising in competition with modern, purpose-built vessels.

In an age when the natural expectation of life of ships is tending to decrease, this is no mean record: a record Favoured by Fate, one might say, whilst the other U.S.M.C. projects were veritably Damned by Destiny but . . . were their designs any the better or the worse than those less fortunate projects? Or was it simply that their Fairy Godmother's wand sparkled as it touched the money-bags of American Export Lines, whilst the wands of the guardian fairies of those other ships enjoyed no such impulse. As some men are said to be born with silver spoons in their mouths, so it is with ships . . .

146. The *INDEPENDENCE* in her original livery, following extensive reconstruction in 1959.

147. *The ATLANTIC, ex-BADGER MARINER, bought by the American Export Lines after two of the 'Four Aces' were withdrawn from service.*

148. *The CONSTITUTION.*

XXID DESIGN FOR THE TRANS-PACIFIC SERVICE OUT OF SAN FRANCISCO – THE PXE (LATER P5–S2–E1)

Chapter Sixteen has already detailed the story of the pre-1939 War P–4–P design for the Pacific service, for which three vessels were originally contemplated, and of how the two 24-knot ships which were then substituted for them were finally abandoned when the United States entered the war. Certainly the effects of Pearl Harbour and all that followed after it scuttled any ideas which the U.S.M.C. may still have entertained for progressing them, although the indications are that the scheme was already almost moribund – perhaps due to the first cost of any such vessel and, if this form of passenger liner/aircraft carrier did not materialize in the event, its demise can be applauded from a purely aesthetic standpoint, if for none other!

Once the war was over, the U.S.M.C. were considering the Pacific route once again, in consultation with the American President Lines, with the object of operating a service out of San Francisco with calls at Honolulu, Yokohama, Shanghai, Hong Kong, and Manila, with a similar return voyage.

In the years preceding the war, the trans-Pacific route had been worked by the American President Lines' *President Hoover*, *President Coolidge*, *President Cleveland* and *President Taft*. The *President Hoover* was lost in December 1937;* the *President Coolidge* was sunk in October 1942 in the Pacific, the *President Cleveland* in the following month off Morocco,

---

*The *President Hoover* had been bombed by Chinese warplanes in August 1936 when they mistook her for a Japanese ship, although she was, at the time, evacuating refugees from Shanghai. In December of the following year, when bound from Kobe towards Manila, she ran into considerable fog and rain off Formosa and, at 1.00 a.m. on the 10th, she went onto a reef some 600 yards off Hoishoto Island and, listing and stuck fast, she was never salved, but broken up where she lay by Japanese breakers. Her back had been broken several days after the stranding. Her 453 passengers and 408 crew were all rescued. At the time she had 7,000 tons of cargo, including 2,000 bags of mail, aboard.

149. *A cursory glance might lead one to suppose that this – the VIRGINIA – was a quite different ship from Pl.141 of the BRAZIL which was reconstructed in 1938, with only one funnel. The VIRGINIA, of course, became the BRAZIL.*

and the *President Taft,* which had been taken over as a trooper, alone survived the war, but she was not returned to her owners. The pre-war schedule operated by these four liners was based on a 56-day round voyage and provided a service for passengers in three classes (first, tourist and Oriental), and also shipped a large volume of freight.

Three different permutations of the required fleets to serve this route were considered, namely: four 18½-knot ships operating on a 56-day cycle; three 23-knot vessels working a 42-day cycle, and two 29-knot ships on a 28-day cycle. The number of passengers per vessel and the amount of cargo carried would, of course, have varied with the type of ship and the speed selected, as, indeed, would the number of freighters carrying cargo only that would have been necessary to operate in conjunction with the lead ships.

After careful comparisons of these several types, based on economic studies which were made, all the indications were that the two large

29-knot vessels would prove to be more satisfactory than the other two combinations. With this object in view, detailed investigations were then devoted to what was designated the PXE design.*

The first consideration affecting the design was that of the weather characteristics which she might encounter, and all the evidence showed that the proportion of fair weather which could be anticipated would be much higher than on the trans-Atlantic run and that such seas as would be encountered would be longer, with a longer period, and more in the nature of a ground swell. For this reason, it was considered that it should be possible to adopt smaller vessels of less displacement tonnage than would be acceptable on the North Atlantic route. This important conclusion had also been borne out by the actual performances of certain types of vessel which had given a good account of themselves during the war in the Pacific theatre, although unable to provide such sea-kindly performances when operating in the Western Ocean.

Once peacetime operations were functioning normally again, it was believed that full advantage would be taken of bunkering at suitable locations in the Phillippines but, in the meantime, it was accepted that it would be very imprudent to design a ship which was dependent on a doubtful supply of fuel and that sufficient tanks for bunkers would, therefore, have to be provided for a round trip of some 14,500 miles at the designed service speed of 29 knots. Thus, due to the large amount of fuel which might be carried, the ship's expected dead-weight would be relatively large for the high speed anticipated.

During the pre-war design era, the acceptable speed to length ratios † for large passenger liners did not usually exceed 0.9 or 1. However, ferries in the English Channel (to which reference has already been made when considering the P3−S2−DA1 design for the South American route‡), reached a value of 1.2, whilst large super-liners, like Cunard's *Queen Mary,* had achieved a value of 0.94 when steaming at around 30 knots. Thus, if the shaft horse-power was to be maintained at a reasonable figure and the vessel able to operate with an equally reasonable fuel consumption, it was proposed that the PXE's length should be calculated to be less than 900 feet.§

The proposed principal statistics of the PXE were as follows:

*See page 316.

† Used purely in relation to wave-making calculations. See Glossary under Froude No.

‡ See page 223.

§ 274.32 metres.

Waterline length . . .	895 feet
Beam	85 feet
Depth to strength deck . .	71 feet
Longitudinal co-efficient . .	0.57
Power plant	Geared steam turbines
Designed displacement . .	37,500 tons
Fuel oil capacity . . .	9,500 tons
Fresh water	800 tons
Swimming pools . . .	200 tons
Passengers, baggage, crew and provisions	1,000 tons
Dry cargo	1,350 tons
Reefer cargo	150 tons
Total deadweight . . .	13,000 tons
Designed speed . . .	29 knots
Designed shaft horse-power .	100,000
No. of screws	2
Designed steaming radius . .	12,500 miles
Number of passengers . .	1,000
Number of crew . . .	496
Bale capacity	150,000 cu. ft.
Reefer capacity . . .	15,000 cu. ft.

In view of the climatic nature of this semi-tropical route, it was thought to be desirable to avoid the use of inside state-rooms wherever possible, and that the installation of outside ones would be rendered the more easy by the outstanding proportions of the vessel — a great length and a comparatively narrow beam. On the other hand, from the point of view of the passengers' comfort, it was essential to ensure that the designed beam should be sufficient to ensure a satisfactory period of roll.

For the P4–S2–41 trans-Atlantic design, it had been proposed that the discharge of cargo should be by the use of masts and kingposts with derricks operated by winches through open hatches. However, in the case of the DA and the PXE, because there would be only small amounts of cargo to be carried and because each ship's beam would also be smaller, it was considered that side-port cargo-handling would be the most practicable in these two types, and that the PXE should depend on numerous

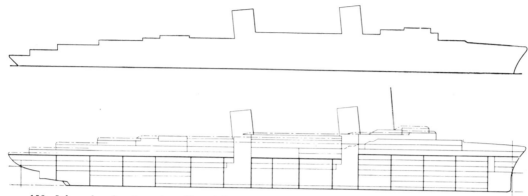

150. *Inboard and outboard profiles of the PXE design of 1945.*

side-ports through which cargo could be discharged by a new type of cargo-handling gear previously suggested for use in the P3–S2–DA1. In this manner, any topside cargo gear would be eliminated, as would any trunked hatchways. Thus the accommodation for the passengers could be extended further forward and aft, although it was felt that they might be uncomfortable if they were berthed *too* near the ends, when the effects of pitching would be accentuated.

Results from model tests in the Washington ship tank had predicted that the use of twin skegs would not be an advantage to the proposed hull configuration, which would have been of full form, but that twin rudders could be a possible alternative which warranted further studies.

The PXE, being a twin-screw vessel, would have been designed to have two boilers per shaft, from considerations of pure simplicity and also of saving space, but, owing to the high horse-power (50,000) required for each shaft, as proposed they would have been the largest marine boilers ever built and would themselves have required special design considerations. The advantages gained by having a small number of boilers were that the associated auxiliaries would have been reduced in number, too, thus simplifying the piping, uptakes and boiler mountings, etc., besides having an influence on all round convenience in the engine room layout.

In the designs which had been put forward for the P4–S2–41 and the DA, the propulsion machinery had been situated amidships and, in each case, there had apparently been ample justification for this location. However, the PXE, which was intended for the Pacific, would have had a much greater length than the other two vessels, so that it was feasible, in theory, to place both machinery compartments in the after third of the vessel. This location would have had the double advantage of reducing the length of propeller shafting, as well as placing the funnels far enough aft to obviate most of the smoke and funnel smut nuisance normally experienced when they were placed in the more conventional position amidships – or almost so. This line of thought seems to have been 'in the pipe-line' before the advent of the *Southern Cross, Canberra* and *Northern Star,* although its origins actually went back much further, since the early Matson vessels *Lurline* of 1908 and the *Wilhelmina* of 1909 might be said to have pioneered this concept. However, in fairness, it must be stated that these two vessels were primarily cargo-passenger ships rather than passenger-cargo liners.

Nevertheless, investigations into stability in a damaged condition revealed that the three-compartment standard required in a vessel of the PXE's length could not be obtained so satisfactorily with the machinery located aft as when it was amidships, and for this reason the engine placement did follow the pattern set in the P4–S2–41 and DA designs after all.

Due to the side-port cargo-handling method which was selected, deck obstructions would have been reduced to a minimum. One advantage of this clear profile was that large areas of such unobstructed decks could be utilized to their fullest advantage for passenger recreation but, equally, the disadvantage was that the apparent wind created by a liner steaming at high speed, especially when added to the effect of a strong head wind, could render such large unprotected areas unsuitable for the purpose of recreation, or even of promenade.

In consequence, it would have been necessary to have provided special forms of wind protection on these open decks.

In 1945, aluminium was more readily available and less costly than before the War, and this material was therefore considered for extensive use in the PXE's top-side structure, since it would have given the added benefit of reduction in weight.

An important consideration in this respect was that, if the vessel was to be entirely or partially 'turtle-backed' with the exception of the fore-castle, the use of light metal would have to be applied liberally. Where it would have been undesirable to have provided a turtle-back feature, palisades or similar structures would have had to have been utilized. These features would have contributed in a marked degree to the radical appearance of the PXE class.

It was thought that the anticipated post-war traffic on the Pacific route had been estimated accurately, as there was no direct competition with the Japanese at that time and there would not be any for some years to come. So long as this situation prevailed, it was clear that, of the various interests which would be capable of carrying the expected freight and passenger traffic across the Pacific, the one which possessed the fleet which had borne the lowest capital cost could be expected to earn the highest percentage profit on its capital investment. In other words, when comparing all the possible fleets involved, and assuming on the one hand that they had equal cargo capacities and on the other that their operating incomes would be approximately equal, then the capital and fixed charges would be most advantageous for that fleet in which the capital costs had been the lowest.

Moreover, it had been gleaned from detailed economic studies that, if expected traffic on the route would support ships of acceptable displacements, cargo would be carried most profitably at up to — but not exceeding — 18 knots, but that the optimum passenger-carrying speeds would have to be faster: in the order of 28 to 30 knots. This latter speed was postulated because the overhead charges for victualling passengers were so much higher and because, if they were too long at sea, they would, literally, eat up the profits.

For these reasons, the final choice of design for the PXE was for two 29-knot passenger liners with limited space for high grade cargo to operate across the Pacific on a bi-weekly sailing schedule. These two vessels would be supplemented by C3-type cargo ships. This fleet was not only seen to be the ideal one, but to represent both the least capital investment and the greatest earning capacity for the future.

The following year, in 1946, the Maritime Commission initiated another proposed design for operation by the American President Lines

(A.P.L.). Bearing the designation P5−S2−E1,* these twin-funnelled liners were presumably intended for A.P.L.'s round-the-world service and, as if to bear this out, were dubbed the 'Great Circle Liners'. The designation letters indicated that they would have been twin-screw vessels driven by steam turbines, with a waterline length between 800 and 900 feet and, in fact, their estimated overall length was 942 feet.† They were expected to carry 1,248 passengers in three classes, and detailed plans prepared by the Maritime Commission disclosed extravagant and luxurious public rooms and amenities.

To all intents and purposes, the P5−S2−E1 was a modified and re-vamped version of the PXE and it is interesting to note that, in her profile, the type of smoke-deflecting cowls intended for her funnel tops were those originally wind-tunnel-tested and considered for use in the United States Lines' *America* in 1939. Tenders for the two P5−S2−E1 liners were invited by 20 September 1946 but, in the event, they were never forthcoming because, in the interim, the ships had fallen victims to President Truman's austere budget cuts of that year.

Although the U.S.M.C.'s PXE and P5−S2−E1 designs were good and financially viable concepts for the immediate post-war years on the Pacific, and although there is no doubt that the A.P.L. endorsed these recommendations whole-heartedly, they were never pursued apart from the requests for tenders on the latter design. As stated, this was partly due to considerations of financial restraint, but it was also influenced by the change of wind in the politics of China which, by that time, was in a state of serious civil war.

Instead, the A.P.L. purchased from the Bethlehem Alabama Shipyard two of the last emergency P2-type troopships whilst they were still under construction, with appropriate specifications for them to be finished off as luxury liners. In 1947, they took delivery of the *President Cleveland* and, a year later, of the *President Wilson*. The A.P.L.'s approach may have been to fill the vacuum on this route as detailed by the Maritime Commission, but not with such an ambitious project as they had had in mind originally. As it was, these two *Presidents* were America's first two post-war passenger liners. The P2 design had already proved itself in all theatres of the war and in all weather conditions, so that, in effect, these two vessels were 'de luxe' versions of this troopship design. They each

* See page 316.
† 287.12 metres.

had a gross tonnage of 15,456, and an overall length of 610 feet:* they could carry 550 passengers in three classes and their turbo-electric power plant could sustain a cruising speed of 19 knots. As originally envisaged, their itinerary was from San Francisco to Honolulu, Yokohama, Hong Kong, Manila and return and both ships completed twenty-five successful years on this route before being sold in 1972.

This was a model case when some, but not all, of the recommendations laid down by a government body were followed up with action.

Even though the very conceptions of the PXE and P5–S2–E1 designs were dead, a further proposal for a super-liner on the Pacific route was to emerge some 12 years later, as will be seen.

*185.93 metres.

151. The new PRESIDENT CLEVELAND of 1947.

152. *Seen passing the Statue of Liberty, the MANHATTAN which, with her sister, the WASHINGTON, (See Chapter XXIA, 1st para), were the biggest ships built in the United States at the time of their launch in 1932/3, being 24,289 tons gross. They proved to be most successful, if with few claims to beauty. (But see the WASHINGTON later in life — Pl.190)*

XXII THE LIBERTY LINERS

In 1949 an attempt was made to resuscitate the 'Yankee Clippers' scheme for two massive cabin-liners, which had previously been proposed in the late 1930s, when it had come to nought. A company, called Liberty Liners Incorporated with offices on Broadway, New York, and on K Street, Washington, D.C., was set up to promote the project, and it made a new approach to the Government in an attempt to win its support for the construction of these vessels, primarily by stressing their auxiliary potential. Paul Chapman and Theodore Ferris – no less! – were in fact urging the United States Government to approve and finance the creation of two high-speed, emergency troop transports and aircraft carriers which, when not commandeered for military purposes, would be operated commercially on the North Atlantic route by Liberty Liners Inc., without any Government subsidy once they were in service.

The liners were exactly as they had been devised before the war, except that prices had risen sharply. Unfortunately, estimated construction costs had spiralled to $100 million each, while the one-way passage fare, exclusive of meals, had doubled to $100. Nevertheless, based on this fare and the estimated earnings on weekly sailings with only 50% of the passenger capacity filled, Chapman and Ferris calculated that two such ships would not only manage without the need for an 'operating-differential', but would make a respectable profit to boot.

Once again, Chapman and Ferris met with no success but, resolute as ever, they decided to modernize and re-sculpture their design completely to bring it into line with the latest ideas whilst, at the same time predicting the forthcoming competition which passenger ships were likely to face in the challenge from air transport, they also contrived further novel features to ensure the viability of their proposed super-cabin-liners.

This took them until March 1951, when the two giant vessels were still basically the same as before. Their overall length was still designed to be 1,254 feet, although the gross tonnage was reduced, as they now had one deck less. This was the uppermost one, with its 'cathedral' windows, which had originally been intended for aeroplane storage space but, in spite of its elimination, it was not expected that the auxiliary aircraft-carrying capability would be affected adversely.

In appearance, however, the liners had changed considerably. A revised artist's impression depicted them with a single modern mast above the bridge, replacing the two conventionally placed masts of the earlier design. The two funnels had acquired a streamlined rake and a distinctive upward trend of the sheer line forward, starting beneath the fore part of the midship superstructure, gave the vessels a sleek and racy look, while the fifty-eight double-banked lifeboats had been raised from the main to the promenade deck.

The passenger accommodation and troop-carrying potential were naturally rather less since the cabin space had been reduced, but there was the hint of one interesting innovation in the form of cafeteria-style restaurants in addition to the traditional dining saloons. With such an arrangement, the proponents declared: *'The passengers will have a means of controlling their expenses at sea.'*

Each vessel was planned to have a dry cargo capacity of 375,000 cubic feet and a refrigerated storage capacity of 100,000 cubic feet. It was proposed that cargo and mail stowage would be through the sides of the ships, using 'gear of the extensible-boom type', rather like the gantries used today in the handling of container cargoes.

These new Liberty Liners would have been of entirely fireproof construction, completely enclosed and air-conditioned throughout. The hull was designed to three-compartment safety standard with 17 main water-tight bulkheads.

The propulsion machinery would have been located in two independent, widely-separated engine rooms and consisted of four double-reduction geared turbines designed to develop 280,000 normal shaft horse-power to give a sustained sea speed of 34 knots. Steam would have

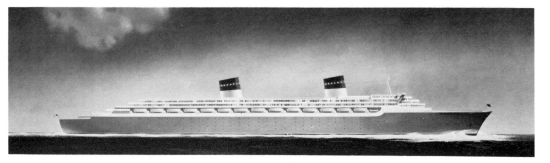

153. An artist's impression of one of the Liberty Liners in 1952.

been furnished by eight boilers at 925 p.s.i. and 1,000 degrees Fahrenheit.

To promote their scheme still further, Chapman and Ferris engaged a top-ranking public relations firm to 'plug' the super-liners. They had a mock-up of a typical cabin suite built, complete with private bathroom and wall-to-wall carpeting. Further, they explained how the construction of the two monster liners would provide much employment for thousands of industrial and shipyard workers, as well as for 1,700 seamen, whilst additionally providing the United States with two liners which would be the envy of the whole world.

In order to finance the project, however, Liberty Liners Inc. still depended on receiving Federal aid. At this time, the Government-subsidized *United States* was nearing completion, albeit designed to the United States Navy's specifications, but nevertheless she was America's first giant passenger steamship which was entirely the product of the effort of the United States. The fact that Government money had already been spent on this enterprise was one which partly jeopardized the success of the request for similar financial assistance from Liberty Liners Inc. on the one hand, but debate over the proposed size of the ships also caused problems on the other.

It is difficult to convey in mere words alone just how immense these ships would have been. As successive super-liners have entered service, their arrival has been accompanied by surfeits of publicity material to illustrate their vastness and magnitude in suitably dramatic terms: how their length, or the total weight of their rivets, contrasted with the height of this, or the mass of that, famous monument or landmark; or how their miles of electric cable equated with the distance between two particular cities, and so on. It is quite impossible to draw such comparisons for passenger liners that were never built, but some impression of their enormous proportions can be conveyed when the unbuilt vessels like the Liberty Liners are compared with those giants which were afforded this copious form of salesmanship, viz:

	G.R.T.	Length (overall) Feet	Metres	Horse-power/ Screws	Comments
Normandie	83,425	1,029	313.64	165,000/4	
Queen Mary	81,235	1,019	310.59	210,000/4	
Queen Elizabeth	83,675	1,031	314.25	210,000/4	Largest ever built
United States	53,330	990	301.75	240,000/4	Fastest ever built
France	66,350	1,035	315.47	160,000/4	Longest ever built
'Yankee Clippers'/Liberty Liners	100,000	1,254	382.22	380,000/4	(380,000/5 in 1961)
Amerika/Viktoria	90,000	1,070	326.14	300,000/5	
Bretagne (Yourkevitch design)	100,000	1,148	349.91	280,000/4	

Where the Liberty Liners proposal was concerned, the sponsors explained that they had designed ships of such unparallelled dimensions in order that they would have engines big enough to give the required speed, whilst still able to carry sufficient passengers to make them successful economically even if they were utilized at only half their capacity. As for their tremendous length, this was required to enable them to span three, or to straddle two, 600-foot heavy-weather Atlantic waves, thereby reducing the effects of pitching and effectively making them steadier ships, even in extreme conditions.

However, whether because they already had money invested in one project aimed at elevating America's maritime prestige, or whether because of the unprecedented size of these two liners is not known for certain but, yet again, the Federal Maritime Board was unable to recommend that the Maritime Commission give its support for the construction of two such vessels.

This ended the final fling of Chapman and Ferris and both died soon afterwards. Theodore Ernest Ferris' death occurred in May 1953 and Paul Wadsworth Chapman's in the following year. As to the former, his name lives on in maritime history for his many successes and innovations in other forms of ship design, particularly in the two World Wars, but,

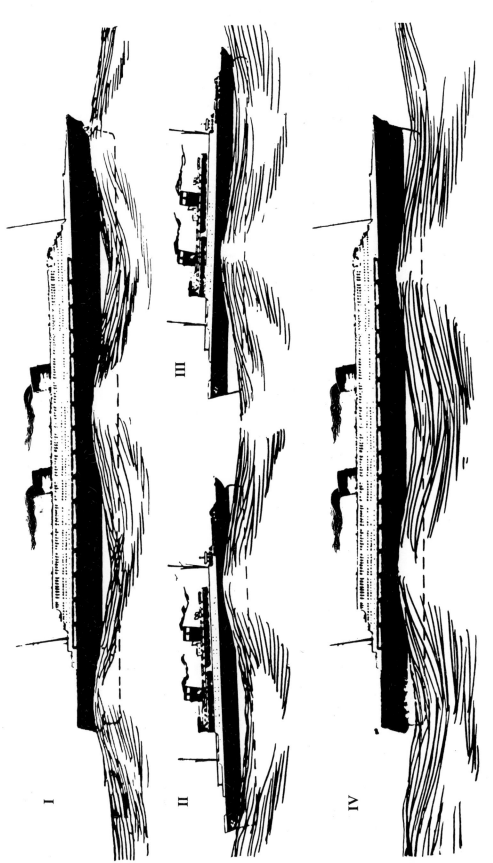

154. Sketches illustrating the behaviour at sea of a 1250-foot ship (I & IV) compared with that of a 700-foot vessel (II & III) under 'heavy weather' conditions of the North Atlantic. The length of seas (horizontally from crest to crest) is 600 feet: their height, from crest to trough (vertically), 36 feet.

although extremely successful before embarking on maritime affairs, Chapman cannot be said to hold the same distinction in this field, since his actual achievements were negligible. Certainly the influence of both men made its impact, even though it may be difficult to demonstrate that it led to any positive results.

Nevertheless, they were both men possessed of enormous resolution, fortified by their unswerving confidence and beliefs in their grandiose conceptions, which were not only intended to be commercial ventures but were equally initiated from a deep-seated sense of patriotism for the greater prestige of the United States. If ever two men might have borne the motto *'Never say die'*, these were those two, and, in modern parlance, they were men who could 'think big'. Such vessels as they proposed have never been built, and the likelihood that they ever will be constructed is now very remote. Nevertheless, their schemes were no mere pipe-dreams and it may be said with truth that they were 'Damned by Destiny'. That is the title of this book, determined after much soul-searching. It might have been 'Liners which Never Were', and that, too, fits the Chapman/ Ferris conceptions yet, as pointed out on page 209, those liners which never were might well have come into being. If, perhaps, the *United States* had not been under construction when the Liberty liners were proposed, one wonders whether they might not have materialized . . . who can say? Had they been constructed and had gone into service, Chapman and Ferris would have gone down in history as two names with which to conjure, for this alone. Fate and Fortune are inextricably intertwined.

Nevertheless, the question of the size of passenger vessels, like those proposed by Liberty Liners Inc., is an interesting one. Certainly there are valid arguments in favour of such monsters, but the logic of building them becomes disputable when one considers that their vast size would immediately prevent their navigation of the Panama Canal and, perhaps of lesser consequence, the Suez Canal, since the passage of the former, at all events, is a point of enormous strategic value in their adaptation to military work, as well as having great commercial merit if and when the occasion should arise. The smaller *United States* was able to pass through both canals. Another point which may be remarked, when viewing in retrospect the intervening years – years in which Chapman and Ferris were already dead – and particularly those in the last decade, when virtually all passenger liners were employed to a greater or lesser extent on cruises, is that the outsize super-liners would have been precluded from using many ports and desirable anchorages due to their excessive draught. Indeed, in this context, it may be noted that a sight not infrequently seen in the Solent some years ago was that of the *United States* steaming up Southampton Water while the *Queen Elizabeth* or *Queen Mary* lay at anchor down at Cowes Roads, having to wait the deeper water of the full tide.

Certainly Chapman and Ferris could not have foreseen the switch from passenger-carrying on liner (scheduled) services to cruising, but there has always been a school of thought which maintained that there must be an optimum size for a super-liner which should not be exceeded, if only for the reasons cited above, since any such ship must be expected to be diverted for service in time of war. There is some validity in this contention, even though those who subscribe to it may not agree precisely what that optimum size should be, but recent developments in merchant shipping might be said to alter the complexion of the argument.

When the *Great Eastern* was launched, she was by far the biggest ship in the world, and she retained this distinction — being far ahead of her times — until exceeded by the *Oceanic* in 1899. Although she had a chequered career, the *Great Eastern* was built as, and intended to be, a passenger liner. From the *Oceanic* onwards until well after the 1939-45 war, the biggest ships in the world were always passenger liners and, incidentally, on the North Atlantic route. Whatever their era, those in the top echelons were invariably very much bigger than other merchant vessels and, by their very nature, with increasing upperworks and decks as the years rolled on, apart from their vast array of boats etc., they seemed to be all the more impressive when compared with the run-of-the-mill merchant ships, which did not increase in size proportionately over the period. We have already commented upon the sort of statistics which were quoted so often in respect of the great liners, in an effort to titillate the imagination, and it must be admitted that artists' impressions of — say — the *Queen Elizabeth* or the *Normandie* fitted into, and overlapping — perhaps — Trafalgar Square in London or Times Square in New York, do provide a clearly demonstrable idea of their size.

Let us take another example. If we consider just the hulls of these two ships and assume that they were to load cargo, then they could have loaded four or five of the largest cargo ships in trade at the time of the 1939 war. In this connection, we have spoken of displacement tonnage at intervals in our text, although this was a form of measurement seldom used of merchant vessels, except in their design stages. Until 1939, the biggest tankers were some 18,000 deadweight tons. This is not to say that, if such an hypothetical exercise as to load four large cargo ships into an Atlantic liner were to be undertaken, they would not need to be cut into sections, or subjected to some equally hypothetical crusher, in order to make them 'fit', but the example provides the measure of the vast disparity in size between the large cargo ships of the day and the super-liners.

Today the boot is very much on the other foot. Passenger liners have tended to decline in size from their pre-war peak, whilst the larger merchant vessels have reached sizes in terms of tonnage which were unimaginable before the Second World War, and range, in some instances, from a quarter of a million to over half a million tons deadweight, whilst their lengths extend up to 1,359 feet.* It will have been noted that 1,000-foot liners were long the goal of ship designers' ambitions and, in the event, this length was only exceeded in four of them that were actually built. The super-tankers and Very Large Crude Carriers are intensely functional, superficially resembling monstrous and gigantic barges with box-like accommodation units aft, together with a funnel or two. This box of accommodation is, in fact, a great deal bigger than it looks, for it only represents so small a portion of the total length, and is often equipped with a lift between its many decks. (How old square-rigger men must turn in their graves at this development!) Nevertheless, although we are not necessarily comparing like tonnages, the fact remains that, in terms of capacity, these largest cargo vessels of the modern age could accommodate six or seven of the original *Queens,* or five of the proposed – gigantic – Liberty Liners!

The largest vessels afloat today are tankers, and of these the biggest in terms of deadweight is the *Pierre Guillaumat* of 274,838 gross tons and with a capacity of 555,031 tons d.w.† That is, a load of 555,031 tons will bring her down from her light condition to her summer freeboard marks and, in general terms, is the amount that she can carry. Her length is 1,359 feet – over a hundred feet longer than the proposed Liberty Liners and

---

*414.22 metres.

†A 16-knot vessel, she is powered by four turbines delivering 6,500 s.h.p.

some 40% longer than the *France!* She is owned by the Compagnie Nationale de Navigation. Another tanker, not far behind her, is of 553,662 tons deadweight, with a greater gross tonnage of 275,276. Calculated displacement tonnages have been quoted extensively in these chapters and, in the case of a large, express passenger liner, the displacement and the gross tonnages tend to be very much the same. In the case of tankers and bulk carriers, the gross tonnage is roughly half that of the deadweight, or even less.

It is not within the scope of our theme to discuss the merits or demerits of these vast bulk cargo-carriers or container ships, their advantages or their disadvantages. The basis for their existence lies in the economic truth, so well appreciated by the proponents of the 100,000-ton super-liners, that the larger any unit of transport, the more economically viable she will be, always providing, of course, that she can be kept fully employed and turned round in port with expedition. Thus it must remain a matter of speculation whether, had these enormous cargo ships appeared before the North Atlantic passenger trade was virtually killed by the flying machine, Destiny might have been kinder to some of the grandiose projects which form the burden of this book. There have always been men ahead of their times — men like Brunel, for example — but the majority of them have become lost in the mists of time simply because their peers were less far-sighted and too timid to back their ideas.

Certainly Theodore Ferris and Paul Chapman died with their great dream unrealized and unfulfilled, but it was not the end of that dream. In 1961, a final, ephemeral bid to get their ships, designed ten years previously, into service was made by two close colleagues, William Perott and Walter M. Ballard, who had been associated with Chapman ever since his early days with the United States Lines.* More recently, Ballard, who had been the design director for the interiors of the liners *Manhattan* and *Washington,* had managed the offices of Liberty Liners Inc. on K. Street, Washington, D.C. These gentlemen proposed the construction of the two ships as designed, but with the replacement of the original propulsion system by one combining nuclear reactors and steam turbines. This would have developed a total of 380,000 shaft horse-power, giving a maximum speed of around 40 knots with five propellers.

Nothing came of their efforts either, and it seems that the only thing

*Page 99.

which the Chapman/Ferris projects lacked was the necessary financial support to build the liners. Nevertheless, the American drive for giant passenger liners was soon to have a new champion.

155.

156. *Two sketches of the Liberty liner design, the top one showing the vessel in conventional guise, the lower one with her funnels telescoped, her ventilators collapsed and with her masts lowered, providing a flying deck runway measuring 140 × 800 feet.*

XXIII THE CANTOR PROPOSAL.
THE *PEACE* AND *GOODWILL*

On 5 April 1956 a New York hotelier, Mr. Hyman B. Cantor, who was President of the Carter Hotel Group, read an address to the Propeller Club of the United States at the United States Merchant Marine Academy, Kings Point, New York. His subject concerned the construction of two trans-Atlantic super-liners to inaugurate ocean travel to Europe for a one-way fare of $50 (£17) and it seemed that a successor to Paul Chapman and Theodore Ferris had arrived on the scene to perpetuate the American dream of a giant liner.

In his address, Mr. Cantor stated that he had been thinking in terms of accomplishing this goal for the past twenty years, but had seen no way of financing such a project until a year previously. At that time, early in 1955, the Government had made it possible through certain amendments to the Maritime Financing Act.

Upon receiving his copy of the amendment, he had seen the possible means of financing two super-liners to make the trans-Atlantic crossing. He foresaw a way of providing ocean travel which the American wage-earning classes could afford by utilizing mass-handling methods, and with the regular American Merchant Marine, yet without an operating subsidy from the Government.

The United States, he averred, had a reasonable amount of passenger ship accommodation available for the upper financial strata of its people, but little or no transportation existed for the lower income groups. Cantor's ships were to provide such a feature to a virtually untapped market and, instead of catering to the Waldorf-type clientele in the manner of the existing liners of the day, they would offer, instead, ocean passages done in the full American commercial tradition at 'Times Square' prices, permitting fares to Europe within the economic reach of almost everyone.

Originally his plans called for two ships, each of 100,000 tons, 1,250 feet* long and with a capacity for 9,200 passengers but, since the Coast Guard regulations would not permit the carriage of over 6,000 passengers in any one vessel, the plans had to be revised several times in order to conform to this ruling. After these modifications had been incorporated, and following a tremendous amount of work, he eventually evolved a scheme incorporating all of the following features:

His final plans were for the construction of two 90,000-ton trans-Atlantic Ocean super-liners, to be named the *Peace* and the *Goodwill* to carry passengers to Europe for a one-way fare of $50 (£17) minimum. These were to be the largest and fastest ships afloat, each to have a length of 1,150 feet† and a 34-knot cruising speed. Their beam would have measured 135 feet and their draught 34 feet. The two ships were expected to travel between the United States and Belgium in four days, with accommodation for 6,000 passengers and with a crew of 1,350.

The $50 one-way fare would include the transportation and berth only. A single-class catering service was planned, with a large kitchen at the centre of each ship servicing a 1,500-seat cafeteria as well as a 1,000-seat formal dining room. In addition, there would have been self-service canteens of automat style, with food and beverages at economy prices, located on each guest deck. Four bars and cocktail lounges were also planned for each of the liners.

The passenger cabins would have been prefabricated by the Pullman Company and laid out in two- and four-berth rooms, each with a private bath, television and air-conditioning.

Each of the two ships would have had two indoor swimming pools, a skating rink, two theatres, outdoor sports equipment, a concert hall and facilities for religious services. Also planned were shopping centres, where goods from both sides of the Atlantic would be sold at reasonable prices.

The vessels were designed to be unsinkable with twenty air-tight

* 381 metres.
† 350.52 metres.

compartments in the hulls and, in time of war, they could be converted immediately to aircraft carriers or to division-strength troopships.

The top deck would have been a flat, clear space, 450 × 80 feet, abaft the funnel, and this would have been used as a sports deck for outdoor activities and would also incorporate a swimming pool. Below this there would have been a glass-enclosed aircraft hangar space two decks deep, which would normally be used as a convention hall with seating capacity for 4,000 people, but it would have featured roll-away doors to enable the space to be divided into meeting rooms for smaller groups.

During off-season periods, the intention was that business groups on both sides of the Atlantic would be contacted to make passenger bookings in order to hold conventions and business 'junkets' aboard the two vessels. Hyman Cantor planned to utilize his long hotel operating experience to arrange two-week packaged vacations at low cost. Voyagers would be offered tours, with all expenses included, for as little as $330 (£110), of which $33 would be paid in cash and the balance in ten monthly instalments, an idea pioneered by the United States Lines in 1940, when they had been compelled to send the newly completed *America* cruising, due to the war in Europe.

Cantor himself headed a group of investors with $25 million in available cash, plus a working capital of $5 million. Since the repayment of a Federal loan towards construction costs was guaranteed in 20 years, an operating subsidy from the Government would not, therefore, be required.

His estimates were that the construction of the two liners would take two years, and he let it be known that reservations for passages would be accepted only after the keels had been laid. Whilst this may seem to have been somewhat optimistic in this age when projects are so prone to fall behind schedule, it was once quite a common practice, and bookings were made on this basis for the maiden voyages of the *Olympic* and the *Titanic,* to cite but two instances.

After numerous reappraisals, the final 6,000 passenger, 90,000-ton ship design seemed to be the most practical, in that it provided ample public space and had complete sports and recreational facilities. There was no question, in Mr. Cantor's opinion, but that there was an extremely intense and general need for travel accommodation of this type.

Although there were always critics of mammoth ships *per se,* there was also the valid concern that they might outgrow the port-handling facilities available to them, but apparently it was felt that these vessels would not be too large on this count, since they would be loaded from their sides, making the length of the piers at which they would berth relatively unimportant.

Hyman Cantor envisaged the operation as a 'Ferry Line' linking New York and Belgium. Initial considerations had covered three ports as the European terminal, namely: Zeebrugge in Belgium, Flushing in the Netherlands and Milford Haven in the United Kingdom. The reasons for the selection of Zeebrugge were that Belgium did not have a passenger line of its own and that the officials there had been very co-operative. The operational base for the company would have been at Boston, Mass.

Cantor pointed out that the ships already in service at that time operated with a steward servicing six or eight rooms in the first and second classes. This same steward made the beds; cleaned the cabins; did the valet work such as pressing clothes; shone the shoes; ran errands, acted as room service waiter and even dispensed pills when a passenger was sick but, as a result of all this activity, he only made up some fourteen to sixteen beds a day. For his part, Cantor was looking for a more efficient production approach and had arranged with the unions for a target of sixty-five beds per maid *per diem,* and they had agreed to this in return for the concession that there would be no overlap of jobs. A maid was to be maid: a waiter a waiter; a doctor a doctor, and so on. Through this more productive method, he was confident that he would be able to reduce the crew requirements considerably.

As an example, he quoted the *United States,* a ship with 1,700 beds and 1,062 crew, and the *Queen Elizabeth* which, with 2,200 beds, utilized a crew of 1,600.* Compared with these, his super-liners would have had 6,000 beds and, according to the manning scales that he had arranged with the unions, there would be less than 1,350 crew. In other words, there would be a ratio of four passengers to one crew member as opposed to about one and a half passengers to one crew in the existing large liners. However, neither caviare, pheasant nor like delicacies would be offered as part of his service!

The laundry would all be done ashore and, because of the great volume involved, a discount of 40% had been offered from land-based

*i.e. Total crews – not just the catering departments, in which the savings were much more dramatic.

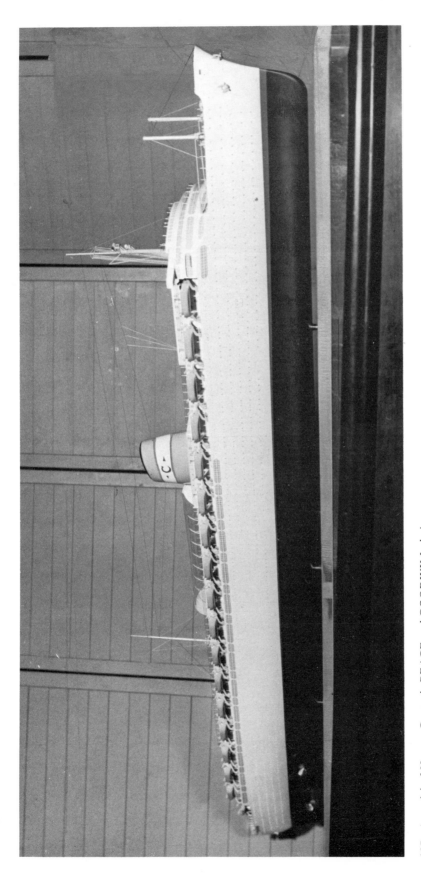

157. *A model of Hyman Cantor's PEACE and GOODWILL design.*

commercial laundries. Most of the food would be pre-cooked, frozen or prepared in advance, and served on individual trays which would be discarded over the ships' sides,* thereby eliminating preparation aboard, and this would be an enormous amount of help. Two men in each watch would be able to keep twenty canteens supplied with food, and each of these canteens, in turn, could supply hundreds of passengers.

Cantor's detailed plans, along with the stress and strain studies, were put on display for the inspection of the Propeller Club audience. He stated that he had been asked by European shipyards to build the ships over there, with the offers of very favourable financial inducements to do so, but stressed that he himself was an American and that this was a strictly American concept. He continued that most of his business would emanate from the United States and, for these reasons, he preferred that Washington should help him to close the deal in his own country.

As for the Merchant Marine officers of the future, Cantor saw an opportunity in his enterprise to restore the glory of the American passenger fleet to their advantage because he felt that, in one fell swoop, his project would accomplish passenger ship supremacy for the United States and supply permanent employment for 2,700 merchant seamen, in addition to 4,000 shipyard and construction employees while the ships were being built, simply by the application of the American concept of mass-handling.

In conclusion he reiterated that no Government operating subsidy would be necessary for his ships and that he hoped that the loan guarantee would be favourably received and set in motion very soon, in order that contracts could be signed for their construction.

Apparently the U.S. Maritime Commission liked Mr. Cantor's proposal, and preliminary plans were sent to the United States Navy Department for their approval, since the two vessels would be used as troop transports or aircraft carriers should the need arise and they were, therefore, classified as 'special purpose vessels'.

In 1954 the estimated cost of these proposed liners was $200 million (£65 million) if they were to be built in the United States but, owing to large wage increases and rises in the price of steel, by August 1956 this figure had risen to $270 million (£90 million).

This posed the question of where the liners would be built, as United

---

*Had his scheme been fulfilled, there would doubtless have been an outcry from ecological lobbies, particularly if the trays were of plastic – and thus indestructible.

States Navy approval would be necessary if Mr. Cantor was to benefit from a construction subsidy of between 40% and 50% but, in turn, this would be conditional on them being built in an American yard. On the other hand, if they were built in a foreign shipyard, they would have been much cheaper but, in that case, there would have been no Government subsidy. Representatives from a German shipyard visited Cantor about the building of the ships, but nothing concrete materialized as a result.

The proposals for the *Peace* and the *Goodwill* remained a subject of much interest in passenger shipping circles for the next three and a half years, by which time another American tycoon, Mr. Edgar Detwiler, had arrived on the scene with some proposals of his own to rival Cantor's ideas. (Edgar Detwiler's project is dealt with in Chapter XXV.)

Hyman Cantor's grandiose and bold scheme culminated in September 1959 when, in the midst of rumours that he had negotiated contracts with Deutsche Werft A.G. at Hamburg for the construction of two 90,000 g.r.t. liners, it finally transpired that all that he had done was to come to an understanding with the yard that, if and when he had found the money and had made all the other arrangements necessary, they – probably like many other shipyards – would be happy to build the ships. According to one report, Cantor had discussed the matter with Dr. Erhard, the West German Finance Minister, in an attempt to conclude an agreement with the West German Federal Government over the cost of the building of the ships. It seems that he was prepared to sign a contract with the Deutsche Werft shipyard involving $168 million (£56 million) if the German Government would guarantee 70% of the building expenses. In this context, and since this supposition may require clarification, the explanation is provided by a letter written by Cantor shortly afterwards, in which he said: *'We even signed a contract'* (for the *Peace* and *Goodwill)* *'with the Deutsche Werft shipyard at Hamburg, subject to the German Government providing primary mortgage financing, but negotiations on this never materialized.'*

By this time a company named Sea Coach Transatlantic Liners Inc. had been formed to manage the project, and Cantor wanted his 'Hotel Dixie' super-liners, as they had been dubbed, to be in service by 1962 and 1963. Deutsche Werft quoted 36 months to build each ship, but against this there was a competitive bid from a Japanese yard of 30 months per ship, with primary financing provided by the Japanese Government. However, the terms of this contract, in respect of amortization, were considered to be too onerous for the company and, since it was felt to be imprudent to proceed on such terms, this solution to the building of the ships had to be abandoned.

After that set-back, nothing more was heard of Hyman Cantor's proposals. Just how seriously his scheme should be viewed in retrospect may be uncertain, but he certainly did a great deal of talking and a lot of interested and well-known people listened to him at the time. The fact of the matter was that one practical problem associated with these proposals of 1956 and 1959 was the unfamiliarity of Cantor himself with ships and naval architecture, although he was well versed in hotel management and catering matters. The famous naval architect, Vladimir Yourkevitch, the designer of the *Normandie,* acted as his consultant.* In this capacity, he must have been much discomforted by day-to-day changes of service speed by as much as three knots for such reasons as: *'By getting them in before lunch we can save a meal',* or *'This will mean two more round voyages in the year.'* The consultants were accused of making difficulties when they explained that such large speed increases might require almost a doubling of power, thereby resulting in a severe reduction in the space available for accommodation!

It is nevertheless interesting to note however, that as we enter the 1980s, the largest profit-earning liner, the *Queen Elizabeth 2,* owned by Cunard, was part of the major holding group, Trafalgar House Investments, itself a large hotel and catering organization. Similarly, it is ironic to observe that, on 28 September 1977, Freddie Laker inaugurated his 'Skytrain' service between Gatwick and New York, based on cheap one-way fares of £59, thus succeeding in doing by air what Hyman Cantor had failed to accomplish by sea.

In late 1978, Cantor revealed that he was investigating other liner operation possibilities. These involve the utilization of two large scale ships with huge public rooms and suitably adapted interiors for conventions and public meetings, like the *Queen Mary* in her role at Long Beach. He declared that *'this would be very profitable',* but whether any concrete outcome eventuates from this proposal, or whether it, too, will be 'damned by destiny', remains to be seen while this book is being written.

*The influence of his *Bretagne* design was quite evident in that for the *Peace* and *Goodwill.*

XXIV A SECOND *AMERICA* AND THE *PRESIDENT WASHINGTON*

Abid to obtain approval for the construction of the contemplated sister ship to the *United States* began in 1956, and this scheme was closely linked to another project involving a new trans-Pacific super-liner for the American President Lines. Both vessels, looking very similar indeed to the earlier *United States,* were designed by the Gibbs brothers, although it seems that the A.P.L. apparently were not happy with this and were looking for an appearance which reflected the advances made in the years since the previous liner was built. The two projects were linked by the fact that they formed integral parts of a bill presented by Representative Herbert C. Bonner, the North Carolina Democrat and the Chairman of the House of Representatives Merchant Marine Committee, before the 85th session of Congress. The eventual failure to appropriate funds for their construction was yet further evidence of the vacillating attitudes concerning giant liner ownership within the American Administration.

The United States Lines' vessel was requested as a replacement for the *America,* which was then nearly twenty years old and due to be superseded at this age under the terms of the Federal subsidy agreements. The new liner, which would probably have borne the same name, was virtually a duplication of the *United States,* although construction costs had increased by 60% since she was built, but plans for her National Defence auxiliary capabilities included the provision for possible installation of a nuclear propulsion unit, as an alternative to the traditional steam generation plant.

158. An artist's impression of the PRESIDENT WASHINGTON.

The American President Lines' ship, which was in fact given a name –
the *President Washington* – was some 10,000 tons smaller with an
estimated gross tonnage of 43,000, an overall length of 956 feet* and a
passenger complement of 1,450 divided between three classes. The *President Washington* was also considered for the installation of nuclear
instead of plant/boilers for military reasons and, as a twin-screw ship,
would have had the very creditable speed of 29 knots.

Competitive tenders for the two liners were requested, and in each case
the lowest came from the New York Shipbuilding Corp. at Camden, New
Jersey, who quoted around $109 million (£36 million) for the sister to the
United States and $97½ million (£32½ million) for the *President
Washington,* although construction of the latter vessel was at first considered to be most likely to be undertaken on the West Coast. The progress of the Bill for the two liners was fairly smooth at first, but then a
difficulty arose between the United States Lines and the Federal Maritime
Board with regard to the subsidization of the extra speed required for

*291.39 metres.

their new vessel. The Company argued that their experience, gained from the operation of the *United States,* showed that a vessel, designed with a great emphasis on auxiliary requirements and carrying engines with an excessive margin of reserve speed, was an uneconomic proposition. They wanted, therefore, to have the commercial speed of the new liner set at 28 knots, with the Government paying for the cost of increasing the speed above this figure. The Federal Maritime Board, on the other hand, argued – with some reason, as may be thought – that the average speed at which the *United States* had been operated was 31.5 knots, and that this should therefore be the service speed of the new vessel. This divergence of opinion very unfortunately prolonged the negotiations over the two ships and, as a result, the legislation for approving their construction fell as a casualty of budget pruning in the first session of the 85th Congress.

Matters had reached a head again by 20 March 1958 when the House of Representatives Merchant Marine Committee once more recommended the construction and sale of two super-liners. The committee proposed that one of them should equal the size and grandeur of the *United States* with a capacity for 2,000 passengers, while the other would ply a major Pacific route and would accommodate 1,400 passengers. In effect, this was an echo of the new *America* and the *President Washington* proposals, and had a familiar ring about it.

By this time, however, the cost of the new running mate for the *United States,* to replace the old *America,* had risen to around $128 million (£42½ million), which would include her defence features, together with luxury facilities and appointments. There was no total cost quoted for the Pacific liner, but estimates were thought to be approximately $200 million (£67 million) as a minimum for both vessels.

The proposal was that the United States Lines should purchase the larger liner for $47 million (£15½ million) and the President Lines the smaller one for $34 million (£11⅓ million), or 45% of the domestic construction costs in each case, whichever should be the greater. These sale prices to the companies would be fixed but, if shipbuilding and outfitting costs rose above contract specifications, a provision would be made whereby any cost differential between the fixed sale price and that of final construction costs would be borne by the Government.

It seems that this provision was in line with Congressional legislation that any new passenger liner would have to be ready for troopship duties in times of national emergency. Any construction and sale operations would still be subject to the approval of the Federal Maritime Board. The Bill, which was basically the same as that originally sponsored by Herbert C. Bonner, still required that the repayment terms from the companies should be in accordance with the existing laws but, nevertheless, the terms were felt to be liberal ones. In this context, the payments made by the respective operating companies would not include U.S. Navy specifications or costs of features added to the vessels to this end, since these would have to be met at the Government's expense.

The contracts for the two ships now depended entirely on Congressional action on separate maritime appropriation bills which went before the Senate and the House of Representatives. In the event, the construction of both vessels *did* finally receive authorization by Congress and was also fully endorsed by the President. These hurdles having been cleared, the schemes now seemed to have no further obstacles before them and merely awaited the actual allocation of Federal funds. By 1961, however, there had still been no provision for money in the administration's fiscal budgets and, at this point and despite their contractual obligation to the U.S. Government to build replacement tonnage for the *President Wilson* and the *President Cleveland,* the American President Lines shelved their project for a new liner and terminated their arrangements with the lowest-bidding shipyard, with which no formal contract had been signed.

The United States Lines, on the other hand, pursued its intention of building a sister-ship to the *United States,* although they appeared to have abandoned the initial design proposal which was, as previously stated, virtually a duplication of the famous record-breaker. In 1963 they authorized the Gibbs brothers to prepare a study for a 'super-*United States*' but nothing developed from this either. Then, in 1965, they approached the Gibbs again to produce designs for 'a new *America*', but this also failed to gain Government approval for a Federal subsidy, even though the Company was still under its obligation to replace the old *America* which, by this time, had become the Greek *Australis*. (Since the 1958 bill before Congress was in respect of both the Atlantic and Pacific vessels, it automatically broke down when the President Lines renaged on their obligations and, for this reason, the subsequent moves on the

159. *William Francis Gibbs and Frederic H. Gibbs in their office. The names of these two inspired brothers have appeared intermittently in the text ever since the days of the BOSTON and BALTIMORE proposal.*

United States Lines' projected vessel were subject to separate and un-related applications for Federal approval and aid.) The reason for this persistent reluctance to aid contract replacement programmes on the part of Congress lay in the ever-increasing shipbuilding costs. So long as these programmes were projected as loss-making operations requiring massive long-term subsidies, the Government was not, it seems, prepared to press shipping companies into fulfilling those contractual obligations which had been undertaken in a different financial climate.

Today, of course, the very idea of constructing a new United States

Lines super-liner is patently absurd, for the *United States* herself has been laid up in a state of idleness until recently, and is now scheduled to re-enter service in a cruising role.

During the years that the United States Lines lobbied Congress for the financial support to build a consort for the *United States* (probably with a feeling of some frustration in the light of the fact that approval *had* been given to such a ship in the 1958 bill, and it was no fault of theirs that their ship had not materialized as a result of it), another quite different bill to appropriate the construction costs of giant passenger liners was laid before Congress, albeit with an equal lack of success.

The instigator of this latter bill was a Republican Senator, John Ray of New York, who called for the approval of the building of two 90,000 gross ton all-Tourist Class liners for the Department of Commerce, which would then sell them to any interested operating concern, including the United States Lines! He advocated two vessels having a length of 1,150 feet* and a speed of 35 knots, each being intended to carry up to 6,000 passengers at low-rate fares, and to be operated like commercial hotels, lacking the splendour, grandeur and elaborate cuisine of the real luxury liners. Senator Ray's proposals were received with even less enthusiasm than the original ones put forward by the United States Lines and, it seems, were never sufficiently tangible to warrant inclusion in this book.

Around this time it was rumoured, without much evidence to support the story, that the Sovtorgflot – the managing organization of the Soviet merchant service, was planning the construction of an 85,000 gross ton liner. As usual, Russia was a 'dark horse' about her merchant and naval plans, and little could be ascertained about the ship's design or intended service. Whether or not there was any fire beneath the smoke of that particular rumour, it seemed to fade into the impenetrable mists and mysteries behind the Iron Curtain, and represented the merest interlude for speculation in a period dominated by projects of American origin.

*350.52 metres.

XXV THE DETWILER PROJECT – THE *UNITED NATIONS* CLASS

In the winter of 1958/9, plans were announced for the intended introduction of four 120,000-ton passenger liners on the trans-Atlantic
route, each of which would carry 8,000 passengers. Mr. Edgar
Detwiler, President of the American-European Travel Project Inc. of
New York, proposed that these vessels, to be called the *United Nations,
New Yorker, Lisbon* and the *Hollander* (alternatively to be named the
Mayflower), would be built in the Netherlands and would possibly trade
under the Portuguese flag. Their projected speed would enable them to
cross the Atlantic in about 3½ to 4 days, and the charge for the all-in fare
would be less than $162 (£54) – the lowest ever available!

Mr. Detwiler had apparently been planning to carry large numbers of
American tourists to Europe in enormous one-class ships ever since 1929,
and he hoped that, following the signing of the building contracts, the
ships would enter service in 1961. Following these sudden announcements, which displayed Detwiler's initial enthusiasm, the story became
more complex and involved as it proceeded. At the time, the estimated
cost of each of the ships would have been more than $90 million (£30
million), and he was confident that the money would be raised from
'International sources'. The preliminary design of the liners had been
prepared by Mr. John Wright, an American naval architect, and this was
seen during a visit to the United States by Mr. Cornelis Verolme, the
Chairman of the Verolme United Shipyards in whose yards it was proposed that the ships should be built.

In order to cater for such a mammoth undertaking, the first step was the formation of a Dutch shipping, holding and financing company called American European Lines N.V. in the autumn of 1959, one of the reasons for which was that it was proposed to man the vessels with Dutch and other Europeans, thereby incurring lower wage bills and other operating costs than under the United States' flag. No contract had been signed at this stage, and the major problem which lay ahead was the actual financing of the project. In the meantime, Mr. Detwiler had assured potential backers that arrangements were being made not only to finance the proposed vessels, but also to cover the cost of the ocean terminals which would have been necessary both in the United States and in Europe to accommodate liners of such gargantuan proportions. The cost of each fully equipped vessel, including the interest payments involved in financing the construction period and other expenses, the operating capital and a pro-rata proportion of the cost of the ocean terminal facilities was estimated to be some $128 million (£43 million) per vessel. The necessary equity to provide operating capital, amounting to $34½ million (£11½ million) per vessel, was said to have been arranged already.

The outstanding balance for each of the liners would be paid on an instalment basis at the various stages of construction. The ships would be managed and operated by a Dutch company and, as such, would be registered under Dutch law and be required to fly the Dutch flag, and not the Portuguese, as originally planned. It will have been noted that Hyman Cantor had had to amend his original idea of carrying 9,200 passengers to 6,000, to conform with the U.S. Coast Guard regulations, and that each of the successive American schemes had settled on this figure of 6,000 passengers for this very reason. Now, of course, by operating his vessels under a flag which was not under the jurisdiction of the U.S. Coast Guard, Detwiler was enabled to set his target for the higher figure of 8,000 berths.

His holding company entered into a contract with Hardy, Tobin & Co. Ltd., a firm of consultant naval architects, marine engineers and ship surveyors in London, to draft the final designs for the vessels of his proposed fleet − since it was no less! − and, in this connection, Detwiler had frequent meetings with Mr. A. C. Hardy, the Director of the consultancy.

160. Edgar Detwiler had many irons in the fire. When this picture was taken in 1960, he was returning from signing a 5-year agreement between his finance company and the Congo Republic to develop and finance its resources.

It was then revealed that much of the design for the ships, besides the broad economic strategy of the scheme, was based on the 'Liner of the Future' concept which had been outlined by A. C. Hardy and Pierre de

Malglaive as far back as 1937. (Chapter XX.) Consequently, Hardy, Tobin & Co. were given the responsibility for both the architectural work and interior design of the four passenger liners. In appearance, the two designs are not altogether dissimilar, the principal difference being the substitution of the retractable funnels and unusual exhaust arrangements of the 'Liner of the Future' for a funnel placed aft in the Detwiler ships. There are even similarities in the dimensions of the two designs and in the type of power plant selected.

The *United Nations, New Yorker, Lisbon* and the *Hollander* were to be one-class liners with the following main particulars, viz:

Tonnage (gross registered)	108,000/120,000
Length overall	1,275 feet (388.62 metres)
Beam	130 feet
Speed	35 knots
Power plant	Turbo-electric
Shaft horse-power	300,000–400,000
Number of passengers	8,000
Number of crew	2,000

The turbo-electric drive selected for the main propulsion of the *United Nations* class would have used two land power station type of turbo-alternerators which would supply five double-armature motors each coupled to a propeller. Mr. Hardy considered that it was then ten years too early to consider the installation of nuclear power plant in such ships as a viable proposition.

Special features planned for each Detwiler vessel included a large theatre to seat 1,200 people: four different kinds of night club: eight different areas in which to dance; a cinema seating 800 persons where the latest international films would be shown, and eight dining rooms of varying standards accommodating 4,000 people at a time with first-class food and service. In addition, a number of snack bars, American-type soda fountains and different types of tea, coffee and cocktail lounges would be provided. There would be no cafeteria-type service as originally envisaged in the Cantor project.

Facilities would have been provided for many kinds of entertainment, for sports (in the form of swimming pools, etc.) and for recreation, while tax-free goods would have been available in a comprehensive shopping complex of about fifty shops. There would also have been many rooms with the capability of mounting large conference and convention groups.

These proposed liners would have been completely air-conditioned. Each stateroom was planned to be of the lounge type, with its own bathroom and would have accommodated from one to four people. Indeed, the accommodation and facilities to be provided by each ship would have somewhat exceeded those of the world's largest hotels of the time. It was estimated that the building of the first vessel would take about three years and the following sisters about two years each.

The intention was that two of the vessels would have operated regularly on the North Atlantic between New York and Amsterdam, with intermediate calls at Cobh* and Plymouth, while the other two would have plied on the more southerly track between New York and Lisbon, with occasional voyages to Italy. Each of the four vessels would have been interchangeable between these routes, depending on the volume of summer or winter traffic available.

The estimated round-trip fare for a family, or for a social or student group of three of four people, in a private stateroom with bathroom and including meals was to have been about $175 (£58) per head, but the same facilities for two people would have been $200 (£67) each. Special terms, such as hire-purchase arrangements, were to have been made available to passengers to assist them with the passage cost and associated tours, if required.

Detwiler had foreseen the building of marine ocean terminals, which would have been required in conjunction with these huge liners, in order to expedite the embarkation and disembarkation of their passengers and the handling of their cargo, and had predicted that there would need to be a complex combination of railway, 'bus, coach and heliport termini with a car-parking capacity for 10,000 cars. In addition, he planned that hotels, motels and a complete tourist and shopping centre would have to be available and, to provide for layouts of such complexity, he calculated that six piers and over thirty acres of land would be needed. However, Detwiler promised that all these facilities would be made available at Amsterdam and at Lisbon — and this is not to make any mention of the need to widen the North Sea Canal to Amsterdam to allow the passage of

*Cork (in fact, at Queenstown).

his enormous vessels! During the early part of his various negotiations, he had had talks with the Port of Rotterdam authorities about the use of Europort as the Dutch terminus, since this was one of the few ports able to accommodate such large vessels, and it is not entirely clear what the objections may have been, although it might be safe to presume that the area of land required did not accord with the Europort scheme as already determined. On the other hand, the River Tagus at Lisbon was deep enough to take the vessels and possibly presented less of a problem on the score of the size of the ships.

It was predicted that, when the four proposed liners were all in service, they would have been able to carry 900,000 round-trip passengers each year between the United States and Europe, and that the spending potential of this number of tourists might amount to some $500 million (£167 million) while they were in Europe.

We have already considered in previous chapters some very ambitious schemes, upon the viability of which readers may have formed their own opinions and, in the full knowledge of the way that events have shaped after these various proposals were made – and died – they may conclude that some would not have proved to be viable. This would be a perfectly valid conclusion, particularly in the case of the later, post-war schemes, although it must be remembered that the various entrepreneurs and their backers did not possess crystal balls and that, although the threat of air-transport as a serious competitor to the passenger liner was certainly looming, no-one could then have guessed just how great that threat was to prove to be, nor the sudden collapse and withdrawal from regular service of so many splendid passenger ships. In order to take a balanced view of these proposals, it is necessary to project oneself back in time to the years when they were being considered without prescience of what the future might hold and, having accomplished this rather difficult operation and setting aside the knowledge of those factors which *did* subsequently occur to sabotage the economics of passenger ship operation, it will be found that, in general terms, the various schemes did seem to be perfectly reasonable, and the reasons for their foundering were usually because the initial costs could not be raised or due to other factors which have been described and which were not immediately concerned in any lack of confidence in them. Indeed, as has been shown, they received the

161. It was generally circumstances, and not the ships themselves or their promoters, which determined their destinies. Had – say – the first World War broken out ten years earlier, it is easy to suppose that the TITANIC and OLYMPIC (above) and their sister, the BRITANNIC, would never have come into being. Similar arguments can be used of many famous vessels.

support of influential men of high intelligence and, in some instances, of genius.

So it was in the case of Edgar Detwiler. His was the most ambitious scheme of all: not only because his ships were to be the largest and because there were to be more of them, but also because the ancillary requirements, in the sense of his vast ocean terminals, were the most grandiose yet conceived. Moreover, he was the last of the proponents of the great American 'dream' – the last to try to place the United States at the forefront of the Atlantic passenger trade – and it might be thought that, by the late 1950s, the writing was on the wall where concepts of this sort were concerned. In fact, this was not the case although, had he come forward ten years later, it is doubtful if anyone would have listened to him. As it was, he received the support of some very influential and respected men in the field of shipping. Mr. Cornelis Verolme of the Verolme United Shipyard at Rotterdam, now part of the Rhine-Schelde-Verolme Group, felt that the project was 'extremely serious' and if, in the event, the building contract had been signed, the order would have been worth a total of $340 million (£122 million) and would have achieved a record as the largest shipbuilding order ever placed up till that time. Of course, in citing him, it might be argued that he had a vested interest in the project: an interest which would have enhanced the profits and prestige of his firm almost beyond measure, but no business man of his acumen and experience was likely to undertake such an operation unless he had full confidence in its successful outcome, for the ships were not going to be built over-night, and it is difficult to imagine a more alarming situation than to have such enormous vessels well on the way to completion and then to find that the purchasers could not proceed. These were not vessels which could be 'sold off' elsewhere, and much confidence was required to undertake to build in the first place, regardless of the possible rewards which might accrue from the venture.

A somewhat cynical reader might argue that Mr. A. C. Hardy, another party who gave the scheme his backing, had an equally vested interest. A marine engineering and naval architecture consultant of very high standing, he was a sincere man who had already been convinced of the viability of very large Atlantic liners for over twenty years. He did a great deal of work on the project, for which he was presumably paid, but, once again, it must be remarked that it does not help any man's reputation to back a failure, and if Hardy was a naval architect *par excellence,* he was on a plane which did not ignore the economic considerations involved in the ships he designed. Even the Chairman of the Board of Directors of Mr. Detwiler's American-European Travel Project Inc. was no less a man than the former Prime Minister of the Netherlands, Professor P. S. Gerbrandy, while the Holland America Line, in collaboration with the Fugazy Travel Bureau Inc., was involved as potential ship managers or charter operators. K.L.M., the Dutch airline group, were said to have been negotiating the helicopter service planned for each terminal, using the recently developed Fairey Rotodyne, because of its capacity, speed and low running costs. (3 U.S. cents − or 2½d − per passenger mile in those days!)

Again, it might be argued that all these people and bodies had something to gain, but it was nevertheless considered worth expending a good deal of time and money investigating their several roles. Sadly, like

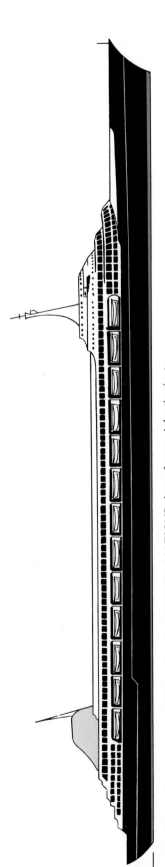

162. *The profile appearance of Edgar Detwiler's UNITED NATIONS class of trans-Atlantic giants.*

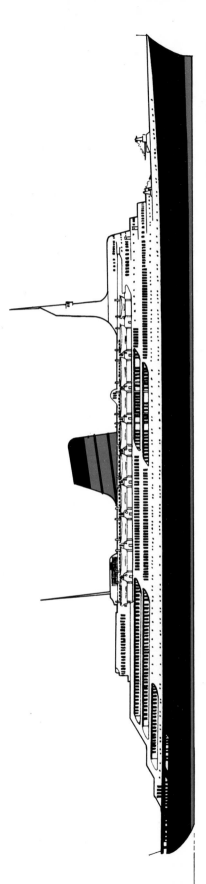

163. *Profile of Cunard's ill-fated Q3, based on drawings dated 30 March, 1961, when the funnel design was not finalized. The artist's rendering is the most likely configuration.*

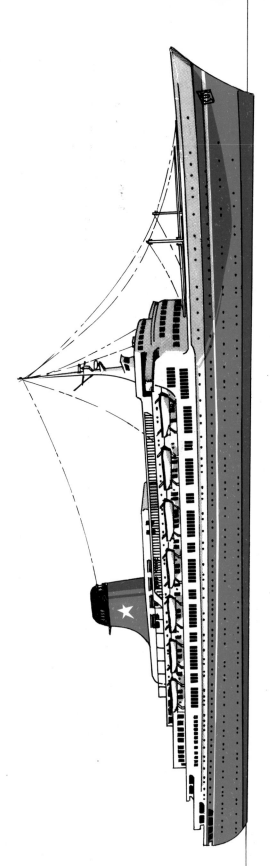

164. *Design for the Achille Lauro replacements for the ROMA and SYDNEY, which were cancelled before any work had started on them. (See Chapter XXVI)*

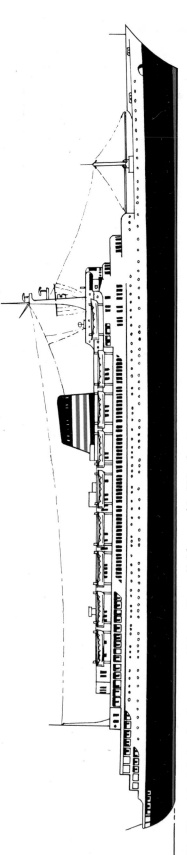

165. *The original design for the proposed Nippon Yusen Kaisha vessel (p.279 refers.)*

Hyman Cantor's proposal, the one important ingredient that Edgar Detwiler lacked was vast financial backing. However, his case was not the same as Cantor's, nor many of the other endeavours to build and operate the 'might-have-been' liners, since, in the first place, he was going to operate under a foreign flag, and thus, if able to increase the number of passengers to be carried, he had in the same movement abandoned all claims to enhancing the national prestige of his country and, since the ships were obviously not on call to the United States in the event of a national emergency, he had forfeited any hope of Federal aid. Nor, by the very nature of his proposed operation, could he hope for aid from any other Government, and he was thus left with the remaining option of raising money by the sale of stock in the markets of the world, but this, too, had the disadvantage that the capital so subscribed would not show any return for some considerable time until the ships were actually completed and in service. Taking the situation as it obtained at the time, this seems to have been the great weakness in the structure of Detwiler's embryonic empire. Even if some magic wand had been waved and the money had been available to enable the ships to be duly built, and taking account of the developments in the passenger ship situation in the years which ensued, it is difficult to escape the conclusion that, however statistically impressive they might have been, they would have proved to be the whitest of all white elephants in the event, for they were much too big to have been diverted to successful cruising roles.

Sporadic reports about the four giant liners continued right up to the end of 1959, after which there was silence. One of Mr. Detwiler's associates was quoted as saying that the trouble with him was that he started things and would put in a lot of his own money, but that when things really got going, he bowed out. This may or may not be fair comment, and it is certain that Detwiler *did* put in a great deal of time and money in the first instance, but the fact was that the furthest the negotiations ever reached with Verolme United Shipyards was the exchange of 'letters of intent'; a fact which may seem to substantiate the comment made by Detwiler's colleague. Beyond this, no further substantial progress was made.

Other problems which may well have militated against the advancement of the project were, in the first place, the question of the land

266

transportation capable of handling 8,000 passengers each trip when they embarked and disembarked at their various European terminals and, in the second, the matter of what would have happened to such ships during the winter 'off' season never seems to have been resolved.

There is one aspect of both the schemes of Hyman Cantor and Edgar Detwiler which should be borne in mind, and which must have fortified both of these entrepreneurs in the validity of their proposals. Perhaps rather surprisingly, more people actually crossed the Atlantic by passenger ship in 1958 (which was virtually in the centre of the periods in which these gentlemen were so much to the fore) than in any other year before or since. Despite this interesting statistic, shipping was in a state of decline, and the fact of the matter was that the increase in trans-Atlantic aircraft passenger travel was even more remarkable. The figures for the passenger liners may have looked to be superficially encouraging, but those for the Air Lines were the salient ones, since these represented a clear writing on the wall when predicting the future. Yet . . . it is easy to make such a comment today in the light of all that has actually occurred in the ensuing two decades, but prescience of the future is quite another matter, and thus judgement on these schemes can only be passed on the basis of the information available at the times when they were initiated.

As already mentioned, the Detwiler project was the last of the great American liner dreams which were never realized but, before leaving the New World, we should record another unusual proposal which emanated from a Canadian source in 1961.

The proponent was a Mr. Garry Reschka, a 26-year-old German immigrant who had arrived in Quebec on 15 August 1958, after running a small hotel. He intended to build four 45,000-ton liners to be named the *Progress, Confidence, Pacific Whale* and the *Sea Hawk* – a rather strange combination – which would carry 3,000 passengers each, at 34 knots on an apparently unspecified route. Certainly this scheme did not get very far, and the names of the ships are about all that survives from it, since Mr. Reschka's appearances in public life came to an abrupt end in November 1961, and the matter is not one which merits further comment, only being included here to complete the roster.

XXVI CUNARD LINE'S Q3 &
THE *ROMA* AND *SYDNEY*
REPLACEMENTS

While the smoke of the various American schemes was clouding the sky, there was considerable activity on the building front on the other side of the Atlantic, particularly amongst the Continental lines. In consequence, the Cunard Line was compelled to give consideration to the replacement of the *Queen Mary* and the *Queen Elizabeth,* the former being twenty five years old that this time. The result was the famous, if unfortunate, Q3 *Queens* replacement project.

Cunard had reserved a berth at John Brown's shipyard on Clydebank in 1957 for a vessel to replace the *Britannic,* the last White Star unit in the fleet, but did not proceed with her in the event and, at that time, took no further action concerning new vessels for their express service than to indicate that they were also contemplating two large liners which would cost about £20 million each.

As it turned out, the Company had the two *Queens* so extensively over-hauled, including the fitting of new cabin suites, lido areas and fin stabilizers, that it was widely believed that they might possibly remain in service for many years. Furthermore, there were other suggestions, designed to prolong their service lives by improving their performance, being made at this time. One such proposal came from Mr. Arthur P. Pedrick, a prolific inventor with a certain knowledge of high speed hull principles and techniques. He claimed that the *Queen Mary* and the

Queen Elizabeth could be kept in service longer by improving their speed with boundary air lubrication which would reduce both frictional and wave resistance. This would have been effected by feeding compressed air to their underwater hulls through hundreds of small holes, the power required to compress the air coming from a slight uprating of their engines' power output.

This idea was too complicated to detail here in full but Pedrick's plan included the provision of a false side, or sheet, on either side of the hull and parallel to it, bonded in such a way as to be airtight, but attached to the ship's hull along its top edge by a sort of bellows, or diaphragm, in such a way that, when expanded, it would form a reservoir of air. The air holes in this false side which were necessary to provide the required slip-stream for improved efficiency would be positioned at different levels so that, when the false side was drawn in flush against the hull, it would to some degree act as a valve, sealing the air holes in the hull. The mathematics of this suggestion* were extremely involved, but Pedrick claimed that the power requirements to provide the compressed air would have been so small that there would not have been any need to have turned it off, even in port, when a lower output would have been sufficient to balance the air and the water pressures. There is no doubt that Pedrick was both a genius and an eccentric, and that the majority of people found themselves out of their depth when trying to follow all the details of his schemes. While this proposal was mathematically feasible, it was never put to the test, largely because it was overtaken quite swiftly by other developments with surface effect vessels (i.e. hovercraft, hydroskimmers and hydrofoils).

How much credence Cunard may have attached to this or to similar suggestions which were being discussed in engineering and technical journals of the day is purely academic, since the underlying problem was not the speed of the two vessels but the very age of their hulls. At all events, the Cunard Line took no further action in the matter until 1960, by which time the Compagnie Générale Transatlantique and the Holland America Line had forged ahead with their new *France* and *Rotterdam* respectively, while the United States Lines, in this period at least, had also achieved reasonable headway in their moves for a second *United States*. All of these vessels were to be subsidized annually by a considerable

*Patent Specification 997,737 – *Reduction of Hydrodynamic Drag of Water Buoyant Vessels,* published 7 July, 1965.

amount, while the rapidly ageing *Queens* received no similar financial assistance although, rather optimistically, Cunard had stated earlier that they would not need Government economic aid for their replacement liners anyway.

By 1960 this rapidly changing situation had become a cause for great concern to the Cunard Line. It would be difficult enough for them to keep abreast of these foreign competitors, let alone to maintain that degree of supremacy on the North Atlantic which they had enjoyed since 1945, and, to make matters worse, the cost of building the two new ships had risen sharply due to their own prolonged procrastination over the issue. When the Company finally approached the British Government with their problem, they had to talk in terms of £40 million worth of aid towards shipbuilding costs, since it was by then estimated that each ship would cost something in the region of £28 million – an increase of 40% on the original figure quoted. The *France,* in contrast, was expected to cost the C.G.T. the equivalent of £25 million.

The Government was sympathetic to the Cunard Line's request and set up the independent Chandos Committee to advise on the best way of finding a solution to the Company's difficulties. Their discussion centered on a proposal for two liners of approximately 75,000 gross tons with an overall length of about 1,000 feet* and a service speed of around 30 knots. (In 1959, Cunard's chairman, Colonel Denis Bates, had intimated that the replacement ships for the two *Queens* could be up to 80,000 gross tons and as long as 1,040 feet.†)

At the same time the P. & O. Line suggested a partial amalgamation with the Cunard Line in the event of no acceptable or adequate monetary help forthcoming from the Government. Their idea was that one ship should be built for a joint company for operation on both the North Atlantic and Australian routes at their respective peak periods. This scheme which, in essence, was similar to another proposed merger of interests in 1946, was likewise rejected. In the first place, Col. Bates had expressed his firm belief in maintaining an all-the-year-round North Atlantic service, but Cunard were also worried about the P. & O. Line's involvement with air transport because, around 1955, Saunders-Roe (now British Hovercraft Corporation) of East Cowes, on the Isle of Wight, had carried out a design investigation, closely linked with this

*304.8 metres.
†316.99 metres.

166. Col. Denis Bates.

shipping operator, for a massive, 670-ton five-deck flying boat designated the P192.

This enormous aircraft, measuring 318 feet* in length and having a 313 foot wing-span, was so big that a man could have stood upright in the wings to service the engines during flight. Its 24 Rolls-Royce 'Conway' by-pass turbo-jet aero engines would have given 18,500 pounds thrust each at take-off and a cruising speed of 389 knots at 35,000 feet would have been possible. There would have been accommodation for 1,100 passengers – a normal liner-load – or space for 67,600 cubic feet of cargo. Although the P192 was designed specifically for an overland route to Australasia, the P. & O. nevertheless opted to retain their traditional passenger liner service.

Meanwhile the Chandos Committee made its first recommendation to the Government to the effect that financial aid for Cunard's new ship programme should be in the form of a loan rather than a subsidy, which was the decision that had been expected. The subsequent decisions were

* 96.93 metres.

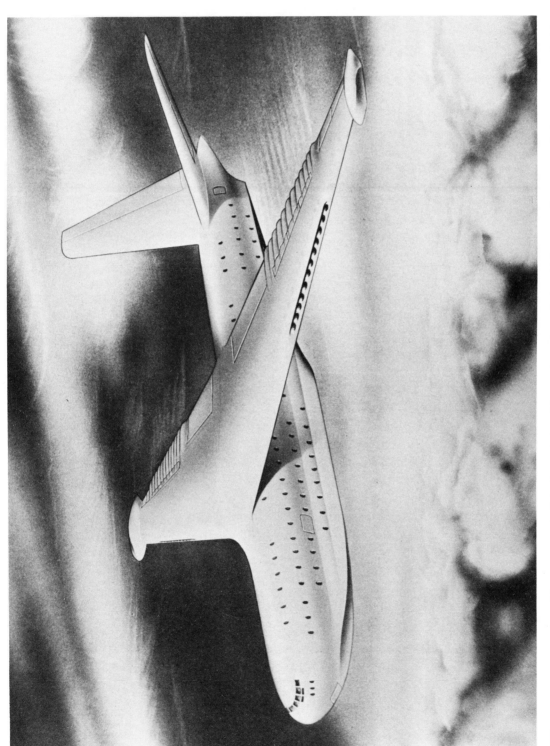

167. *An artist's impression of the monster P192 flying boat, designed for service to Australasia, which was another project which never came to fruition in the event.*

168. The revised appearance of the Q3 in 1961, from a builder's display model.

to be the crucial ones from the Company's point of view and were then eagerly awaited.

Rather ironically, however, an unexpected and ill-timed development at this point was Cunard's decision to exercise *its* rights to operate aeroplanes when it took over Eagle Airways in September 1960, renaming this firm Cunard Eagle Airways. This move prompted the Chandos Committee, in circumspection, to reappraise their recommendations for the amount of Government aid that should be made available to the liner replacement programme for what had now become the shipping side of Cunard's widened operations. Hence their advice was that a Treasury loan of £18 million at 4½% over 25 years should be made to enable the Cunard Line to construct only *one* 75,000 gross ton vessel with a capacity for 2,250 passengers. This seemed to be a fair and reasonable compromise proposal in the circumstances and, with the Cunard's acceptance and following the production of a design specification, tenders for the liner's construction were invited during March 1961. It was anticipated that an order for the new ship, which immediately became known as the 'Q3' or the 'Queen 3', would be placed by the autumn of that year at the latest.

The lowest tender for the Q3, of £28 million, was from a consortium of Vickers Armstrong Ltd. and Swan, Hunter & Wigham Richardson, and it was intended that the liner would be built on Tyneside.

As originally envisaged in drawings dating from 3 March 1961, the Q3 would have had a fairly typical hull form and superstructure with partially open promenade decks. The one unusual feature was the twin-funnel arrangement combining a conventional broad-based funnel aft with a funnel-cum-mast, or 'mack' as it is described in America, above the bridge. The shape of the conventional funnel had not been finalized, but the authors believe that, taking account of contemporary trends, the Cunard had in mind something resembling the funnel shape of the Italia Line's *Leonardo da Vinci*.

Only a few months later, a completely different outboard profile for the Q3 was unveiled in a builder's display model. All the superstructure was now enclosed for complete air-conditioning and the fore-deck had a turtleback configuration for heavy weather wave dispersal. The forward 'mack' was retained, though with a slightly modified shape, and the after funnel was now of similar form.

The Q3's dimensions were 990 feet* length overall, and 116 feet breadth. Her draught was designed as 35 feet, while her gross tonnage was expected to work out at nearer 80,000 than 75,000. She would have been a quadruple-screw vessel driven by geared turbines producing 200,000 shaft horse-power. Steam conditions were planned for 850 p.s.i. and 950 degrees Fahrenheit. It is interesting to note that, with a similar machinery arrangement to the earlier *Queen* liners, the Q3 would only have had eight boilers compared with twelve in the *Queen Elizabeth* and twenty-seven in the *Queen Mary*. Provision for eventual nuclear propulsion was made in the design, as it was in the case of the *France*.

With only one such replacement liner, the Cunard Line could no longer expect to be able to dominate the North Atlantic passenger trade but, nevertheless, with a ship of this calibre, they should have been able to compete with other lines on equal terms.

Everything seemed to be set fair for proceeding with the Q3 when the Cunard Line, quite unexpectedly, made another move which further endangered the realization of the newly proposed liner. On 19 October 1961 they decided to postpone the order for her indefinitely.

This postponement was partly due to poor trading results for the Cunard Group in 1961, but also because the Company's directors were not entirely happy with the design of the new ship. Colonel Denis Bates,

*301.75 metres.

who had died on 13 September 1959, had been succeeded as Chairman by Sir John Brocklebank in early 1960, and he was fundamentally in favour of a dual-purpose ship, whilst regarding the Q3 design as a recipe for disaster. He felt that a ship of her type – a high-speed luxury liner suited only for the North Atlantic service – was not the ideal vessel for economic operation in what was then becoming an unprecedentedly competitive business: a belief since confirmed by the problems experienced by the *France*. In addition, the Q3 investigation had established quite conclusively that advances in marine technology had reached the point where the required passenger complement and speed could be achieved in a smaller twin-screw ship.

Thus the revised Cunard's requirements called for such a liner of reduced size, suitable for off-peak cruising in both the Atlantic and the Pacific, and thus able to negotiate the Panama Canal, and with construction costs nearer to £22 million. Described as the Q4, this specification ultimately resulted in the *Queen Elizabeth 2*.

The immediate dilemma confronting the Cunard Line late in 1961, however, was that the granting of Government aid for a new ship was subject specifically to a vessel of the Q3 type being built. Although this condition was abrogated subsequently, it was Cunard's failure to place such an order in 1961 that finally necessitated the cancellation of the project.

Viewed with restrospection, the failure of the Q3 can hardly be considered to be the Cunard Line's equivalent to the White Star Line's ill-fated *Oceanic* of the 1920s, for their super-liner did finally appear in the form of the *Queen Elizabeth 2,* which was clearly a more appropriately designed ship with a creditable success record throughout the difficult years since her entry into service. After a year's silence following the cancellation of the Q3, Sir John Brocklebank spoke further on the Company's replacement policy when he addressed the shareholders in July 1963. He then promised a decision on the Q4 in 1964, and it was on 30 December of that year that an order was placed: the *Queen Elizabeth 2* entering service in April 1969.

It is well worth while comparing this latter ship with other contemporary liners in order to illustrate the advantages in her design which had been advocated by Sir John Brocklebank. Measuring 66,863 gross tons and

169. Sir John Brocklebank.

963 feet* in length overall, her draught, at 32½ feet, is less than that of the much smaller *Canberra*. The draught of the *France* is 34½ feet, that is: the same as that of the *Canberra,* which has suffered on the cruise circuit as a result of this disadvantage since the shallow waters of certain Caribbean Island ports deny her essential berthing facilities.

For purposes of making the transit of the Panama Canal locks, the *Queen Elizabeth 2* has a beam restricted to 101 feet – 15 feet less than the Q3 – and, in addition, she has a high capacity distilling plant enabling her to make longer sea voyages on routes other than the North Atlantic. The *Queen Mary's* fresh water tanks limited her time at sea to six days!†

*293.52 metres.

†That is: when on passenger service. Passengers are extravagant with water. Although the numbers aboard and the time at sea were sometimes greater in the war when she was trooping, the usage of water per capita was considerably less.

After reading thus far, through the chronology of the years, the reader may well have misgivings about the terms 'giant' and 'super-liner', since the words are used much in the context of the times of the individual ships, and the use of the word 'giant', taking account of the monsters which never left their drawing boards, might be held to be as loose in its application as the proverbial 'length of a piece of string'. Nevertheless, the *Queen Elizabeth 2* will take her place in the record books as the last 'giant' liner to be built, if we make the yardstick any such vessel of over 50,000 gross tons, but the Q3 was undoubtedly the last of the truly enormous passenger liner projects, and she was also the last giant liner to be conceived specifically for the North Atlantic route. Albeit stillborn, she ended a chapter of maritime history which has never failed to excite the imagination.

It is true to say that few of the liner projects contained in this book (which is exhaustive within the tonnage limits imposed) have been designed for any other routes than the North Atlantic. This was simply because the most luxurious and ambitious ocean transport was synonymous with the world's most illustrious sea route but, as aeroplane traffic between America and Europe increased and the sea traffic reciprocally declined, attention was focussed briefly on other sea passages on which some shipping companies still saw a future in the large ocean passenger carrier.

The Italian Company, Achille Lauro, established in 1923 as Flotta Lauro of Naples, which operated a service between Europe and Australia, was seeking two replacements for the old *Roma* and the *Sydney* in 1962. Details are, unfortunately, rather scarce, but two 30,000 gross ton vessels were ordered from Ansaldo's Leghorn (Livorno) shipyard and given the yard numbers 1604 and 1605. Each of these liners was to be a twin-screw turbine vessel with a service speed of 27 knots and able to carry approximately 1,700 passengers. Achille Lauro hoped to have these new liners in service by 1965 and 1966 respectively and in all probability, following the trend of current Italian design, they would have looked somewhat similar to the *Guglielmo Marconi* and the *Galileo Galilei*. However, in 1964, the order for the two ships was cancelled before much work was done on them.

The cost of building new ships was considerably greater than that of

170. The Q3 was finally immortalized in the QUEEN ELIZABETH 2, seen here leaving Southampton.

converting and streamlining two existing ones and, when the two Dutch liners *Willem Ruys* and *Oranje* came on to the market for disposal, due to poor results from their round-the-world service, Achille Lauro bought them instead of building their new vessels and re-built them into the *Achille Lauro* and the *Angelina Lauro* respectively. This was a more minor episode in the continuing saga of thwarted schemes, for which the over-riding reason was simply that it was a sign of the times. The times *were* hard where the passenger liner was concerned. The evolution of transport from one country to another, involving the crossing of seas or oceans, has occasionally been accelerated by some fundamental change as, for instance, when steam superseded sail. Yet the sailing ship was a long time a-dying and, for long, was able to compete with steam while running in parallel and on equal terms, until she was gradually forced into trades which were uneconomic for the supplanting, screw-driven vessel. The passenger liner expired much more quickly before the modern, highly developed aeroplane and, being so specialized in her form, she had virtually nowhere else to turn. Changes never take place over-night, but the death of the passenger liner in the true sense of the word — as a vessel which plies on a regular schedule — occurred in a remarkably short span of maritime chronology, and the Italian decision even to convert two existing vessels, rather than to build from scratch, was to some extent a bold gesture in the very shadow of death, although it is true that, at that time, they held the emigrant contract and, in this sense, enjoyed the patronage of the Australian Government, but this contract was transferred to the Chandris Lines in 1970. Apart from those relatively few ultra-prestigious vessels which enjoyed Government patronage and subsidy, the *raison d'etre* of shipowning was to earn profit, even if it so often takes a low priority in shipping histories. By the 1960s, with the ever-spiralling costs of construction and the increasing cost of money, quite apart from higher wage bills and so much else, and with flying machines, for all their drawbacks, having caught the public imagination, it is small wonder that Nos. 604 and 605 never advanced to their very keel plates in their Livorno yard.

XXVII THE NIPPON YUSEN KAISHA PROJECTED LINERS

Sometimes it is difficult to pin-point precisely when a scheme started, but it can be said that a very ambitious project in Japan originated in November 1953, when the urgent need for two large Pacific passenger liners was stressed in a plan entitled *The Establishment and Promotion of the Tourist Industry Council and its Execution,* which was presented to the Prime Minister by the Tourist Industry Council for the Cabinet.

More or less concurrently, the Nippon Yusen Kaisha were considering a construction programme within the context of reviving its passenger shipping trade and, although they had not yet invited any tenders for the liners they envisaged, they were going to great lengths in planning their interiors and developing their external appearance in keeping with the ever-changing fashions, in readiness for the moment when it would be possible to start building them. However, since the implications of financing large new liners would have been extremely difficult for a single private enterprise in the severely depressed Japan of the 1950s, particularly after the discontinuance of the war indemnity for high-cost reconstruction projects, they lent their weight to the arguments of the Tourist Industry Council in urging that the realization of the ships should be regarded as a national undertaking.

Even more pressure for action on these Pacific ocean-going liners came in January 1956, when the Liberal Democratic Party's Special Committee for the Tourist Industry held a conference on *Basic Elements*

Concerning the Promotion and Planning of the Tourist Industry. The result of this was that, in August of that year, the Japanese Cabinet issued a statement in which it supported the concept of the building of the passenger liners but, as it turned out, these were but empty words and no action eventuated from them.

The Nippon Yusen Kaisha had figured in the centre of this drive for new Japanese passenger tonnage from the very beginning and, sensing that success was, perhaps, now not too far away, they organized internal company changes in preparation for ordering the ships. In February 1959 they set up the Passenger Ship Arrangements Chamber and in that August formed the Passenger Ship Planning Section. These departments immediately set to work on the final design of the proposed liners and, in due course, they released a specification for them as well as an artist's impression which depicted a handsome single-funnelled vessel. With a gross tonnage of 33,400, the other principal statistics were a length of 689 feet,* a beam of 92 feet and a draught of 30 feet. Geared turbines driving twin screws would have given them a service speed of 24½ knots. The Passenger capacity was for 1,200 persons, divided between 200 first-class and 1,000 Tourist.

While 1959 was a very busy year within the Nippon Yusen Kaisha, it was also a significant one in the campaign to persuade the Japanese Government to approve the construction of the ships and to make adequate financial appropriations for them. The fact was that the Olympic Games were scheduled to be held in Tokyo in October 1964, and it was obviously important to place the liners in commission in time for this event and, to this end, the completion target date for the first vessel was set at July 1963, and a year later for the second. The implication of the Olympics brings to mind the previous project involving the *Kashiwara Maru* and *Izumo Maru,* which were also planned with the same event in mind.

In the meantime, pressure for action was mounting from all quarters, with deputations from the Japan Shipowners Association in May 1959, the Yokohama Municipal Assembly in June and even from branches of the Japanese Chamber of Commerce in both Honolulu and Los Angeles. Finally, influenced by such an overwhelming weight of both public and professional opinion, a close examination of the ships' design and

*210.01 metres.

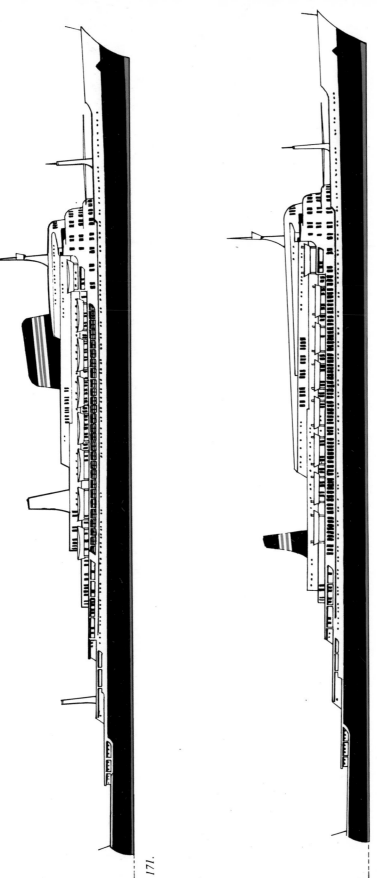

171.

172. *If there had been as much activity in building the proposed Nippon Yusen Kaisha vessels as there was in the company's drawing office, much might have resulted from it! Here are two more of the designs, which were continually being amended to 'keep up with the times'. These should be compared with Pl. 165.*

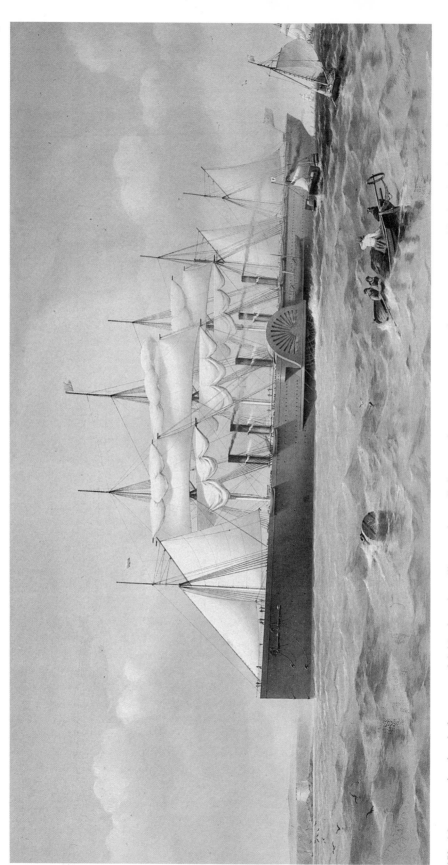

173. *Many completed and often successful ships have been illustrated, usually because they were germane to the contemporary shipping situations and, to some extent, influenced those projects which were doomed in the event. Of these some, like the QUEEN MARY and, to a less extent, the NORMANDIE, might well have qualified for inclusion as being 'Damned by Destiny', but escaped that fate. As for the GREAT EASTERN, which we illustrate once more, she did not reach our lower limit of 20,000 tons, though she was gigantic in her day, but, set in the perspective of her era, her conception was the most prodigious of all the dreams — and it was a dream that was realized!*

174. A spirited artist's impression of one of the twin N.Y.K. liners as originally conceived.

operating potential was carried out by the Ministry of Transportation. As a result, they were able to recommend that the budget for the fiscal year 1959/60 should include provision for a two-ship programme of the type proposed by the Nippon Yusen Kaisha. The budgetary appropriation requested amounted to 2,375 million yen,* which covered direct expenditure, treasury loans and indirect investments.

Nevertheless, the realization of the new Nippon Yusen Kaisha liners was not achieved, in spite of this Government involvement and endorsement. No money for the ships was included in the budget for 1959/60, and it was not until 1962/3 that an appropriation of any sort was made for passenger liner projects of any kind, and then it amounted to a mere 15 million yen† for investigating the expense of passenger ship reconstruction.

The officials of the Nippon Yusen Kaisha felt that the patriotic resolve for national reconstruction had been abandoned in this instance but, as they required such ships for their own domestic purposes in order to restore their long-interrupted passenger services, they considered other ways and means of raising the funds required. These included Public Holding Corporation and Joint-Stock Corporation financing systems, but none achieved the desired results. The Japanese Government, for its

*£2,339,901. This was a time when Japanese shipbuilding was so cheap in relation to other countries that it was attracting some 90% of the world's new ship construction.

†£14,749.

175. During all the debate and procrastination, the new N.Y.K. liners . . .

part, explained that there was a need for an overall strengthening of maritime traffic in all its forms, and that money could not be concentrated on a single cost-intensive project. This was the official policy which, on the face of it, was based on a certain common-sense and, despite every effort, it remained unshaken and no Government budget to help to finance the big passenger liners ever came into existence. However, much as one may agree with the rationale of the Cabinet's point of view, it is difficult to ignore the inescapable conclusion that a great deal of fruitless effort would have been avoided had it not taken so long to reach its decision, apart from the fact that, aside from economic considerations, the N.Y.K. were quite correct in their opinion that the policy of reconstruction on grounds of a patriotic national revival had been allowed to drop.

The fact of the matter was that, throughout this long, indecisive period, the Nippon Yusen Kaisha had been pursuing various improvements in the design of their ships, taking account of the changes in shape which were coming into being all over the World. Subsequent renditions showed a gradual transition of the liners' profiles from the original form through to a stage where there were twin exhaust flues aft and a conventionally-shaped dummy funnel forward of them, rather like the new Moore McCormack sisters *Argentina* and *Brasil*. Later still, the dummy funnel was eliminated completely and the bridge deck and associated structure extended aft. The twin exhaust flues themselves were now painted with the Company's colours. At the same time, paintings

176. . . . underwent several metamorphoses on the drawing boards.

depicting the planned public rooms and exterior facilities were also released, and these highlighted the very superior standard of appointments that were intended for the vessels.

Although the Nippon Yusen Kaisha still remained hopeful that the construction of the liners might take place, the issue was more or less resolved against them in the end with the publication of a Japanese Government policy statement in 1963. Entitled *Two Laws of Maritime Traffic Reconstruction,* this document posed the question whether or not passenger service reorganization was attainable – or even desirable. It left the construction of new passenger ships as a problem to be resolved in the future by which time, in the event by the late 1960s, it no longer required deliberation due to the replacement of passenger travel by aircraft.

Oddly, another Japanese company, the Toyo Yusen Kaisha, also featured on the projected liner scene at about this time. This firm's plans involved the construction of a 50,000 gross ton, triple-screw passenger ship with a speed of 35 knots for service between Japan, Australia and the United States and, depending on the availability of a Government subsidy, it hoped to have the vessel in operation by 1967. As might be expected, the Japanese Government did not offer any financial inducements and, in consequence, the huge liner did not materalize. Had she been built, she would have been by far the largest liner to have been owned by a Japanese shipping Company.

The Toyo Yusen Kaisha subsequently expressed considerable interest in the two Cunard cruise vessels, the *Carmania* and *Franconia,* when they were on the market in 1972 but, in the interim, they were finally sold to Russia and renamed *Leonid Sobonov* and *Fedor Shalyapin* respectively, and the Japanese dreams of large post-war liners were finally dashed, since the ensuing years were not conducive to even dreaming on this subject.

The early 1960s was a relatively fruitful period for new passenger liner schemes, considering the ever-increasing encroachment of air transportation. New ships were built for the Atlantic by the Canadian Pacific Lines, Italia Line and the Zim Israel Line, while Lloyd Triestino completed the *Galileo Galilei* and *Guglielmo Marconi* for the Australian route and Union Castle introduced the *Tranvsvaal Castle* on the Cape run. Other new liners included Home Line's *Oceanic,* Costa Line's *Eugenio C,* a new *Kungsholm* for Sweden and the *Sagafjord* for Norway. Yet this was but a temporary respite, for the general decline in passenger shipping services continued unabated, and soon many of these ships were to be dependent solely on cruising to earn an income and, indeed, it is interesting to speculate whether their several owners would have ordered them at all had the situation prevailing when they were completed been the same as that when they were laid down. Certainly the conditions at this time caused various other germinating schemes to be nipped in the bud. Many of these amounted to no more than announcements of intent, but one or two of them are worthy of more detailed comment.

One particularly interesting project, of which very little is known, also originated in the Orient, in the Chinese People's Republic. As a result of research into nuclear ship projects in the mid-1960s, naval architects at Vickers Ltd at Barrow-in-Furness discovered that Communist China was planning to build a 20,000 gross ton nuclear passenger liner for service between Tsientsin and Shanghai. This ship was apparently intended primarily for the transportation of migrant workers and would, therefore, have had only dormitory accommodation. Although there is no official or authenticated documentation available, and, incidentally, even this information cannot be substantiated by Lloyds, the experts at Vickers (now part of the British Shipbuilders) remain convinced that such a vessel may possibly already exist or that she may yet be constructed. As to her existence, it would surely be incredible that she had escaped notice if actually operational but, if they are correct, even to her proposed construction, such a ship would be only the second passenger-carrying nuclear vessel after the United States' *Savannah*.

Yet another project which reappeared in the 1960s was Russia's elusive giant. First mentioned in 1958 with a gross tonnage of 80,000 and destined for the New York express service, her construction was supposed to have been started in 1961. However, by 1963 the ship had been scaled down to 50,000 gross tons, although most maritime journalists viewed even these reports with much scepticism. In 1965, two years later, a more detailed and plausible report stated that a geared-turbine vessel of around 25,000 gross tons was under construction at the Admiraltieski Shipyard at Leningrad. The secrecy with which Russian officialdom enshrouds itself makes it impossible to even speculate on the rise or fall of this scheme, but it is certain that nothing emerged from it – at all events in the form of a passenger ship, for the only new liners to be added to the Sovtorgflot fleet in recent years have been the five units of the *Aleksandr Pushkin* class, all built in East Germany. The whole Russian system is so very different from the conditions which exist in the West, and it might be thought that, in some respects, such a project as even the original 80,000-tonner, once agreed, might have more hope of survival since, for one thing, there is not the same likelihood of a situation where a private enterprise shipowner becomes embattled with its government in matters of subsidy since the Government is, in effect, the shipowner, whilst the national budget is not dictated by entirely the same considerations. Perhaps there never was the necessary unanimity of opinion amongst those concerned, but it is not a matter on which the authors can begin to offer any balanced opinion, although the fact that the American stevedores union was threatening to refuse to handle Russian ships at that time could have been a relevant factor.

As the 1960s drew to their close, very few passenger liners remained employed full-time on scheduled services. The prevailing economic and political climates, worsened by the oil crisis of 1973, hastened the departure of many still youthful ships to the breakers' yards. Others turned to full-time cruising, and this, in itself, generated a boom in the construction of vessels purpose-built for this expanding and lucrative market, and even Metro-Goldwyn-Mayer, the Hollywood film conglomerate, was reported to be planning a series of 20,000-ton cruise ships prior to its partial liquidation in October 1973. It is therefore apposite that our final chapter should conclude in this theatre of passenger ship operation.

177. *The AUSTRALIS, seen here, was originally the AMERICA of 1940, being bought by Chandris Lines in 1964 and used on the Australian run and for cruising. Her funnels had been heightened since originally built, and now she has a cowl to obviate the ever-present smut menace on passenger liners. She suffered further sales but was, at this time, the last of the pre-war vintage of Atlantic liners still in commission.*

XXVIII KLOSTER REDERI'S
SEMI-CATAMARAN CRUISE VESSEL

The cruising boom of the 1970s, precipitated by the need to keep passenger shipping employed profitably, distinguished itself from other similar periods of intense activity in this direction in a number of respects. Whenever passenger figures became low or depressed, or when certain ships were past their prime, shipowners were prone to resort to cruising as a temporary expedient, which was the primary reason on all such occasions in the past. By this time, however, the situation was rather different, since although the reason was the same, the liners which had become diverted from their normal schedules were, in fact, being diverted into cruising roles permanently and, whereas the need had been apparent for distinctive dual-role ships in the 1950s and 1960s, this form of shipping business, by now highly competitive and catering for a more discerning and sophisticated clientele, had created a demand for specially designed cruise vessels.

At the same time, with the involvement of Public Relations experts, cruise itineraries were no longer the rather haphazard schedules which had characterized them in the past, when the voyager was tempted by a few exotic place names, interspersed with monotonous days at sea. Instead, carefully planned cruise circuits had been evolved, in order to provide the cruise passenger with the maximum amount of sight-seeing and the least amount of transition time between the various stopping-off points. The three most popular areas which emerged were the Mediterranean, the Baltic and the Caribbean. The latter undoubtedly headed the list, primarily catering for the American market, and it had been mainly exploited, quite uncharacteristically, by the Norwegians.

Amongst the first major companies to recognize the potential of cruising the Caribbean waters out of Miami, Florida, was Klosters Rederi A/S of Oslo, which operated under the name Norwegian Caribbean Lines, and it was for this company that a new and most unusual cruising vessel project was first announced in the late 1960s.

The Norwegian Caribbean Lines commenced operations from Miami in 1966 with the small passenger cruise vessel-cum-car ferry *Sunward*. This vessel was first complemented by, and later replaced with, three larger passenger ships, namely: the *Starward,* which entered service in December 1968, the *Skyward* which followed her exactly one year later, and the *Southward,* whose first cruise was early in 1972. The two latter ships, each measuring 16,500 tons, were virtually twice the size of the *Sunward,* thus indicating the remarkably rapid growth of the Kloster Company's cruise business.

By this time, however, other Norwegian companies had appreciated the significance of Miami as an operational centre and were also beginning to establish themselves there. The first of these to arrive was the Royal Caribbean Cruise Line in November 1970, followed closely by Norwegian Cruiseships and the Royal Viking Line in 1972. These contenders for the business were quite apart from such foreign competitors as the Cunard, Home and the Holland America Lines. As a result of this situation, Klosters Rederi decided to embark on a programme of new construction which would augment their already popular fleet of ships. In the first instance, they ordered a sister-ship to the *Southward* from the same builders, Cantieri Navali del Tirrenio ed Riuniti in Italy. Although planned to bear the name of the company's inaugural ship, the *Sunward,* this vessel, like the *Southward,* was contracted on a fixed price basis, but the builders ran into financial difficulties and asked Klosters to pay an additional £10 million. This they refused to do, with the result that the contract was terminated and the new *Sunward* was taken over by the P. & O. Lines and launched and completed to their specification as the *Spirit of London.*

Klosters' other new building scheme, for a completely unique cruise vessel, now took precedence over everything else. First mentioned in

178. Knut Utstein Kloster.

1969, it was being revived as part of this expansion programme. Designed specifically for the Caribbean cruise circuit, she was probably the most revolutionary ship conceived for many years and would have introduced more new features into a single vessel than had ever been attempted previously.

Described in detail for the first time in May 1972 when Klosters announced their firm intention to build her, the proposed ship would have had a semi-catamaran hull: that is, a conventional bow and fore section but a double-hulled stern.* The reduction in her length/beam ratio resulting from this would have reduced her rolling characteristics radically, especially in beam seas. Apart from the advantages of this additional stabilization, and even of classification, Klosters also intended to exploit the proposed ship's unusually broad configuration to the maximum in the planned passenger facilities. As to the classification benefits inherent in such a design, Mr. Cedric Barclay, a former technical employee of Klosters, offered some explanation in saying: *'The cost of a catamaran would be prohibitive. In a passenger vessel, the only saving*

*Prior to the collapse of the Court Line in late 1974, the Appledore Shipyard in North Devon were tentatively scheduled to construct a full catamaran-hull ship for it. This proposed vessel does not fall within the scope of this book since she would only have been of approximately 10,000 gross tons.

likely to arise would be in the fire-fighting classification of one of the hulls, if not intended for passenger use.'*

Amongst the facilities proposed were a partial glass bottom through which the marine and coral life below the surface might be viewed; a vast sun deck terraced around a large swimming pool and an extensive inside sports area with numerous tennis courts. The most spectacular of the interior attractions was a huge, all-purpose room on the uppermost deck covered by a clear bubble-dome which would permit, late at night, the observation of the stars in order to gain an appreciation of their role in celestial navigation – a kind of floating 'Planetarium' in fact,† which could also be used for dancing, cabarets and other activities.

An artist's impression of the proposed cruise-ship which was released to the press exhibited all the space-age characteristics we have described, while it also revealed a certain resemblance to the liner *Oriana* in the bow and bridge areas. Painted on the bow was the name *Elysian,* conjuring up the Elysian Fields of Greek mythology, whither favoured heroes were borne without passing through death to dwell in a state of sustained happiness and bliss. This may have been only a working name for the project, as Klosters have maintained a consistent naming policy in all their undertakings, even to bestowing the title *Landward* on the construction programme for their new office block in Miami. If, however, the name *Elysian* had been given to the planned semi-catamaran liner, it would have represented a dramatic break from the Norwegian Caribbean Lines' tradition of having names ending in *'-ward'.*

Measuring 20,000 to 22,000 gross tons, the futuristic semi-catamaran's passenger capacity would have been nearly 1,000, with the construction costs being estimated at £20 million in 1972. In commenting on the ship, Mr. Knut Utstein Kloster, the Chairman of the parent company, Klosters Rederi, said: *The broad beam would allow for the greatest flexibility of facilities and freedom of passenger movement on any cruise vessel afloat.'*

The Norwegian Caribbean Lines were undoubtedly very enthusiastic about their latest enterprise, but spiralling costs, compounded by the 1973 oil crisis, forced them to defer the project temporarily. Most observers held the view that it had been cancelled completely at that time.

In fact, this was not the case. Almost two years later, in July 1974, press

*i.e. The rules are less stringent about hull sub-division, the provision of sprinklers or smoke detectors, the situation of hoses and extinguishers, and the installation of bilge injection pumps in these circumstances. But, of course, these circumstances did not apply, since the evidence is that both *hulls were to be used for passengers.*

† As to the navigational use of stars (used mainly in the semi-twilight when the horizon is visible and the stars hard to discern to the naked eye), one wonders whether the passengers were to be treated to preliminary courses in spherical trigonometry and navigation!

179.   Even though her twin hulls are not immediately apparent in this artist's rendering of the ELYSIAN, it shows her to have been the most radical departure from conventional liner design for over a century.

announcements indicated that the scheme had not been abandoned. The Norwegian Caribbean Lines' Miami-based Sales Vice-President, Mr. Bruce Nierenberg, declared that a suitable shipyard was being sought and that the final decision on whether to proceed with the vessel would be made that September. He added: *'If the go-ahead is given, the ship could be in service by late 1977.'* However, the optimism of the summer made a marked contrast with the gloom in the Company's Miami offices that autumn when Knut Kloster announced his decision to shelve his ambitious plan to build the world's first semi-catamaran liner yet again.

The reasons were entirely financial and a common enough problem – inflation and sky-high operating costs. As Knut Kloster put it: *'Even with full ships, today we are not making much money.'* Despite this statement, there were apparently still firm intentions to keep the project alive, and Knut Kloster confirmed this when he said: *'The plans have not been dropped, but it is difficult to see how it could be justified from a prudent business point of view to build a ship which, due to tremendous inflation and price increases in the past two or three years, will probably cost four or five times as much as* (each of) *our present ships.'*

Since that time the economic climate has not improved sufficiently to favour the resumption of the project, with construction costs rising higher than ever. Another ominous factor was the return of all the data relating to the *Elysian* to the Company's office at Oslo in 1977.

Klosters Rederi were nevertheless quick to scotch any rumours that the semi-catamaran cruise vessel scheme was finished. That her construction might yet proceed became evident from statements made by Knut Kloster in a communication on the subject of the ship in 1978, when he remarked, *inter alia, '. . . the project is still very much at the sort of "fluid" planning stage with a highly uncertain prospect for realization.'* More optimistically, he further stated: *'All the particulars* (of the ship) *are preliminary, and subject to a lot of future changes.'* Al Wolfe, the Norwegian Caribbean Lines' Director of Public Affairs, added his own sanguine observations: *'I would be very reluctant to say that it* (the ship) *has been permanently shelved. We continue to hope that, at some future date, conditions will permit us to pursue it.'* One pertinent new factor, unforeseen at that time but certain to have had a significant bearing on the prospects for the *Elysian,* was the purchase by the Norwegian Caribbean Lines of the former

180. The EL YSIAN had a certain resemblance in her bow and bridge areas to the ORIANA, the last big passenger liner to be built for a regular trade, seen here in her original Orient Line livery as she left her builder's yard at Barrow-in Furness.

French luxury liner *France* for Caribbean cruise duties in June 1979.

Re-named *Norway,* the former C.G.T. North Atlantic vessel, one of the last great ships built in a spirit of 'jingo-ism' to show the flag, was extensively re-furbished for her new role at the Hapag-Lloyd AG shipyard in West Germany. As part of this programme, previously enclosed promenade decks were opened up and numerous additional recreational and dining facilities were installed.

In the light of this, it was difficult to endorse the optimism of the Norwegian Caribbean Lines' officials regarding their project for a semi-catamaran cruise vessel. An investment of the size involved in the purchase of the former *France* would take some considerable time to be recouped, apart from the fact that the Company expressed a desire to buy another similar-sized vessel should the *Norway* prove to be very successful.

181. While there was a boom in cruising, liners on regular runs were fighting a losing battle. The AUSTRALIS, ex-AMERICA, prepares to leave Southampton on her last regular run for Chandris Lines in 1977.

Two years later, the *Norway* was established in her new cruise service although, up to that point, she had only been a qualified success. Nevertheless, it now seems to be extremely unlikely that the *Elysian* will ever be constructed, at all events in the form originally suggested. This is not to suggest that either the Norwegian Caribbean Lines or one of the other leading cruise operators will not introduce an equally revolutionary ship in the future: a ship which will change the trends of cruise vessel design irreversibly, while remaining cheap enough to construct to be considered a viable concept in the first place. The future prospects for luxury cruising seem to be excellent – a view supported by the number of vessels on order or under construction for this specific purpose, there being no less than seven of more than 25,000 gross tons in the Spring of 1981, and inevitably this boom will generate a demand for more specialized ships like the *Elysian*. This contention is borne out by the revelation in 1979 that the

Royal Caribbean Cruise Lines of Oslo, another of the Miami-based operators, were themselves developing specifications for the 'ideal cruise ship of the 1980s', in conjunction with Wartsila of Helsinki. Only time will show the outcome of this endeavour.

It is, perhaps, significant that our review of those vessels, for which so much was promised and yet which never came to fulfill those promises, concludes in the present day with an ultra-modern cruise ship, well illustrating how such unrealized schemes for new ships have been a persistent feature throughout the entire era of screw-driven ocean travel. Such is the very nature of progress for, while many new ideas will succeed, there will always be the inevitable victims of inauspicious circumstances. The liners themselves may have been eliminated in that great lottery of life, which affects them as much as men, but they were all part of the stuff upon which progress and future innovations are based, and they contributed to this end almost as much as those more fortunate vessels which were launched into their chosen element to race the passenger highways of the oceans. They were all a part of the phenomenal development of the great passenger liner in the hundred-odd years of her existence, and thus as entitled to their place in history as the famed Blue Riband holders. Had they been commissioned, there is no reason to suppose that they would have been found wanting, for all the conclusions must lead to a quite opposite opinion. In no sense were they failures, as embryo ships, but merely victims of man-made circumstances: burgeoning buds of the oceans which were blasted by the chill winds of Chance before they could burst into blossom.

182. *The ships which formed the projects in this book took many forms. One generation of readers might consider the older ones to be antiquated: another might think others to be too futuristic to be taken seriously, but almost all had in common that they were, generally, in advance of the designs of contemporary ships which were actually built, to trade successfully, in many of their features. Some of these features became incorporated in later vessels, while others never came to pass, but these vessels were usually extensions of the fashions of their times. Only the GREAT EASTERN, of the liners illustrated in this work, crossed yards and, gradually, masts and funnels decreased in number and ships became, in some sense, squatter. Perhaps they lost character thereby, but they gained it in other ways. What they lost in sheer splendour, especially in the first-class accommodation, they gained in function and safety. The QUEEN MARY (Pl.120) was exceptional in so large a ship in having such beautiful proportions and so fine a seat in the water, but the variations in form in the passenger liner since – say -- the turn of the century have been manifold and perhaps because, in some sense, she was representative of the transition from the 4-masters and 4- funnellers to those with single funnels and single – or even no – masts, we shall accord this page to the German IMPERATOR, later BERENGARIA, for the German ships of her era bore their own charisma.*

EPILOGUE

We have come a long way since the *Great Eastern* of 1859 and the *Spirit of the Age* proposal, but it is a measure of the progress throughout the century and a quarter which has elapsed that there exists today a car ferry of comparable proportions to Brunel's mammoth, namely Finnline's 23,000 gross ton, 692-foot *Finnjet*. Sad to relate, it may be only in such vessels and small cruise ships that the vestiges of the world's once great passenger liner fleet will be perpetuated, for the conventional passenger liners have virtually disappeared from the ocean highways.

As we have illustrated, the reasons for the failures of these ill-fated liner schemes have been manifold, but in recent years even the completed liners have no longer been able to withstand the combined pressures of the jet-engined aeroplane and of escalating oil prices. Indeed, the erosion of the scheduled-service passenger liner's livelihood has reached the point where traditional ocean travel has virtually become a thing of the past. The echoes of the rumbling wheels of the tumbrils became louder and louder while the growing parade of proscribed ships passed towards the breakers as the 1970s progressed, and even relatively young liners were pensioned off in retirement.

Displaced by another form of transportation, ocean passenger liners are on their way to join the other nostalgia-evoking memorabilia of yesteryear. For those who achieved their purpose, there are memories, many and varied, but for the schemes that were Damned by Destiny there is only the speculation on 'what might have been'.

Yet, in conclusion, it must be remembered that a great part of their reputation rested on their very size and speed: two attributes which were a constant in each decade even if both increased with the passage of the years until the ships reached the very zenith of their splendour, which was always so much greater than in other, less exotic forms of merchant vessels. Now the palm has passed to more humble types. Often they are as fast, and their sizes are sometimes almost astronomically greater. It is not a question of ships being in decline, but of a change of emphasis in the priorities of their functions.

Destiny is like tossing a coin. On the obverse is the Smile of Fortune, on the reverse the Cold Hand of Fate. In the case of the projects for great liners, the coin usually landed with the Smile of Fortune uppermost; sometimes it landed on its edge and spun for an unconscionable time before falling one way up or the other, as in the case of the *Queen Mary,* whose partially constructed hull lay so long awaiting a verdict on her future, whilst, sometimes, the coin dropped with the reverse side sealing her doom.

Many of those which 'won the toss' became legends to be handed down in the annals of maritime history for posterity. Those which lost the toss are recorded in this book, and were none the worse than the others for their lack of fulfillment, since it was only by chance that some became completed, and the *Queen Mary* – one of the most illustrious of ships – came within an ace of being included within our roster. Of those which fell by the wayside, it cannot be said that they failed as a result of the ambitions which they represented (although there are always critics of any new and revolutionary design!), but often because forces beyond the spheres of maritime interest conspired against them – changes in Governments: International crises; War: general Economic conditions; National Policy, or any one of many factors which were not directly related to the proposed ship herself. It is easy to imagine that, had many of the liner proposals been made at different times, some of the successful vessels would have failed to become built and would have earned a place in these pages, whilst others of those which we have included would, instead, have become household names as they raced the passenger lanes of the oceans.

Speculation is an idle pastime which can be pleasant, even if it may touch on an aspect which we have mentioned only very cursorily, namely: the dangers inherent in the old adage about putting too many eggs into

183. *The partially constructed hull of the Cunarder No. 534 – later the* QUEEN MARY *– on the stocks at John Brown's shipyard on Clydebank, with all work stopped, while her fate lay in the balance. This aerial view does not demonstrate how she towered over her surroundings.*

one basket, which is why Hyman Cantor had to revise his passenger numbers in order to conform with the U.S. Coast Guard's regulations, based on this very principle. Technical advance in recent generations has been almost past belief: ships now have navigational aids linked to satellites in space; they can see through fog, there are closed circuit television screens on the bridge and there is so much else of the push-button age but . . . they are still manned and operated by human beings. Reference to the Casualty Reports will demonstrate that technical advance is no panacea for safety and, as already mentioned on page 46, mankind has not kept pace with the advance in its machines. Had some of those vast ships which we have described gone into service, it is safe to speculate that most would have been attended by success. It is easy to cite the triumphs of the past, but it is folly to forget the disasters and, should some of the super-liners have become involved in tragedy, the mind can only boggle at its possible magnitude.

Thus there is a more sombre side to speculation. Nevertheless, these ships represented, within their eras, the grandest scale of maritime thought of their times and they sharpened the edges of naval architecture, to make their imprints, often enough, on successful vessels which succeeded them whilst, at the same time, influencing the very nature of ship management.

John Wolcot's famous line *'Better be damned than mentioned not at all!'* may have been well enough within its context – addressed to the Royal Academicians – but it would be a gross injustice if those ships which so successfully contended for the Blue Riband of the North Atlantic, together with their peers, were to remain as legends, whilst those others, no whit worse in their conceptions and which have formed our subjects, were to vanish into the misty realm of half-forgotten myth. Not only would some of them have eclipsed the greatest liners ever built within human history, but some would have ranked amongst the man-made wonders of the world. Their only fault lay in that they lost the game of Chance, that the dice were loaded against them or that they 'lost the toss' – term it how one will! Non-existent ships can never be legends in the heroic sense but, if we have rescued the grandeur of these schemes from the nebulous penumbra of mythology, we shall have achieved our purpose.

'It is not the critic who counts, not the man who points out how the strong man stumbles or where the doer of deeds could have done them better. The credit belongs to the man who is actually in the arena; whose face is marred by dust and sweat and blood; who strives valiantly; who errs and comes up short again and again; who knows the great enthusiasms, the great devotions, and spends himself in a worthy cause; who at the best knows in the end the triumphs of high achievements; and who at the worst, if he fails, at least fails while daring greatly; so that his place shall never be with those cold and timid souls who know neither defeat nor victory.

THEODORE ROOSEVELT

COMPLETE LIST OF LAUNCHED AND COMPLETED PASSENGER LINERS WHICH NEVER ENTERED SERVICE

Vessels marked with an asterisk (*) are all below 20,000 gross tons, and do not therefore figure in the text.
Those with no asterisk have been considered in depth in the text, and are included here to complete the roster.

Name	Date Launched	Date Finished	G.R.T.	L.O.A.	Notes
PRINCIPESA JOLANDA* (Lloyd Italiano)	21/9/07	—	9,200	486	Capsized when being launched. Scrapped incomplete. Intended for Genoa–Buenos Aires service.
BRITANNIC (White Star Line)	26/2/14	12/1915	48,158	903	Completed as hospital ship.
STATENDAM (Holland America Line)	9/7/14	4/1917	32,234	776	Completed as troopship *Justicia*.
AUSONIA* (Soc. Italiano di Servizi Marrittimi)	15/4/15	—	11,300	518	Planned for first German aircraft carrier in World War I. Sold for scrapping incomplete in 1922 when builders (Blohm and Voss) and owners could not agree price due to high German inflation. Negotiations between owners and builders 1919/20. Intended for Genoa–Alexandria–Venice service.
AOTEOROA* (Union Steamship Co. of New Zealand)	30/6/15	1916	14,744	550	Completed as auxiliary cruiser *H.M.S. Avenger*. Torpedoed and sunk 14/6/1917 by U69.
AURANIA* (Cunard Line)	16/7/16	3/1917	13,936	540	Completed as troopship. Torpedoed and sunk 4/2/1918 by UB67. Intended for London/Liverpool–Boston/Montreal service.
CONTE ROSSO* (Lloyd Sabaudo)	2/12/17	9/1918	15,000	565	Completed as aircraft carrier *H.M.S. Argus*. Scrapped by T. W. Ward, Inverkeithing 1946/47. Intended for Genoa–Buenos Aires service.
STOCKHOLM (Swedish America Line)	29/5/38	—	28,000	675	Burnt out 19-20/12/1938.
STOCKHOLM (Swedish America Line)	10/3/40	10/1941	29,307	675	Ran trials but delivery blockaded. Sold to Italian Government 11/1941 and converted to troopship *Sabaudia*.

Name	Date Launched	Date Finished	G.R.T.	L.O.A.	Notes
VATERLAND (Hamburg America Line)	24/8/40	—	41,000	824	Destroyed by fire in air raid while incomplete 25/7/1943.
KASUGA MARU* (Nippon Yusen Kaisha)	19/9/40	9/1941	17,127	590	Completed as aircraft carrier *Taiyo*. Torpedoed and sunk 18/8/1944 by U.S.S. *Rasher* (sister ships *Nitta Maru* and *Yawata Maru* converted to aircraft carriers *Chuyo* and *Unyo* respectively, but both saw limited commercial service). Intended for Yokohama–Hamburg service.
ZUIDERDAM* (Holland America Line)	1941	—	12,150	518	Sunk incomplete in air raid 28/8/1941. Scuttled 22/9/1944. After second salvage considered as not worth repairing. Scrapped 1948. Intended for Rotterdam–New York service.
MIILE MARU* (Nippon Yusen Kaisha)	12/4/41	9/1941	11,739	535	Completed as troop transport. Torpedoed and sunk 21/4/1944 by U.S.S. *Trigger*. Intended for the Kobe–Vancouver–Seattle service.
IZUMO MARU (Nippon Yusen Kaisha)	24/6/41	7/1942	27,500	722	Completed as aircraft carrier *Hiyo*.
KASHIWARA MARU (Nippon Yusen Kaisha)	26/6/41	5/1942	27,700	722	Completed as aircraft carrier *Junyo*.
GOKOKU MARU* (Osaka Shosen Kaisha)	1941	9/1942	10,348	537	Completed as auxiliary cruiser. Later converted to troop transport. Torpedoed and sunk 10/10/1944 by U.S.S. *Barb*. Intended for Japan–Europe service.
AKI MARU* (Nippon Yusen Kaisha)	15/5/42	10/1942	11,409	535	Ex-*Mishima Maru*. Completed as troop transport. Torpedoed and sunk 26/7/1944 by U.S.S. *Crevalle*. Intended for the Japan–Australia service.
AWA MARU* (Nippon Yusen Kaisha)	24/8/42	3/1943	11,249	535	Completed as troop transport. Torpedoed and sunk, despite diplomatic immunity (flag of International Red Cross) 1/4/1945 by U.S.S. *Queenfish*.* Intended for the Japan–Australia service.
PRESIDENT JACKSON* (American President Lines)	27/6/50	12/1951	12,660	533	Completed as troop transport *Barrett* (T-AP 196) due to the Korean War. Transferred to New York State Maritime College in 9/1973 as a training ship and renamed *Empire State V*.
PRESIDENT ADAMS* (American President Lines)	9/10/50	9/1952	12,660	533	Completed as the troop transport *Geiger* (T-AP 197) due to the Korean War. Laid up in April 1971.
PRESIDENT HAYES* (American President Lines)	19/1/51	12/1952	12,660	533	Completed as the troop transport *Upshur* (T-AP 198) due to the Korean War. Transferred to the Maine Maritime Academy in 1973 as a training ship.

*Allied prisoners-of-war on the Japanese dockside were well aware that Japanese hospital ships sometimes discharged pig-iron, etc. on arrival back in their own country. The authors do not know if the Allied command was equally aware of this fact but, if so, it could put a different light on the sinking of the *Awa Maru*. Nevertheless, the *Queenfish* is reported to have mistaken the *Awa Maru* for a warship in poor visibility.

184.

185. The PRINCIPESA JOLANDA is the first vessel listed in Appendix 1. Ready for launch, with her masts and
funnels stepped, as was common Italian practice, the ship was dressed overall as crowds gathered for the gala
event. As she ran down the ways, nothing seemed amiss to the bystanders, but . . .

186.

187. . . . seldom did a ship make a more public exhibition of herself for, as soon as she took the water, she slewed
round and took a heavy list, going right over very quickly. It was said that the sliding ways caught fire but, when
one considers the short time it took to reach the water, it is not unreasonable to suppose that there was rather
more to the story.

188.

189. *At all events, the pictures show how the PRINCIPESA JOLANDA's launch ended and that was, in fact, the end of her brief career, which was certainly spectacular, if nothing else, and her performance might well have been billed as 'A Shipyard Manager's Nightmare'!*

APPENDIX 2

UNITED STATES LEGISLATION CONCERNING THE MERCANTILE MARINE

(A) The 1920 Merchant Marine Act

Known as the 'Jones Act', the 1920 Merchant Marine Act was passed on 5 June 1920. It repealed the emergency war legislation relating to shipping, reorganized the U.S. Shipping Board and extended its life, and authorized the sale of Government-built ships to private operators. The proceeds of such sales, up to a limit of $25 million, were to be used for loans to private companies for the construction of new vessels. The Shipping Board, acting as a caretaker body, was empowered to propose the establishment of shipping routes for the purpose of promoting mail and trade services and to operate such routes until such time as private interests had taken over.

(B) The 1928 Jones–White Act

This Merchant Marine Act, known as the 'Jones–White Act', was passed on 22 May 1928. It, too, was designed to encourage private shipping, and increased a construction loan fund from $125 million to $250 million from which private builders could borrow up to 75% of the cost of constructing, re-conditioning or remodelling an approved vessel. It also permitted the sale of Government-owned ships at low prices, and liberalized long-term mail-carrying contracts.

(C) Repeal of the 18th Amendment

The 18th Amendment to the U.S. Constitution (Prohibition Amendment) prohibited the manufacture, sale or transportation of alcoholic drink. It was declared ratified on 29 January 1919 and became operative on 16 January 1920.

It was repealed with the adoption of the 21st Amendment on 5 December 1933. Whilst this legislation extended far beyond the Mercantile Marine, its effects within the context of passenger liner traffic, when vessels of all nations except the United States could supply their passengers with alcohol, were obvious, since those who preferred a 'dry' ship were very much in the minority.

190. A picture taken of the WASHINGTON after her funnels had been heightened, as was also the case with the MANHATTAN. (Comparison with PL. 152 is interesting). This vessel did sterling work trooping during the war.

APPENDIX 3

EXPLANATION OF THE UNITED STATES MARITIME COMMISSION (U.S.M.C.) SYSTEM OF DESIGN CLASSIFICATION

In order that the codes used to describe passenger liner designs in Chapters XVI and XXI may be fully understood, this Appendix has been included as an explanation of the working of the U.S.M.C. system of designatory letters and numbers. It should not be regarded as definitive because the system was under development from its very inception and there remain certain unanswered inconsistencies in its operation. Nevertheless, this Appendix can be considered as being both complete and accurate for the purposes of this book.

As set forth in the 'Merchant Marine Act of 1936', the United States Maritime Commission was created as a replacement for the U.S. Shipping Board and its primary function was to launch a massive long-range shipbuilding programme for the revitalization of the American Merchant Marine. Commenced in 1937, the initial target of this programme was to produce 500 new ships at the rate of 50 vessels annually but, as War approached, the targets were continuously revised until, by 1945, over 5,700 standard design ships of various types had been constructed.

Even while this prolific shipbuilding production was under way the U.S.M.C. was planning for the future in the preparation of replacement designs as the first of a number of moves aimed at maintaining this newly created fleet. The various passenger ship elements of this first replacement/development programme, intended to be started immediately after the end of World War Two, form the subjects of Chapters XXIA–D. Subsequent replacement exercises were initiated periodically by the United States Maritime Administration (MARAD), the successor to the U.S. Maritime Commission from 1950.

All vessels designed by the Maritime Commission and the Maritime Administration can be identified by a coded type classification. Similarly, most privately designed vessels can be recognized in this manner, having likewise been allocated a type classification, not because they were standard ships but because their construction was invariably controlled and financed by one or other of these Government bodies, e.g. the *America, Constitution, Independence* and the *United States.*

As the U.S.M.C.'s inaugural shipbuilding programme progressed, it was divided into three parts, viz. the 'Peace' programme, the 'War Emergency' programme and the 'Victory' programme. Vessels of the 'War Emergency' programme bore the prefix letter 'E' to their design classification, while those of the 'Victory' programme were prefixed with the letter 'V', e.g. EC2–S–C1, the Liberty ship, and VC2–S–AP2, the Victory ship.

TWO-GROUP CLASSIFICATION

The original system of type classification, used for designs of the U.S.M.C. 'Peace' programme, consisted of two groups of letters and numbers. The first such group indicated the type of vessel by a letter and the design service speed by a number.

Type of Vessel		Design Service Speed
C = CARGO	1	14 kts
	2	15 kts
	3	16 kts
P = PASSENGER (Express & Cargo)	1	16 kts
(usually over 100 passengers)	2	18 kts
	3	20 kts
	4	22 kts +
R = REEFER (Refrigerated Cargo)	1	14–16 kts
	2	16–18 kts

T = TANKER	1	?
	2	?
	3	?

The second group, of letters only, commencing with 'A', expanded on the ship's application or distinguished groups of ships having specific features or equipped with particular types of engine, arrangements, e.g. P & C – cargo vessel with extensive passenger accommodation; SU – vessel with direct drive Doxford diesels built under licence by Sun Shipbuilding & Dry Dock Company.

Unfortunately, not all of these letters or their meanings are known but it is believed that 'A' and 'P' represented respectively 'Atlantic' and 'Pacific'. In this context, the classification P–4–P (Chapter XVI), perhaps more correctly written as P4–P, though only rarely so, indicates a passenger vessel of over 22 knots designed speed for service on the Pacific Ocean, for this was the intended theatre of operations for the design.

In addition to the two principal groups of characters in the two-group system of classification, occasionally the first letter or letters of the shipyard were given, producing a sort of hybrid three-group system, e.g. C3–IN–P & C, a quartet of cargo passenger liners completed as troopships by the Ingalls Shipbuilding Corporation.

From the very outset, all hull designs in the U.S.M.C. 'Peace' programme were allocated design numbers, although these were, as far as can be determined, never actually indicated in the designatory classification in its original two-group form. In passing, design number '1' was the United States Lines' *America,* designed by the Gibbs brothers, but she did not receive her full classification until some time later, then being designated P4–S2–1. From this it is apparent that her classification was determined from the later three-group system.

The practice of allocating design numbers was continued beyond the 'Peace' programme. It is recommenced at number '1' for the first of the 'War Emergency' designs but at some time during the Second World War, probably under the 'Victory' programme, the sequence of numbers was replaced by one made up of letters and numbers. It should be noted here that, during wartime, designs from various programmes were being drawn up simultaneously.

THREE-GROUP CLASSIFICATION

Experience showed that most ships built under the 'Peace' programme exceeded their design speeds, when in service, by considerable margins. It was therefore concluded that a classification based on the vessels' predicted performance was not a very accurate means of identifying the design. Besides this, it was also apparent that two vessels of similar specification but with quite different designs could be easily confused under the two-group system. For instance, had the *America* and the P–4–P vessels both been destined for service on the same sea route, then they would have borne identical classifications in spite of their quite different designs.

A modified, three-group, system of classification was introduced in 1941, because of these less satisfactory aspects of the original system, and this incorporated the hitherto unrevealed design number.

Of the three groups, the first, comprised of letters and numbers, indicated the type of vessel by a letter and the approximate waterline length by a number, this being considered a more tangible yardstick by which to express the size of the ship.

Type of Vessel	Waterline Length – ft.					
	1	2	3	4	5	6
C = CARGO	under 400	400– 450	450– 500	500– 550	550– 600	—
L = GREAT LAKES ORE CARRIER	under 400	400– 450	450– 500	500– 550	550– 600	600– 650
N = COASTWISE CARGO	under 200	200– 250	250– 300	—	—	—
P = PASSENGER (Over 100 Passengers)	under 500	500– 600	600– 700	700– 800	800– 900	900– 1,000
R = REEFER (Refrigerated Cargo)	under 400	400– 450	450– 500	—	—	—
S = SPECIAL SHIP	under 200	200– 300	300– 400	400– 500	—	—
T = TANKER	under 500	500– 600	600– 700	—	—	—

As to the second group, again made up of letters and numbers, this provided basic information on the type of propulsive machinery and the number of screw propellers featured in the design.

Type of Machinery	Single Screw		Twin Screw		Triple Screw		Quad. Screw	
	Passengers —12*	+12†	Passengers —12*	+12†	Passengers —12*	+12†	Passengers —12*	+12†
STEAM (Reciprocating & Turbine)	S	S1	ST	S2	?	S3	?	S4
MOTOR (Diesel)	M	M1	MT	M2	?	M3	?	M4
TURBO-ELECTRIC	SE	SE1	SET	SE2	?	SE3	?	SE4
DIESEL ELECTRIC	ME	ME1	MET	ME2	?	ME3	?	ME4

The third group in the modified system, indicated the particular design of the type of ship and any modifications thereof.

From 1941, when the three-group classification was introduced, the designs were listed in numerical sequence.

From circa 1943 an alphabetical series was adopted, the first design being 'A', the second 'AB', and so on until 'AZ', followed by a 'B' sequence, 'C' sequence and so on. Variations in the basic design were shown by a number which was appended to the letters.

In 1950, as the Maritime Commission was replaced by the Maritime Administration, a further change was made in the style of design identification. Once more a numerical sequence was reverted to, with modifications to the basic design now indicated by a letter following the number, i.e. '1a', '1b', '1c', etc.

From this detailed breakdown it is possible to both decipher the type classifications referred to in Chapters XXIA—D as well as to determine the approximate period in which the individual designs were commenced:

Chapter XXIA: P4—S2—41

This indicates a passenger vessel with a waterline length between 700 and 800 feet, propelled by twin screw steam turbines. Design number 41, commenced between 1941 and 1943.

Chapter XXIB: P3—S2—DA1

This indicates a passenger vessel with a waterline length between 600 and

*—12 = under 12.
† +12 = over 12.

700 feet, propelled by twin screw steam turbines. Design DA, first modification, commenced between circa 1943 and 1945, when the U.S.M.C. post-War programme was launched.

Chapter XXIC: The *Independence* Class (U.S.M.C. Code P3−S2−DL2)

This indicates a passenger vessel with a waterline length between 600 and 700 feet, propelled by twin screw steam turbines. Design DL, second modification, commenced between circa 1943 and 1945.

Chapter XXID: P5−S2−E1 (Formerly PXE)

This indicates a passenger vessel with a waterline length between 800 and 900 feet, propelled by twin screw steam turbines. Design E, first modification commenced between circa 1943 and 1945. The type classification PXE represents one of the unanswered inconsistencies mentioned earlier. However, if written in the form P-X-E it is perhaps possible to unravel it. Clearly a passenger vessel, it would have been the basic E design. At the early stage that this classification was allocated, the length and engine arrangement may not have been finally determined, the 'X' representing an unknown quantity in these circumstances.

In conclusion, and for comparison, the other major American passenger liner designed and constructed under the auspices of the U.S.M.C. was the *United States,* whose type classification was P6−S4−DS1.

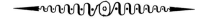

COMPARISON OF ENGINE ARRANGEMENT OF THE Q3
WITH OTHER CUNARD *QUEEN* LINERS

Year	Name	Gross Tonnage	Speed	Propulsion System	H.P.	Boilers	Fuel Consumption (tons/day)	Engine Room Crew	Stm. Cond. (lb. in²/°F)
1936	QUEEN MARY	81,237	28.5	Quadruple-screw, single reduction geared turbines.	212,000	27	1,075	250	400/700
1940	QUEEN ELIZABETH	83,673	28.5	As above	212,000	12	1,050	220	425/750
1960	"Q3"	80,000	28.5	Quadruple-screw geared turbines	200,000	8	800	146	850/950
1969	QUEEN ELIZABETH 2	65,860	28.5	Twin-screw, dual tandem, locked train double reduction geared turbines.	110,000	3	520	93	850/1000

Machinery Notes: Q3 and Q4. When the time came to consider replacement of the QUEENs, consideration was again given to diesel machinery, although the Q3, which was the original replacement concept, was to have a turbine installation with four screws and would have been similar in many respects to the old QUEENs. However, the Q3 investigations made it evident that marine technology had advanced to a situation whereby the required passenger complement and speed could be achieved in a much smaller ship driven by twin screws. Thus the Q4 (QE2) was born. Initially, the Q4 was to have had 4 boilers and 5 generators located in two different compartments, in the interests of safety. In the event, and to reduce overall cost, a revised machinery layout was agreed, embodying 3 boilers and 3 generators. While the final installed power was 110,000 SHP, i.e. 55,000 SHP per shaft, the original design was for 120,000 SHP.

191. *The longest liner ever built was the FRANCE, seen here at the Ocean Terminal at Southampton after conversion to the NORWAY (p.295). Perhaps her purchase by Klosters Rederi finally doomed the ELYSIAN project. This unconventional angle of view demonstrates the fineness of the ship's entrance.*

GLOSSARY
OF GENERAL, NAUTICAL AND
TECHNICAL TERMS

In order that this book may be acceptable to its widest possible reader-
ship, the authors have endeavoured to keep its technical content to a
minimum. However, as some readers may not be familiar with
certain terms and phrases used in the text, the following glossary should
prove to be helpful. Since terminology has tended to change over the
years, we have used those terms which apply today. Thus Length/
Breadth Ratio is preferred to Length/Beam ratio: Block Coefficient to
Coefficient of Fineness, etc.

AFTERBODY: The portion of the hull abaft the greatest transverse section, which is
generally (but not always) the 'midship section', this being a datum of the hull of the
ship. Broadly, the Afterbody is the run and parallel body aft of amidships.

ALTERNATOR: A generator which produces alternating current (a.c.) electricity.

AMIDSHIPS: (1) Used as a naval architectural term within the text of this book, it
means the midway point between the (fore and after) perpendiculars; (2) As a seamanship term it is also used of anything lying in the line of the keel or the centre fore-and-aft
line of the ship.

ANTI-ROLLING TANKS: There is a limit to the extent to which amplitudes of motion
of a ship can be reduced by hull shape, but considerable reductions in roll amplitudes are
possible by other means. From the aspect of comfort, rolling is, in general, the most
objectionable of all ship motions. Anti-Rolling tanks fall into two groups, namely, the
Passive and the Active, viz:

    PASSIVE TANK SYSTEM: These consist of wing tanks containing water or fuel oil and connected across the ship by a U-tube duct or a free surface 'flume'. They are arranged preferably with the duct or flume above the centre of gravity of the ship and as high up as possible. If the vessel is rolling from, say, port to starboard, liquid from the port tank will commence its flow through the connecting duct or flume as soon as the ship has passed through the upright condition and is heeling to starboard. On the return roll, there will be an excess of weight in the starboard tank which will reduce the righting moment and thus effect damping on the return roll. Further damping is provided by the destruction of much of the kinetic energy of the liquid flowing in the flume. For correct functioning, the motion of the tank fluid must lag one quarter of a cycle behind the ship cycle. Since the anti-rolling action is initiated by the rolling itself, it cannot prevent the initial development of a roll, but can only provide a damping moment.

Among the best known of Passive tank systems are Frahm and McMullen anti-rolling tanks.

ACTIVE TANK SYSTEMS: There are various systems available, but in each the essential features are two tanks, one on each side of the ship, in which the water level can be controlled by sensory mechanism. The active tank system, which is still in the development stage, has the disadvantage that, in addition to requiring sensitive control mechanism, it has intermittent power requirements with a high peak demand.

See also: FIN-STABILIZERS and GYRO-STABILIZERS.

BALE CAPACITY: The spaces within the faces of the sparring and cladding fitted on the faces of the ship's frames, above the tank-top ceilings and below the underside of the beams, used for the carriage of bale or general cargo.

BALLAST PUMP: The pump used to transfer water ballast into or out of tanks in the double bottom, or in and out of deep tanks, via an oil separator. Usually has by-passes to enable it to be used in conjunction with sanitary and fire systems etc. Obviously, care must be exercised that pumps which can be used for pumping fuel oil are not connected to − say − the fire main!

BARE-BOAT CHARTER: Also known as DEMISE CHARTER. The charterers (or hirers) of a vessel become virtually the owners of the ship for the duration of the charter. They receive just the ship and are responsible for supplying the crew and for paying all expenses and liabilities.

BAUER-WACH SYSTEM: A method used on large reciprocating engines whereby exhaust steam from the main engines would be utilized in a low pressure turbine which, in turn, would be used on the main shaft in tandem with the main engines. Power increases of up to 30% were claimed by the use of this system.

BEAM: (1) The greatest breadth measurement of a ship; (2) Transverse structural member of a ship's framing, below the decks and supporting them against stresses, whilst checking racking tendencies in the transverse section.

BILGE: Space where drain (bilge) water collects at the bottom of a ship between the keel and the ribs (or frames), or at the sides of a double bottom.

BILGE KEEL: A lesser keel, attached along the 'corners' of the hull externally, usually for 30-40% of the ship's length, to reduce rolling. Its disadvantage lies in the fact that propulsive resistance is increased by some 4%, and slightly more when the ship is pitching.

BLOCK CO-EFFICIENT: A 'Box' standard is useful for comparative purposes, since a vessel is said to have 'fine' or 'full' lines according to the proportion of her displacement to that of a box of the same length, breadth and draft. In other words, it is the ratio of the immersed volume of the ship to the product of her length, breadth and draft. It is a dimensionless number. The *Normandie's* block co-efficient was 0.56 compared with about 0.75 for an average 11-knot 400-foot cargo vessel of that time, demonstrating just what fine lines these great liners possessed. Once known as the COEFFICIENT OF FINENESS, the BLOCK COEFFICIENT can be calculated on a slightly different basis, especially if the displacement is not known, but this is outside the scope of this book, although it emphasizes the need to compare like with like at all times.

BOILERS: Used in a large vessel in which steam is generated from distilled or demineralized water by the application of heat. There are two kinds: water-tube and fire-tube. In the former, there is a series of tubes connected with 'drums' or strong, steel circular bodies in which the water is contained. The heat is outside the tubes. Water-tube boilers are quick in raising steam, flexible in output and compact in space, and for this reason are often operated with a turbine. The steam turbine, in virtue of its internal construction, is better suited to take steam at a higher temperature and pressure than the fire-tube boiler, or Scotch boiler as it is sometimes called, is capable of supplying.

The fire-tube boiler has a series of furnaces connected with a common combustion chamber at the back of the boiler. To this combustion chamber are linked a series of tubes through which the gases generated in the furnace are passed. As they do so on their way to the funnel, they give up their heat to water surrounding the fire tubes. (These boilers work on the same principle as the old steam locomotives.)

As the gases pass on their way, they may also heat up other tubes which give extra temperature to the steam generated and which are known as superheaters.

BOW: The forward end of a ship from where the sides trend inward towards the stem.

BREADTH: (1) EXTREME: The greatest measured breadth of a vessel, measured to the outside of the outside plating; (2) MOULDED: The greatest measured breadth of a vessel, measured inside the inner strakes of shell plating. Both these breadths generally occur amidships.

BULBOUS BOW: A term used of a bow design in which the forward frames are swelled out at the forefoot *(q.v.)* and into a protuberance which is carried forward. This prevents the bow dipping too easily and mitigates pitching, whilst aiding the steering in the case of long-hulled ships.

Naval Architects have striven to reduce resistance ever since the advent of power-driven vessels. Gains can be achieved either by reducing the horse-power required to achieve a given speed, with corresponding reductions in machinery size (and cost,

322

besides fuel consumption), or by increasing the speed for a given horse-power, or by a combination of both. For slow-speed vessels, whose frictional resistance deriving from the underwater portion of the hull comprises about two-thirds of the total, the greatest gains arise from a very smooth surface to the hull. Thus the substitution of welding for riveting enabled the eddy-producing overlaps of the shell-plating to be eliminated whilst, in recent years, careful preparation of the steel plate surface, in conjunction with special, long-life anti-fouling coatings, has reduced the amount by which a ship's speed falls as the surface deteriorates with age.

For high-speed ships, in which the frictional resistance can be appreciably less than the wave-making resistance, the biggest gains are made by reducing the waves generated by the hull, and this is also achieved with the bulbous bow.

A ship's normal wave system starts with the crest slightly abaft the stem, but the distance between succeeding crests and troughs of her own wave system depends on the speed/length ratio *(q.v.)* since, at a V $\sqrt{L}$ of 1, there are 1.8 wave-lengths from crest to crest in the hull length, but only one wave-length if the speed/length ratio is 1.34. By placing the bulb below the waterline, a new wave system is generated which has a trough where the normal bow wave crest occurs and thus, to some extent, the two systems cancel each other out, thereby reducing the wave-making as a whole and, therefore, the resistance.

Additionally, the extra buoyancy of the protuberant bulbous bow below the waterline permits a fining of the angle of entry at the waterline itself, without introducing excessive trim by the bow. A compromise is reached in vessels whose speed/length ratio is approximately 1 and which maintain a reasonably constant load draught, since much benefit is lost when it nears or breaks the surface.

See also: HULL FORM.

BULKHEAD: A vertical partition (or wall), in a thwartship or fore-and-aft direction which separates two compartments. Usually of steel for watertight bulkheads, or insulated steel or asbestos for fire-screen bulkheads.

BUNKER: A compartment for storing fuel, whether coal or oil. As a verb, to BUNKER normally refers to taking in oil fuel. (Taking in coal was normally referred to as COALING, but 'OILING', as a term, had obvious objections, and became 'to bunker oil', and thus 'to bunker'.

CENTRE OF BUOYANCY: See METACENTRIC HEIGHT.

CENTRE OF GRAVITY: See METACENTRIC HEIGHT.

COMBINATION MACHINERY: A propulsion system in which a reciprocating engine attached to a propeller exhausts into a low pressure turbine also driving a propeller. Normally, in such a case, there were two reciprocating engines, both exhausting into a low pressure turbine on the centre screw. This type of drive went out of use with improvement in turbine reduction gears.

COMPARTMENT (WATERTIGHT SUBDIVISION): Ship compartments which have been opened to the sea do not fill with water completely because some space is already occupied by machinery, hull structure or by cargo, etc. A compartment which has been opened to the sea is said to have been 'bilged', and it is essential that there is a factor of sub-division such that there is a reasonable chance that the ship will remain afloat in such an emergency.

See also: WATERTIGHT SUBDIVISION.

CONDENSER: A vessel which converts steam back to water for further use in the boiler feed system. When the steam has done its work in the steam propulsion plant it passes into the condenser. This consists of honeycombs of tubes through which cold sea water passes. Upon its impingement on the outside of these tubes, the steam condenses into water and is drawn off by the extraction pump. The act of condensation produces a vacuum, and in this manner steam pressure is applied at one end of the engine and suction is applied at the other, discharging the steam quickly and increasing the efficiency of the engine in terms of high pressure.

COUNTER STERN (see pl. 15): Also termed an OVERHANGING STERN. The older type of stern, which generally accompanied the straight stem in its latter days, in which the upper works extend beyond the rudder-post, forming a continuation of the hull line. Generally half-round or elliptical in plan view. It required to be so framed so as to support its own weight besides providing structural resistance to the battering of a following sea – two requirements not so applicable to a CRUISER STERN *(q.v.)*.

A modern version of this style of stern was incorporated into the large United States' liners *Constitution* and *Independence*. *The counter stern was, in effect, an extension of the hull above the stern post on which the rudder was hinged.

CRUISER STERN: The more general type used on modern liners, the name may have derived from the type of stern used on cruisers prior to the introduction of the transom stern. In profile, the overhanging end of the ship is carried down towards the waterline in a general curve which finally turns in a forward direction near, or on, the waterline, and then runs forward horizontally until it reaches the main part of the hull at the rudder and sternpost.

The cruiser stern gives a longer waterline length, improving hull flow through the water and aiding the efficiency of the propulsion. It gives better protection to the screws in harbour, particularly suits the incorporation of a balanced rudder, since it is not so subject to hammering by waves, and gives greater buoyancy aft, though in some ships this created an unbalanced couple and caused the bows to dip excessively into head seas. This, however, was a matter of design.

DAVITS: Mechanisms, usually for clearing and lowering (or hoisting) ships' lifeboats. They take different forms. The old radial davits had to be turned outboard, and were guyed. The boats were lowered from a three-fold purchase at their heads. The gantry davits, referred to in connection with the *Britannic,* were more like girder cranes, and later forms allowed a form of davit which lowered the boat by a single wire, and which ran down tracks to put the boat into the lowering position, simply by one man operating

*Pl. 146.

192. The 21,131 gross ton Hapag liner HANSA, ex-ALBERT BALLIN, passing the 4-m. barque POMMERN immediately prior to the 1939-45 war, exhibits a good example of a cruiser stern.

a brake lever, these being known as 'Gravity davits'. There have been other types.

DEADWEIGHT: A form of tonnage, which is in effect the carrying capacity of the ship. It is the difference between the lightweight and displacement tonnages, being the actual weight required to bring a vessel from her light draught to her loaded summer freeboard marks, and includes cargo, stores, fuel, etc.

DIESEL-ELECTRIC PROPULSION: In this form of power plant, diesel (oil) engines are used extensively as prime movers to operate electric generators. These, in turn, drive large electric motors which are directly coupled to the propeller shaft. Diesel-electric plants' main advantages are that they are better suited to machinery areas where space is too limited for boilers and coal storage, or where condenser cooling water is not required for a turbo-electric plant. The initial cost of a diesel-electric power plant of a given size is also less than that of a turbo-electric one of the same size, and this form of power plant in ships provides much better flexibility of operation and of speed control than a straight

*Albert Ballin was largely responsible for the great success of the Hamburg Amerika Line (and thus enhancing German prestige and prosperity) and the ship had been named after him. Because he was a Jew, she was re-named under the era of Nazi lunacy. Mined in the Baltic in 1945, she was salved and taken over by the Russians, as the *Sovietsky Sojus*.

diesel engine drive. The one disadvantage is the expense of maintaining the diesel prime movers.

DIMENSIONS: All dimensions and data quoted for each ill-fated liner scheme are given, where known, in Imperial units (i.e. feet, tons) and not in the recently established Système Internationale d'Unités (S.I. Units). This has been done for three basic reasons, namely: (1) With a few exceptions, the majority of the projects were originally documented in Imperial units and any conversion might have led to confusion; (2) The earlier systems will be more familiar to the majority of English-speaking readers for purposes of comparison and identification; (3) The ton of 100 cubic feet used for gross tonnage measurement will be difficult to replace and will be required for continuing usage pending international agreement.

DOUBLE ARMATURE MOTOR: The method of propulsion proposed for the Detwiler ships. The propeller drive units were to be double armature motors or synchronous motors, which had the advantage over other types of motor that, at normal full power operation, higher efficiency was predicted for a lighter weight.

DRAUGHT – EXTREME: The distance measured from the waterline to the bottom of the keel, sometimes called the 'draught-bottom of keel'; MOULDED: The distance measured from the waterline to the top of the keel.

DRAW WATER, TO: A ship is said to 'draw' as much water as her maximum draught, which is generally rather more aft than forward. A ship must always have more water than her actual draught in which to proceed.

EXCHANGE RATES: See MONETARY.

EXPANSION JOINTS: In the superstructure or deck plating, a sliding joint which permits linear movement between adjacent sections when the ship is subjected to hogging and sagging stresses which might otherwise tend to be destructive.

FIN STABILIZERS: Activated fin stabilizers are a more modern means of reducing rolling and consist of rectangular fins which can be projected from the sides of the ship, and are controlled by two small gyroscopes acting through hydraulic and electrical power. The one is turned upwards when the one on the other side hinges downwards, counter-acting the tendency for the hull to roll.*

FLYING BOAT: A type of aircraft designed for landing on water in which the body itself serves as (and is shaped like) a boat, and is not supported by floats, as in the case of a seaplane.

FOREBODY: The immersed body of the hull forward of the midship section, or point of maximum breadth.

FOREFOOT: The lower part of the stem where it is stepped into the keel.

FREEBOARD: The vertical distance between the waterline and the upper surface of the freeboard deck: that is, the upper deck having permanent means of closing all openings leading below.

*For diagrams and full explanation, see *Origins, Orient and Oriana*, by Charles F. Morris, p. 291 (Teredo Books Ltd., 1980).

FROUDE'S LAW: Froude's Law of Comparison states that, if two geometrically similar forms (i.e. two ships, or a ship and its model) are run at speeds proportional to the square root of their lengths, or of their corresponding speed, then their residuary resistances (i.e. resistances due to wave-making, hull shapes and air resistances) per unit of displacement will be the same.

That is: $$\frac{V}{\sqrt{L}} = \frac{v}{\sqrt{l}}$$ Where V (v) = Corresponding speeds, and L (l) = Waterline lengths.*

In the United States, this Speed/Length ratio is known as the 'Taylor Quotient'.

FUEL VALVE BOILER: This was the term used by A. C. Hardy to describe the Velox Steam Generator, in connection with the Liner of the Future (Chap. XX). The design of the Velox Steam Generator was the outcome of many years' study and research carried out by the Brown-Boveri Company. It was felt at the time that the introduction of the Velox Boiler would represent the first step towards replacing the conventional boiler of the day by an automatically operating steam generating machine.

The Velox units were advocated for marine use due to their light-weight construction, small space requirements and high efficiency, and were recommended for naval use because of their quick flashing capabilities and almost instantaneous response to sudden load fluctuations.

The term 'Fuel Valve Boiler' was used by Mr. Hardy as it was felt that it was the only expression capable of describing in an explanatory manner the device which made external combustion resemble internal combustion.

The Fuel Valve or Forced Circulation Boiler was not really a boiler in the accepted sense of the word, but it was a machine which took water and pumped it through an apparatus which turned it into steam immediately, at a fairly high pressure and temperature. The boiler did not, as was thought mistakenly, depend for its action upon high pressure and high temperature. The real advantage of its operation lay in its ability to turn water into steam quickly and, therefore, to become, in effect, a kind of control valve on the prime mover to which it supplied steam.

Certainly, as far as is known, this boiler had only found a limited marine application up to 1939. In 1934, out of 34 Velox boilers built, only one had been ordered for a merchant ship. This was a 35-ton unit which replaced seven Scotch boilers in the *Athos II*, of the Messageries Maritimes. Apart from this, the French post-war vessels *Ville de Tunis* and *Cambodge* were also fitted with Velox boilers.

GEARING: The steam turbine operates at high speeds whilst the propeller must operate at low speeds. Therefore some form of speed reducer must be fitted between the two, the most popular form being reduction gearing. A speed reduction of up to about 30:1 can be obtained by using a single reduction (S.R.) gearing but, for greater reduction, double reduction (D.R.) gearing must be used.

GENERATOR (A.C.): See ALTERNATOR.

GYRO-STABILIZERS: Roll stabilization by means of gyroscopes depends upon the high-speed rotation of large masses to produce stabilizing couples. Generally consisting

*i.e. A 25-knot vessel, 400 feet in length = $\frac{V}{\sqrt{2}} = \frac{25}{20} = 1.25$.

of an axially rotating body which has rotational inertia ('spin'). The momentum and rotational axis preserve their direction so long as no external forces act upon the gyroscope. Because of this tendency to keep the direction of its axis constant in space, it can be used suitably for the stabilization of movements. There is a reduction of roll of about 50%. It is effective at low speeds (which is not true of a fin-stabilizer *(q.v.),* but the system is heavy, being about 2% of the displacement: has a large power requirement and occupies considerable space in the hull.

The Sperry gyroscope stabilizer has been fitted to a number of vessels, including the liner *Conte di Savoia,* in which the installation weighed 691 tons, or 1.72% of her displacement. The average stabilized roll was about 56% of the free roll over a lengthy period. Whilst this average reduction was appreciable, it was not regarded as being wholly satisfactory. Investigation showed that stabilizing was poor in following and quartering seas, especially when broad on the quarter (i.e. at about 45°).

HORSE-POWER: Power is the rate of doing work, and the horse-power was almost universally adopted as a rate for measuring work. The unit was devised by the engineer James Watt and was his estimate of the rate at which a good horse could work for a few hours, though he deliberately fixed it at a high amount. The Horse-power (h.p.) has now been superseded by the Watt and Kilowatt. Concerning the measurement of the power of marine engines, there are three basic methods which should be considered, viz:

(a) BRAKE HORSE-POWER (b.h.p.): Usually power obtained from an internal combustion engine. It represents the actual work done by the engine in turning some machine, such as a propeller and propeller shaft or, on the test bed, a device known as a water brake. In this case the engine dissipates its energy by turning a paddle against a weight, and thus a measure of the power can be obtained.

(b) INDICATED HORSE-POWER (i.h.p.): Is the measured power per cylinder obtained from steam reciprocating engines and internal combustion engines. The horse-power is actually indicated by a small gear which records graphically the mean pressure in the cylinder at any position of the piston during the stroke. It is actually the horse-power indicated or developed by the engine at the time.

(c) SHAFT HORSE-POWER (s.h.p.): Is the measurement of output of steam turbines and is the power transmitted by the machinery to the propellers. S.h.p. is measured as close to the propellers as possible by means of one or more instruments called 'Torsion meters'. These measure the angle of twist caused in a known length of the shaft by the applied turning moment, or 'torque'.

HULL FORM: The hull design, or shaping of the underwater hull, so as to move the vessel through water with a minimum of power wastage. It is desirable to combine hull form, propeller design and power to give the best results. Hull form performance in the field of Naval Architecture is generally predicted from model tank testing. When the Yourkevitch form of bow is referred to in the text, it indicates the employment of a full underwater form forward, thus claiming improved propulsive efficiency. This form was patented by Vladimir Yourkevitch, the lead designer of the *Normandie,* who believed that the forebody shape of a ship was the most important factor in her wave resistance.

According to him, the wave resistance could be reduced by drawing in the forebody section at the waterline so that the waterlines in that region became more or less hollow. The point of change in waterline shape from concave to convex was determined by a formula based upon the ship's length and speed. The displacement lost by hollowing the load waterlines was regained by fitting a bulb below them. As bulbous bows had been employed previously, the Yourkevitch bow can be considered to be a special case of bulbous bow *(q.v.)*.

The 'U' section bows, referred to in connection with the U.S. Maritime Commission's post-war designs of 1945, were very similar to the Yourkevitch form.

INDICATED HORSE-POWER (i.h.p.): See HORSE-POWER.

JAPANESE LANGUAGE; and the NIHON SHIKI or KOKUTAI SHIKI (Japanese or 'National' System of transliteration): The Japanese language in its written form is constructed of numerous (literally thousands) of syllables based on Chinese ideograms, or characters, which originated in the 8th or 9th century A.D., and which are known as 'Kana'. The kana is further divided into, or comprised of, the 'Katakana' and 'Harigana', the one being a more colloquial and less orthodox form than the other, thereby making it possible to give a particular object two similar meanings but different-sounding descriptions.

This is further complicated by the Romanization of the Japanese language by the method of transliteration, or phonetic transcription: i.e. the word-sound written in Roman characters. Until 1937, the method most widely accepted was the Hepburn system, which was first introduced in the last century. However, in the late 1930s, the Japanese authorities decided upon the implementation, instead, of the Nikon Shiki or Kokutai Shiki for all future transliteration, which had the effect of altering the pronounciation of many words.

KEEL: The keel, or flat plate keel as it is known when referring to steel-hulled vessels, is in reality the middle line strake of the outer bottom plating, and when considered in conjunction with the vertical keel and middle line strake of inner bottom plating, it forms a valuable longitidinal stiffener, or backbone, to the ship.

KEELSON: A fore-and-aft centre line girder extending the whole length of the ship, either above or between the floor plates. The term is usually employed in single-bottom vessels, and referred to as a 'Centre Girder', or 'Vertical Keel' in those with double bottoms.

See also: KEEL.

KING POST: Alternatively known as a 'Samson Post'. A short, tubular mast, usually well to one side of the ship's centre line, and used to support one or more derricks for cargo-handling purposes.

KNOT: All trials, service and cruising speeds are quoted in knots. One knot is a velocity of one nautical mile per hour — a nautical mile being 6,080 feet, which is the length of one minute of arc on the equator or of a meridian. Certain countries work on a nautical mile of 6076.12 feet (1852 metres), but in this book the knot is as previously stated.

KOKUTAI SHIKI: See JAPANESE LANGUAGE.

LENGTH:

LENGTH BETWEEN PERPENDICULARS (LPP): The length measured in feet or metres between a vertical line drawn through the intersection of the load waterline and the forward side of the stem (Forward Perpendicular − F.P.) and a line drawn perpendicular to the intersection of the after edge of the rudder post and the load waterline (After Perpendicular − A.P.). In the case of vessels which had a balanced rudder and therefore require no rudder post, the A.P. is taken as being the centre-line of the rudder stock.

LENGTH OVERALL (LOA): The length in feet or metres from the extreme forward point of the vessel to a similar point aft − i.e. the greatest measured length of the vessel.

LENGTH ON WATERLINE (LWL): Is the length measured on the waterline of a ship when floating in still water at the loaded, or designed, condition.

LENGTH/BREADTH RATIO: On early wooden-hulled ships the ratio of length to breadth (beam) was about 7:1 and sometimes less. Indeed, some East Indiamen built in the eighteenth century had a ratio of 3:1.* There were several reasons for this: a belief that the beam was required to counteract the overturning action of the sails when the wind was abeam or forward of it; to give greater stability when firing broadsides and, not least, a sheer lack of appreciation of ship construction as developed since. Many of the Harland and Wolff steamships were built to a ratio of 10:1, and sometimes 11:1, thus being able to increase the relative payload. This change in practice soon became general in large steamships.

In more recent times the only value of the ratio has been for comparative purposes, to indicate whether a vessel is of fine or of 'beamy' build.

LONGITUDINAL COEFFICIENT: This terminology is used in the U.S.A. Known in the United Kingdom as the PRISMATIC COEFFICIENT. The ratio of the immersed volume of the underwater body to the area of the midship section multiplied by the waterline length. The finer the lines of the ship, the less the coefficient. Passenger ships were generally in the bracket 0.60 to 0.70, whereas cargo vessels tended to be between 0.70 and 0.80.

METACENTRIC HEIGHT: This is difficult to explain briefly without entering into complex fundamentals of naval architecture. It must first be understood that the CENTRE OF GRAVITY of a vessel is the point at which the total weight of a ship and her contents are concentrated − in a sense, her 'point of balance', while the CENTRE OF BUOYANCY is the point through which the resultant upward forces, by which a ship floats freely in still water, is supported. In effect, it is the centre of the immersed bulk of the hull. The Centre of Gravity is a constant for any given condition of lading, but the Centre of Buoyancy will move from one side to the other as the ship rolls. Once the hull is out of the vertical, the METACENTRE is the point of intersection of a vertical

*It is not, of course, suggested that such early ships, of so much smaller size, could have been built to modern length/breadth ratios, for a variety of reasons.

line through the (new) Centre of Buoyancy (B1) with a vertical line through the Centre of Buoyancy (B) when the ship is upright – on an even keel. The Metacentric Height is the distance between the Metacentre and the Centre of Gravity. Once this latter point rises above the Metacentre, the ship is in an unstable condition and will probably capsize.

See also: STABILITY.

MIDSHIP SECTION: The transverse section of the ship at amidships.

MIDSHIP SECTION AREA COEFFICIENT: The ratio of the immersed area of the midship section to the product of the beam and draught. Where the transverse section of greatest area is abaft of amidships, that greatest section is used for the ratio, and this is sometimes known as the Maximum Section Coefficient.

MODEL TESTS: In order to predict, or determine, the lines a vessel should have, the powering she requires, and how she will perform in a seaway, the naval architect uses models to aid his design. In general terms, the model is placed in a large experimental tank, in which it is towed by an overhead travelling carriage at speeds proportional to the designed speed of the ship (see FROUDE'S LAW). Wave-making mechanisms can simulate varying conditions of sea and waves. The carriage is fitted with intricate and delicate instruments which can record the resistance of the model through the water. Calculations are made from the results obtained to determine the power required to propel the real, finished ship. Experimental tanks are also used for other purposes in connection with the performance of the proposed vessel.

MONETARY: Costs and fares to which reference is made in the text are usually in sterling or in American dollars. Sometimes both are quoted, dependant on the source. In these cases, the approximate currency conversion can be assumed to be as follows, viz:

Prior to 1940	£1 equals approx $5.00
1940–52	£1 ,, ,, $4.00
1953–60	£1 ,, ,, $3.00
1960–70	£1 ,, ,, $2.50
1970–80	£1 ,, ,, $2.00

Clearly, these figures are very rough, and were subject to fluctuation. Moreover, in considering monetary values, whether in one currency or another, allowance must be made for the inflation of values over the years. (There is nothing new about this problem – it has merely accelerated in recent times.) Thus it must be borne in mind that, in earlier years, £1 million, or $1 million, represented a greater comparative sum than in each ensuing decade. This is too large a subject to be considered in depth but, reduced to its commonest terms, the value of a loaf of bread (say) in each decade is the best indicator of the value of money.

NAVAL ARCHITECTURE: Was defined as long ago as 1890 as *'The art of designing and projecting plans for the construction of vessels, from rules in accordance with Mechanical and Hydrostatical requirements.'* Nowadays it is much more scientific and supported by a great deal of mathematical data, albeit still leaning slightly on empiricism.

*An Illustrated Marine Encyclopaedia, H. Paasch, 1890.

The body responsible for the profession in the United Kingdom is the Royal Institution of Naval Architects (R.I.N.A.), while in the United States it is the Society of Naval Architects and Marine Engineers (S.N.A.M.E.).

NIHON SHIKI: See JAPANESE LANGUAGE.

PADDLE WHEEL: A form of mechanical propulsion prior to the screw propeller, it usually consisted of a wheel fitted on each side of a paddle steamer in connection with a paddle shaft. Sometimes, in narrow rivers, etc. a single paddle wheel was used right aft. The wheel generally consisted of a cast iron boss from which wrought iron arms radiated and were strengthened by rims and stays. A plate called a 'float' was attached to each arm, sometimes feathering, sometimes fixed.

PASSENGER LINER: Express passenger liners are those built primarily to carry a large number of passengers at the highest economic speed between terminal ports with, possibly, two or three calls *en route*. The largest ships of this class often carried large tonnages of cargo, but the amount was determined by the time that the vessel had available in her turn round time at the terminal port, in order to maintain her schedule.

PAYLOAD: The weight which a ship is capable of carrying.

POWER FACTOR: When considering a.c. motors, the Power Factor is defined as *'the factor by which the apparent power is multiplied to give the true power.'* This may be thought of as 'electrical slip', in the same way that friction affects mechanical movement.

p.s.i. – POUNDS PER SQUARE INCH (lbf/in^2): The Imperial unit of pressure used when referring to the gauge working pressures of boilers.

RADIUS/RANGE: The distance within which a ship is able to operate, determined by the amount of fuel carried (i.e. without re-fuelling or re-bunkering).

RAKED BOW: A bow which is straight, but angled forward from the perpendicular.

REEFER: A refrigerated cargo vessel. Reefer cargo is refrigerated cargo.

REGENERATIVE CYCLE (or EFFECT): The cooling surface in the upper part of the condenser must be sufficiently large to give the rapid condensing of steam to water necessary for high vacuum. A degree of under-cooling is therefore unavoidable. To facilitate matters, a passage free of tubes is arranged in the condenser to allow steam to pass to the lower section. The condensate falling from the tubes above through the steam is re-heated to very nearly its saturation temperature.
See also: CONDENSERS.

RESISTANCE: The ship's propulsion has to overcome three major types of resistance whilst under way, namely: (1) Resistance due to waves which are formed by the motion of the ship herself; (2) The action of the water rubbing against the sides of the ship, called Frictional Resistance; (3) Appendage, or eddy-making resistance caused by the shape of the stern and by projecting parts, such as bilge keels and bossings.

332

r.p.m.: Revolutions per minute.

SCANTLINGS: The thickness and dimensions of all rolled sections: plating, girders and other structural parts of a ship. The various classification societies lay down minimum scantlings, according to the type of vessel, to which builders must adhere if the vessel is to obtain classification.

SCOOPS: A method proposed as an alternative to circulating salt water through the condensers via the pumps. The scoops, which are protrusions on the shell of the ship, would literally scoop up the sea water while the ship was under way, although they would probably have been augmented by sea water circulating pumps while the vessel was stationary or manoeuvering in port.

Condenser scoops were used in the U.S. Lines' *America* (1940). This arrangement, which was an off-shoot of U.S. Naval practice, was found to be satisfactory upon her entry into service and, at the time, was probably of equal efficiency to pumps. It was claimed that scoops had the advantage of saving space and of eliminating the necessity of maintaining two vital and constantly running auxiliaries.

SCREWS: Screw propellers.

SEA-KINDLINESS: A term intended to combine in one expression, so far as possible, the meanings conveyed by safe, comfortable continuity of progress under varying conditions at sea.

s.h.p. (SHAFT HORSE-POWER): See HORSE-POWER.

SHEER: The longitudinal rise (usually curving) of the deck forward and aft from amidships. Generally, the forward sheer is equal to twice the after sheer.

SHELL: The outer hull (plating) of a ship.

SKEG: Protruding metal arm at the after end of a ship, usually to support the rudder and protect the screw. In this case, it is amidships. Twin skegs would be on either side, equidistant from the centre line of the ship. The fin on a surf-board is also known as a 'skeg'.

SPEED/LENGTH RATIO: See FROUDE'S LAW.

STABILITY: This is really too complex a subject to lie within the scope of this glossary, but it is linked with METACENTRIC HEIGHT *(q.v.)*. When the metacentric height is great, the tendency for a ship to restore her equilibrium, if it is disturbed, say, when rolling, is very great and she is then said to be 'stiff'. When the metacentric height is small, the restoring force is correspondingly small, and the vessel is said to be 'tender'. It might therefore be assumed that, the greater the metacentric height, the safer the ship, since her righting moments render her less liable to capsize. However, if a ship is too stiff, she will give short, sharp rolls, and vessels have been known to lose their funnel, or masts, in exceptional circumstances as a result, whilst other damage is not uncommon. In consequence, a ship loading a cargo with a low stowage factor (e.g. a heavy ore which does not fill a ship's holds) must not load it all along her bottom, or she would be much

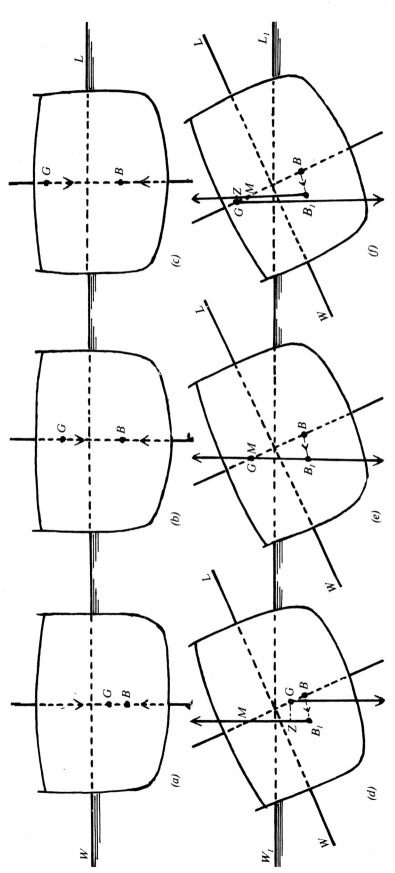

193. *Sketches (a), (b) and (c) show a vessel floating at a constant waterline (WL), but with varying heights to her Centre of Gravity. The GM (Metacentric Height) is calculated when the ship is first built, by heeling her with no ballast, cargo, bunkers, stores or water on board. It will vary subsequently with different conditions of lading and even in the course of a voyage. It is, perhaps, most easy to visualise in the case of a cargo vessel. Thus a vessel loading a heavy ore would need to distribute her weight of cargo between the lower hold and 'tween decks, since the cargo will by no means fill her hold capacity and, if all was loaded in the bottom of the ship, she would be much too 'stiff'. A vessel loading — say — wheat would generally be down to her marks with her holds, roughly, full, but, if loading esparto grass, or a similar light cargo, she would fill her holds and take a large deck cargo and still not be down to her marks. Thus, if anyone were to be so stupid as to load iron ore purely as a deck cargo, the CENTRE OF GRAVITY would be much too high and the ship dangerously 'tender', with little reserve stability. The positions of the point (G) have been exaggerated in the sketches above to demonstrate the point. The lower sketches (b), (d) and (f) show the ship at the same angle of heel. In the first, with a fairly low 'G', the CENTRE OF BUOYANCY (B) has moved to the low side, and the force acting upwards through it cuts the centre line of the ship at the METACENTRE (M), which lies well above 'G', giving a positive stability through the righting arm GZ. In sketch (d) the upward force through B_1 cuts the centre line at 'G', which is also the Metacentre, so that in this case there is no righting arm GZ, and the ship is in a state of neutral equilibrium and, if no other force is applied, will neither come back to an upright position nor capsize but, in the case of (f), the Metacentre falls below 'G', and GZ is negative and, in fact, a capsizing arm. W_1L_1 is, of course, the transverse waterline at the given angle of heel.*

too stiff, but must distribute the weights. A tender ship gives long, slow rolls, often seeming to pause at the end of a roll as if wondering whether to come back. Neither a stiff nor a tender ship is a desirable condition, and both lead to exhaustion and discomfort to those on board. Thus it is essential to calculate the Centre of Buoyancy in relation to the Centre of Gravity in order that the Metacentric Height should be at a reasonable limit consistent with safety, in order to provide the desired stability. (The foregoing comments apply to transverse stability. Consideration also needs to be given to the longitudinal implications.)

STEAM RECIPROCATING MACHINERY: The oldest form of marine power transmission which depends for its operation on the expansive working of steam. If steam is supplied under pressure to an enclosed vessel and allowed to expand, it will push against one of the walls in doing so. If this wall is a piston inside a cylinder, then steam will act on a head of a piston, of which there are several in a row. These piston heads are connected to piston rods that pass through steam-tight flanges at the bottom of the cylinders and go down to where they are connected to the propeller shaft by crank webs that work with a pedalling movement and turn the propeller shaft, known at this part as the crankshaft. As the steam passes from cylinder to cylinder, it repeats this movement, each piston being bigger than the one preceding because the steam, being weaker, works at a lower pressure and more of it is required to force down the piston head.

STEAM TURBINES: These are basically similar in operation to a windmill, with steam taking the place of the wind as a driving force, and with the utilization of many small vanes called 'blades' instead of the large sails of the windmill.

The wheels, with their numerous blades, are mounted on a shaft and are enclosed in a steam-tight casing. The steam from the boilers enters the casing with force, impinges on the blades, and turns the wheels. The movement is transferred to the propeller shaft by gears.

STRAKE: Any particular range of plates, abutting on each other, and of approximately the same width, running fore-and-aft along the whole length of the ship.

STRENGTH DECK: Generally, all decks contribute to the strength of a ship, but the uppermost one (sometimes called the SHELTER DECK) which offers resistance to longitudinal bending is the STRENGTH DECK. It is thicker than the other decks at the line of the hull, to withstand bending moments due to the ship's motion, and is slightly cambered, thereby also providing additional strength to support deck loads. (N.B. Although a strength deck may sometimes be called a shelter deck, a shelter deck is not necessarily always a strength deck, often being a light superstructure connecting the foc's'le head and poop in older vessels, or those structures with the midship section in three-island vessels.)

SUPERCHARGED DIESELS: Generally of the turbo-blower type and powered by the exhaust gas from the actual engine. Air is blown in at the intake side and the products of combustion are swept out of the cylinder after the explosion stroke by the admission of a

194. The leap from the 25,160 tons of the KAISERIN AUGUSTE VIKTORIA to the . . .

volume of air above atmospheric pressure, ready for the next compression stroke.

SUPERHEATERS: See BOILERS.

SUPERLINER: A term used by George C. Gaede, Passenger Traffic Manager of American Export Lines Inc., during a paper presented at SNAME in New York in 1936, who said: *'The word "super-liner" was created to designate the first ship of this character, which was the IMPERATOR, later the BERENGARIA, built in 1912, of a gross tonnage of 52,226 and an average speed of 22.49 knots, for rating purposes in the Conference. The previous largest ship of the Hamburg Amerika Line, the KAISERIN AUGUSTE VICTORIA, built in 1905, had a tonnage of 25,160 and a speed of 16.97 knots. The leap from 25,160 to 52,226 tons suggested the word "super-liner". Later the term was applied to all ships of 50,000 tons or larger. In the trade, therefore, the term has a very definite meaning, although now and then it is carelessly applied to ships of a much smaller tonnage.'*

SUPERSTRUCTURE: The structure or deck-houses built upon the hull. On passenger ships, the superstructure rises in tiers of promenade and other decks, and includes the bridge, small houses and sometimes numerous ventilators and other fittings.

TANKAGE: The capacity within a vessel for carrying its own boiler oil or diesel oil.

195. . . . *IMPERATOR of 52,226 tons, seen unusally without the eagle on her bow, suggested the word 'super-liner'.*

TONNAGE:

(1) DISPLACEMENT TONNAGE: A measure of the amount (mass) of water displaced by a ship floating at a particular draught, equivalent, of course, to the weight of the ship. The displacement, expressed in tons (or tonnes), may be calculated by consideration of the underwater dimensions of the ship (length, breadth and draught) in conjunction with the block coefficient *(q.v.)*. The size of warships is normally expressed in displacement tonnage, but it is used in connection with merchant vessels, particularly liners, in their design stages.

(2) DEADWEIGHT TONNAGE: See DEADWEIGHT.

(3) GROSS TONNAGE: Defined as a measure of the under-deck tonnage with the addition of 'tween deck spaces and other enclosed spaces above the upper deck. Certain spaces are exempt from measurement. The size of many merchant ships is quoted in gross tonnage (particularly passenger vessels), where the ton is 100 cubic feet volume.

During much of the period covered by this book, the regulations governing the gross tonnage measurement in the U.S.A. differed slightly from those in force in the United Kingdom and Europe. Wherever liner projects have been originated in the United States, it is fair to assume that the American method of gross tonnage measurement has been used, and that when European projects are covered, the gross tonnage has been calculated by the British method. For approximate size comparison it is safe to assume that American gross tonnage for completed liners is nominally 25% less than European gross tonnage, but this must be considered to be a rough guide only.

There are variations in uniformity in the measurement of gross tonnage amongst other nations, and the one thing which can be stated with certainty is that, in no case, does it represent the entire enclosed cubical capacity.

There are a number of other forms of tonnage measurement (Net Registered, Underdeck, etc.) which are used for different purposes – sometimes for the levying of dues. The relative proportions of one type of tonnage to another will vary with different types of ships and, indeed, whilst 'Displacement' is the more sensible and normal way of measuring a warship: a cargo ship may be considered in Net Registered tonnage or deadweight, but a passenger vessel is best expressed in terms of gross tonnage, for all the defects in comparison. The whole is a large subject and, for further reading, *Tonnage Measurement,* by Dr. Ing. Luigi Cristiani, from the RINA *Transactions, Vol. 101, 1959,* should be consulted.

TURBINE: See STEAM TURBINES.

TURBO-ELECTRIC DRIVE: Steam is supplied from the boilers to the turbines in the normal way. Instead of being linked to the propeller shafts via gearing, the turbine rotors are directly coupled to electric generators. These generators create the electricity which is fed by cables, switch gear and variable resistances to motors. The rotor of each motor is a propeller shaft. The advantages of turbo-electric drive are that the turbine is unidirectional (i.e. it has no astern blades); elimination of heavy intermediate gearing and finer and more accurate control of propeller speed, which may be controlled directly from the bridge. In the latter, manoeuvering may be effected more quickly and simply electrically than by laborious hand-operated steam inlet valves.

TURTLE-BACK: A deck, the sides of which are very steeply cambered so that water may flow off them the more readily.

WATERTIGHT SUBDIVISION: Passenger ships which carry more than 12 passengers must comply with certain standards of sub-division. The method adopted is to determine a line below which a ship should not sink and, when this is determined, to ascertain the position and length of the compartment which, when flooded, will cause sinkage to that line (and not beyond it). This line beyond which the ship will not sink is known as the MARGIN LINE. From this the 'floodable length', or the maximum length of a compartment which can be flooded without bringing a damaged ship to float at a level below the margin line, can be calculated. However, on large vessels, this length may be divided by a two compartment standard.

The maximum 'permissible length' of a compartment having its mid-length at any point along the ship is obtained from the floodable length for that point by dividing it by a 'factor of subdivision'. The inverse of this factor is the 'compartment standard'. (For example, a ship with a factor of subdivision of 0.5 has a two compartment standard, i.e. any two adjacent compartments can be flooded without any part of the margin line being immersed.)

The requirements for the factor of subdivision – among other features of safety at sea – have been fixed by legislation which, in turn, has been based on the recommendations of various International Conferences on Safety of Life at Sea. The severity of the factor is dependent upon what is known as the 'criterion of service' – a numeral worked out from details of the spaces allocated to cargo, passengers and machinery, etc.

See also: COMPARTMENT.

BIBLIOGRAPHY

Anderson, Roy, *White Star Line* (T. Stephenson, 1964).

Armstrong, Warren, *Atlantic Highway* (Harrap, 1961).

Bathe, Basil W., *Seven Centuries of Sea Travel* (Barrie & Jenkins, 1972).

Barnably, Kenneth C., *Basic Naval Architecture* (6th edn., Hutchinson & Co., 1969).

Baxter, Dr. Brian, *Naval Architecture* (Teach Yourself Books, 1976).

Bonsor, N. R. P., *North Atlantic Seaway* (T. Stephenson, 1955).

Braynard, Frank O., *Lives of the Liners* (Cornell Maritime Press, New York, 1947); *By Their Works Ye Shall Know Them* (Gibbs & Cox, N.Y., 1968); Leviathan, *The World's Greatest Ship* (South Street Seaport Museums, Vols. 1–5, 1973–9).

Breyer, Siegfried, *Battleships and Battlecruisers 1905–70* (Conway Maritime Press).

Brown, David, *World War Two Fact Files – Aircraft Carriers* (MacDonald & Janes, 1977).

Brown, J. J., *Ideas in Exile* (McLelland & Stewart, Toronto, 1967).

Cary, Alan L., *Giant Liners* (Sampson, Low & Marston, c. 1938).

De Kerchove, *International Maritime Dictionary* (Van Nostrand Reinhold, 1961).

Dunn, Laurence, *Passenger Liners* (Adlard Coles, 1961); *Famous Liners, Belfast Built* (Adlard Coles, 1963).

Fraccaroli, Major Aldo, *Italian Warships of World War I* (Ian Allen, 1966).

Gibbs, Cdr. C. R. Vernon, *Passenger Liners of the Western Ocean* (Staples Press, 1952); *Western Ocean Passenger Lines and Liners, 1934–1969* (Brown, Son & Ferguson, 1970).

Gilbert, James, *The World's Worst Aircraft* (M. & J. Hobbs, 1974).

Hardy, A. C., *Ships and Naval Architecture* (Institute of Marine Engineers, 1973).

Hocking, Charles, *Dictionary of Disasters at Sea During the Age of Steam, 1824–1962* (Lloyds, 1963).

Hogg, R. S., *Naval Architecture and Ship Construction* (Institute of Marine Engineers, 1956).

Isherwood, J. H., *Steamers of the Past* (Journal of Commerce, 1966).

Kludas, Arnold, *Great Passenger Ships of the World* (Patrick Stephens, Vols. 1–5, 1975–1977).

340

Maber, Lt. Cdr. John M., North Star to Southern Cross (T. Stephenson, 1967).

Maxtone-Graham, John, *North Atlantic Run* (Cassell & Co., 1972).

Munro-Smith, R., *Elements of Ship Design* (Marine Media Management, 1975); *Ships and Naval Architecture* (Institute of Marine Engineers, 1973).

Lane, Frederic C., *Ships for Victory* (1951).

Newell, Gordon, *Ocean Liners of the Twentieth Century* (Superior Publishing Co., Seattle, 1963).

Okumiya, Masatake, and Horikoshi, Jiro, *Zero — The Story of the Japanese Navy Air Force, 1937–1945* (Cassell & Co., 1947).

Oldham, Wilton J., *The Ismay Line* (Charles Birchall, 1961).

Parker, H., and Bowen, F. C., *Mail and Passenger Steamships of the 19th Century* (1928).

Polmar, Norman, *Aircraft Carriers* (Macdonald, 1969).

Potter, Neil, and Frost, Jack, *The Mary* (Harrap & Co., 1961); *Queen Elizabeth* (Harrap, 1969).

Smith, Eugene W., *Passenger Ships of the World, Past and Present* (George H. Dean, Boston, 1963).

Supino, Prof. Ing. Giorgio, *Land and Marine Diesel Engines* (Charles Griffin, 1915).

Watts, Anthony J., *Japanese Warships of World War II* (Ian Allen, 1966).

Wilson, R. M., *The Big Ships* (Cassell & Co., 1956).

In addition to the books listed above, the following periodicals have been consulted: *Howaldtswerke-Deutsche Werft A.G. House Magazine* — *Janes Fighting Ships* — *Marine News* — *Marine Rundschau* — *The Motorship* — *New York Herald Tribune* — *New York Times* — *Schiffahrte Seekiste/International* — *Sea Breezes* — *Shipbuilding & Marine Engineering International* — *Ships Monthly* — *The Titanic Commutor* (Journal of the Titanic Historical Society) — *Tow Line* (Moran Towing Company's House Magazine) — *Travel Trade Gazette* — *United States Naval Institute Proceedings* — *Washington Post,* and also the *Transactions* of: Institute of Marine Engineers (London) — Royal Institute of Naval Architects (London) and the Society of Naval Architects and Marine Engineers (New York).

INDEX

Names of ships are in italics: those which were either not built or never commissioned are preceded with an asterisk (*), e.g. *Amerika.

342

ADDENDUM

WÄRTSILÄ SWATH DESIGN

196. The Wärtsilä SWATH design.

We are indebted to the courtesy of Oy Wärtsilä ab of Helsinki for the information and sketches in this addendum, all of which has become available since our book was compiled. Wärtsilä have produced this SWATH design for a cruise ship. The letters stand for Small Waterplane Area Twin Hull. Alternatively, she may be called a SSC — Semi-Submerged Catamaran.

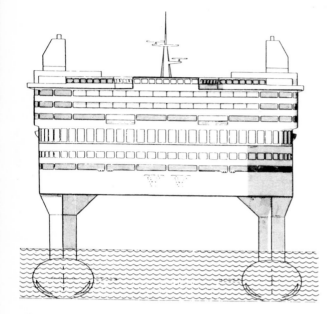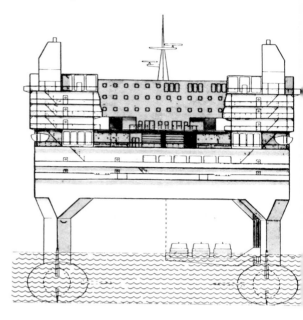

197. *Bow and stern views of the SWATH design.*

Much more revolutionary in design than the ELYSIAN, the hull consists of three basic components, namely: two submar[...] pontoons, containing the engine rooms and propellors, which are attached by two streamlined struts to a superstructure platfor[...] Vibration and noise levels would be quite exceptionally low, and the breadth of deck space in a vessel which is, in effect, [...] catamaran design, would be extremely large in relation to the vessel's size. This beam provides immense possibilities for acco[...] modation, which Wärtsilä intend to exploit to the full. The proposed dimensions of the vessel are 534 feet overall (163 metres)[...] waterline beam of 174 feet and a depth to the top of the struts of 82 feet. Her draught is comparable to a conventional vessel of sim[...] size. On this scale, her gross tonnage would be 44,250, whilst her speed is designed to average 15 knots, this being considered to be [...] economical one for her purpose, though the possibilities of an increase in this design are very great.

On the port side of the lowest deck of the superstructure is a huge, mobile lift of 580 sq. metres in area, equipped with three mo[...] launches (seen in Pl. 197) each with a capacity for 150 persons, and wind-surfers, scuba apparatus and so forth, all of which can [...] launched and boarded within the lee of the struts. The vessel is unique in herself, although the Japanese have experimented with t[...] SWATH design on a smaller scale which did not permit the engines to be accommodated in the pontoons, and the principle, i[...] modified form, is not unknown in oil rigs. Tanks tests on the model have proved to be emminently satisfactory, and the wh[...] project has been co-ordinated with the aid of computers under the leadership of Mr. Kai Levander.

Technically, this is perhaps the most advanced design ever conceived. As to her destiny . . . who can guess? If she encount[...] opposition, it will be that opposition, so manifested throughout the centuries, which stems from some innate conservatism amon[...] shipowners. Thus we include her in this Addendum in no spirit of doubt about her viability or her future, but rather as an interesti[...] comparison with the ELYSIAN.

Balanced on the Horns of Destiny, all work is stopped on the building of the QUEEN MARY.